HEGEL AND MARX

HEGEL AND MARX

THE CONCEPT OF NEED

Ian Fraser

Edinburgh University Press

© Ian Fraser, 1998

Transferred to digital print 2006

Edinburgh University Press,
22 George Square,
Edinburgh

Typeset in Ehrhardt
by Hewer Text Ltd, Edinburgh and
printed and bound in Great Britain by
CPI Antony Rowe, Eastbourne, East Sussex

A CIP record for this book is available from the British Library

ISBN 10: 0 7486 0947 4
ISBN 13: 978 0 7486 0947 5

The right of Ian Fraser
to be identified as author of this work
has been asserted in accordance with
the Copyright, Designs and Patents Act 1988.

CONTENTS

ACKNOWLEDGEMENTS

I would like to thank Andrew Reeve and John Halliday for their constructive criticisms and comments on earlier drafts of this book. Thanks also to Alan Apperley and Peter Burnham for much-needed advice and words of encouragement. The support of colleagues at Nottingham Trent has also been important to me over the last couple of years. Lawrence Wilde has been a great colleague and friend and I am deeply grateful for his interest in my work and for always making helpful suggestions.

Carol Murphy, Vincent Murphy and Brian Brown have always supported my academic endeavours, particularly in the early days when it was so vitally needed. My greatest debt, however, is to Lesley Fraser, whose limitless faith and unstinting support have done so much to make this book possible. The book itself is dedicated to the memory of my mother, Ethel Emily Fraser.

Portions of this book have appeared in the following: 'Beyond Prometheus: Hegel on the Need to be Free', *Politics*, 15, 2, 1995; 'Hegel and Modern Need Theory', in I. Hampsher-Monk and J. Stanyer (eds) *Contemporary Political Studies* (Political Studies Association of the UK, Belfast, 1996); 'Two of a Kind: Hegel, Marx, Dialectic and Form', *Capital and Class*, 61, 1996; 'Speculations on Poverty in Hegel's Philosophy of Right*', *The European Legacy: Towards New Paradigms*, Journal of the International Society for the Study of European Ideas, 1, 7, 1996.

LIST OF FIGURES

LIST OF ABBREVIATIONS

Terms in square brackets and German terms in round brackets are my amendments and insertions unless otherwise stated.

Emphases in quotations are always in the original unless otherwise stated.

The following abbreviations have been used in relation to Hegel's works:

para(s) = paragraph(s)
R = Remark
A = Addition

INTRODUCTION

By the second half of the nineteenth century, Marx noted how it had become fashionable to treat Hegel as a ' "dead dog" '.[1] Marx was so enraged by this that he openly declared himself a 'pupil of that mighty thinker' and emphasised Hegel's relevance for a thoroughgoing critique of capitalism.[2] Ironically, however, as we approach the end of the twentieth century it is now Marx himself who has become the 'dead dog'. The failure of Soviet communism and the positing of capitalism as the only viable form of society has apparently rendered Marx redundant and irrelevant.[3] In this book, I argue vociferously against such a trend by emphasising the importance of *both* Hegel and Marx for comprehending the contradictions of capitalism and for pinpointing moments of trans-cendence beyond such a system. The concept of need is the focal point for grasping these contradictions and transcendent moments. I offer an exegesis that emphasises the strengths of their need theory, defending it against the misinterpretations of many commentators and indicating its cogency for contemporary theories of need.

Why should the focus be on Hegel *and* Marx, though? As Sidney Hook has noted, the Hegel-Marx relationship is 'suggestive of both agreement and opposition'.[4] What emerges from this study, however, is a Hegel and Marx who in general agree rather than oppose each other in their understanding of needs. Such agreement stems, in particular, from their similar dialectical approaches for analysing concepts,[5] a conclusion which goes against the two other main interpretations that oppose Marx to Hegel. One interpretation depicts Hegel's influence as completely negative because it imports mystical idealism into Marx's thought. The expunging of this mysticism is then seen as essential, therefore, if Marx is to become a pure materialist.[6] The other interpretation does actually emphasise the Hegelian links, but finds it necessary to appro-priate Hegel's dialectic materialistically to make it properly Marxist.[7] Chapter 2 will clearly illustrate how the two opposing approaches arise out of a misreading of Hegel which was, ironically, begun by Marx himself. Instead of merely accepting Marx's criticism at face value, as many Marxists do, careful analysis will reveal how misplaced Marx's contentions really are regarding the idealistic nature of Hegel's thought.

Emphasising agreement between Hegel and Marx rather than opposition has important political implications for Marxism. The disastrous effect of the expulsion of any Hegelian influence from Marxist thought led to structuralism[8] and, more recently, the game-theoretic approach of analytical Marxism.[9] The effect of both of these movements on the notion of the subject is particularly dire. In the former, the subject becomes lost in, or the prisoner of, structural determinants; in the latter, the subject is nothing more than the very abstract and disembodied individual that is the necessary starting point for bourgeois liberal thought.

In contrast, I stress the importance Hegel attaches to the subject through his notion of the Will. For Hegel, this Will represents human beings in their interaction with each other as they shape and make their world. Even the materialist appropriators miss this crucial aspect of Hegel's dialectic. Inevitably, this leads them into the error of positing Hegel as a 'mystical idealist' imprisoned within the realm of thought, in contrast to the 'materialist' Marx. Against such a view, I show that Hegel's and Marx's dialectics are not opposite, are not a supersession of one over the other, but are instead intrinsically similar. As such, Hegel offers a materialist understanding of needs which resounds in Marx's own writings. Uniting Hegel *and* Marx, then, as Hegelian-Marxism, is shown to be crucially relevant for understanding contemporary capitalism and the moments that can bring about its rupture and eventual dissolution. Consequently, three main themes emerge that link Hegel's and Marx's analyses.

The first relates to the aforementioned similarities of their dialectical approach for analysing concepts. They analyse forms to deduce their inner connections. In relation to the concept of need, for instance, they analyse the various forms taken by needs and their satisfactions in society through the self-activity of human beings. Many commentators misinterpret Hegel's and Marx's understanding of needs due to a lack of attention to form. Consequently, I will establish that an exegesis based on analysing forms is crucial for a correct understanding of needs within their works.

Second, I illustrate how Hegel and Marx share the same concern for humans to overcome the realm of natural necessity in order to be truly free. Both thinkers see the reduction in necessary labour time within the realm of necessity as a fundamental prerequisite for humans to achieve real freedom. Both see the potential for this development as being dialectically present in human needs and their satisfactions. Out of humans' initial necessity to satisfy their needs, mediations arise. The mediation of labour develops into the further mediations of the tool and machinery, allowing humans to satisfy their needs more productively. On this basis, I argue that both Hegel and Marx see increased automation as a crucial foundation that can enable humans to be truly free. Hegel grasps the labour-saving aspects of increased technology with prodigious pre-science. Marx, himself, echoes and expands on this insight in his own writings. Both recognise the negative use of technological developments which result in the dehumanisation of workers and their descent into poverty. However, they also recognise how the positive and more rational use of technology could eventually allow humans to overcome the realm of necessity and achieve a true realm of freedom.

Third, I argue that Hegel and Marx offer a fruitful contribution to a fundamental debate in modern need theory, namely, the disjunction between universal and particular conceptions of need. The search for objective or universal needs by many modern need theorists often results in the neglect of the particular needs of minority cultures. Alternatively, the attempt to secure particular needs can ignore the diversity of needs within a minority culture and the similarity of needs beyond. Examining the writings of Hegel and Marx on the basis of their method of analysing forms reveals an alternative approach to this problem. They both share an understanding of needs that grasps them in their movement from a universal to a particular form and back again. Both thinkers offer a way, therefore, to try and overcome the impasse that besets modern need theorists, who have a tendency to hold universal needs distinct from particular needs and *vice versa*. I will argue that both Hegel and Marx understand universal and particular needs in their movement and transition from one to the other in their difference and unity. This provides the possibility of perceiving not only the needs of a particular culture, but also the potential mediation of those needs with other cultures. Consequently, Hegel's and Marx's theory of need can offer a cogent contribution to contemporary debates about needs and their satisfaction in a culturally diverse world.

The next chapter examines some of the main issues on needs in contemporary debates. I focus on those problems that have a direct relevance to the subsequent discussion of Hegel's and Marx's need theory. Attempts to distinguish human from nonhuman need, and the conflicts between universal and particular need, are therefore of primary concern. The main conclusion of this chapter is that modern need theory suffers from a tendency to privilege either universal need over particular need or *vice versa*. Further chapters will reveal how Hegel's and Marx's need theory attempts to overcome such a dichotomy.

After a discussion of the dialectic in Chapter 2, Chapter 3 considers one of Hegel's early works, the *System of Ethical Life* – a text that offers a considerable insight into his discussion of needs. I show how Hegel understands needs as taking universal and particular forms in society. The universal concept of need is the 'natural need' for food, drink, etc. – needs that individuals must satisfy in order to live. Hegel then examines the forms these needs take – the particular actualisation of the concept – as individuals attempt to satisfy them. These forms emerge through different stages of need-satisfaction, ranging from immediate through to deferred gratification. Hegel indicates how the mediations of these needs progress from labour to machinery to surplus to money, as society dialectically develops into a 'system of need'. The positive results of this process are human development and the increased productivity gained through labour and machinery. The negative consequences, however, are the development of poverty and domination that result from the natural operations of the free market. Hegel illustrates how the necessity of having to satisfy 'natural needs' leads to immense contradictions – contradictions that humans themselves, create.

Chapter 4 considers the reoccurrence of these arguments in Hegel's last published work, the *Philosophy of Right*. I also develop further Hegel's preoccupation with trying to ensure an escape from the tyranny of natural necessity. Hegel sees the constant burden of having to satisfy 'natural needs' as a fetter on humans' potential to be free. I infer from his comments that technological developments, which allow machines to take the place of humans in the production process, are a way to ensure human freedom. For Hegel, the overcoming of necessity allows humans to satisfy their 'spiritual needs'. The latter do exist as a moment in the realm of necessity and unfreedom, but their proper satisfaction is only possible beyond that realm. The introduction of machines is crucial, therefore, in allowing humans to affirm their 'spiritual needs'.

Hegel's understanding of needs as forms in both of these chapters offers a contrast with the approach of modern need theorists. I show how Hegel overcomes the tendency to privilege either universal need over particular need or *vice versa*. Instead, analysing forms allows Hegel to capture the dialectical movement between universal and particular moments of need.

Chapter 5 amplifies the analysis of the previous two chapters and considers further Hegel's concept of 'spiritual need' through a discussion of his *Aesthetics*. Hegel's emphasis on understanding needs as forms is again evident. Consequently, I show how 'spiritual needs' are a form of 'natural needs.' Hegel indicates how humans have a basic need to objectify themselves in the external world, and the 'spiritual need' for art is one form in which this is accomplished. Hegel also reaffirms his concern to ensure humans' liberation from the realm of necessity in order to reach a realm where they can more fully pursue and satisfy their 'spiritual needs'.

With Hegel's need theory clearly established, Chapters 6 and 7 examine the concept of need in Marx's writings. Chapter 6 defines and explores Marx's core need concepts: 'natural need', 'necessary need', 'luxury need', 'social need', 'socially created need', and 'true social need'. I illustrate how he uses general and determinate abstractions to discern 'natural needs' and the forms these needs take in society. Marx understands all these need concepts dialectically – as contradictions within a unity. The 'inner connections' between these needs result in a circuit of needs which contains various mediations and need-forms that confront workers as they try to satisfy their 'natural needs' in capitalism.

Chapter 7 re-emphasises Marx's understanding of needs as forms by considering what I refer to as higher needs. Marx uses the higher need concepts of 'human need' and 'radical need' to capture the positive moments of humans' realisation of their own essence as truly human beings. For Marx, moments of higher need actually exist in an estranged form within 'egoistic needs' – needs that individuals relate to themselves or to others only through necessity – or in their own right as moments of transcendence in and against capital. Marx emphasises how humans must overcome the realm of natural necessity to achieve a true realm of freedom. In the latter realm, machines take humans' place in the production process, resulting in the reduction and eventual abolition of necessary labour.

Marx's dialectical understanding of need based on analysing forms does not treat universal and particular as separate and distinct, but grasps them in their mediation from one to the other. I establish that many commentators misinterpret Marx as either privileging universal need over particular need or being confused between the two of them. In contrast, attention to form reveals that Marx is grasping the dialectical movement of needs and their satisfactions in and between their universal and particular moments. Human beings, through their self-activity, are the means by which the universal and particular emerge.

Chapter 8 explicitly compares Hegel and Marx on the concept of need in relation to the three major themes: method; freedom from necessity; and their contribution to modern debates on need theory. Both thinkers share the same method of analysing forms that allows us to deduce an efficacious need theory from their writings. Both also emphasise the importance of technology and machines in offering humans the possibility of escaping from the realm of necessity. Only when humans have left this realm can they properly satisfy their higher or spiritual needs and thereby be truly free. Finally, I explain how Hegel's and Marx's dialectical understanding of need makes an interesting and cogent contribution to debates in modern need theory. Comprehending needs as forms provides the possibility of identifying the needs of a particular culture, and the potential mediation of those needs with other cultures. This offers the potential for overcoming the tendency in modern need theory to emphasise universal (objective) needs over particular (subjective) needs or *vice versa*. Hegel's and Marx's dialectical understanding of needs as forms can serve, therefore, as a fertile basis for examining need-satisfaction in and between cultures in the diverse world of today.

The final chapter considers the political implications of the Hegelian-Marxist need theory that has been developed in this study. The experience of need-formation and satisfaction in Soviet communism and the relationship between needs and rights with reference to debates between liberals, communitarians and social democrats are the main areas of focus. Attention to form again reveals the antagonistic basis to need-satisfaction even in a seemingly all-dominating system such as the former Soviet Union. The overemphasis on rights to the detriment of needs in liberal thought is also shown to be misplaced. Instead, rights are shown to be constituted on the basis of need-satisfaction through the contradictory presence of labour in and against the state. The faith that social democratic theorists have in the state constitutionally enshrining a right to certain basic needs is therefore shown to be problematic. Similarly, the desire by communitarians to use the state for propagating 'communal' values is also questionable. Such theorists ignore the fact that the state itself is an antagonistic form which attempts to regulate the social relations of production to ensure the continued existence of capitalism, and which therefore poses severe constraints on achieving desired goals. Additionally, the state can also result in the imposition of certain dominant values to the detriment or exclusion of other minority values.

I now examine some of the primary issues in modern debates on needs. These issues can then serve as a useful foundation for analysing Hegel's and Marx's need theory in subsequent chapters.

NOTES

1. K. Marx, *Capital*, Volume 1, trans. B. Fowkes (Penguin, Harmondsworth, 1988), p. 102.
2. Marx, *Capital*, Vol. 1, p. 103.
3. See, for example, K. Minogue, 'Ideology after the Collapse of Communism', in A. Shtromas (ed.) *The End of 'Isms'?*, Special Issue of *Political Studies*, XLI, 1993.

4. S. Hook, *From Hegel to Marx: Studies in the Intellectual Development of Karl Marx* (Humanities Press, New York, 1958), p. 15.

5. D. MacGregor, *The Communist Ideal in Hegel and Marx*, (George Allen and Unwin, London and Sydney, 1984), has done the most to reassert this interpretation. Antecedents can be found in the following: G. Lukács, *The Young Hegel* (Merlin, London, 1975), and *History and Class Consciousness* (Merlin, London, 1990); C. L. R. James, *Notes on Dialectics* (Allison and Busby, London, 1980, first published 1948); and R. Dunayevskaya, *Philosophy and Revolution* (Columbia University Press, New York, 1989, first published 1973). Dunayevskaya's inclusion does require a caveat. Although she clearly interprets Hegel's dialectic as thoroughly materialist, she, almost paradoxically, still falls back into the materialist appropriation argument (see in particular p. 45). For the recent re-emphasis on the similarities between Hegel's and Marx's method see, for example: A. Shamsavari, *Dialectics and Social Theory: The Logic of Capital* (Merlin Books, Braunton, 1991); G. Reuten and M. Williams, *Value-Form and the State* (Routledge, London and New York, 1989); C. Arthur, 'Hegel's *Logic* and Marx's *Capital*', in F. Moseley (ed.) *Marx's Method in Capital: A Reexamination* (Humanities Press, Atlantic Highlands NJ, 1993). Arthur has captured this movement with the phrase 'new dialectics', in his 'Review of Shamsavari's *Dialectics and Social Theory: The Logic of Marx's Capital*', *Capital and Class*, 50, Summer, 1993.

6. L. Althusser, 'Marx's Relation to Hegel', in his *Montesquieu, Rousseau, Marx* (New Left Books, London, 1982); L. Colletti, *Marxism and Hegel* (New Left Books, London, 1973).

7. For some representative thinkers who take this line see G. Boger, 'On the Materialist Appropriation of Hegel's Dialectical Method', *Science and Society*, 55, 1, Spring, 1991.

8. L. Althusser, *For Marx*, (New Left Books, London, 1969).

9. J. Romer (ed.), *Analytical Marxism* (Cambridge University Press, Cambridge, 1989). For a succinct account of this development see A. Callinicos, 'Introduction: Analytical Marxism', in A. Callinicos (ed.) *Marxist Theory* (Oxford University Press, Oxford, 1989), pp. 1–6.

1

THE CONCEPT OF NEED

Any analysis of the concept of need has to contend with its 'mercurial' and 'difficult-to-fix' character.[1] Modern need theorists approach such a problem by positing a simple need statement of the form: 'A needs X in order to Y.' They then give this skeletal sentence flesh by considering its complex implications, such as: who or what is 'A'? Why is 'X' needed? What is 'X', and is that important for understanding why 'A' needs it? What is 'Y'? Three main issues to consider that arise from these questions are as follows: first, the distinction between human need and nonhuman animal need; second, the relation of needs to wants; third, the division between universal and relative notions of need. These issues are central to contemporary debates in need theory as they arise from the elaboration of the aforementioned skeletal sentence. Even more important, however, is the relevance of these topics to Hegel's and Marx's own discussion of the concept of need, as subsequent chapters will illustrate. For now, we can begin with an exploration of the first issue: who or what the 'A' is in the skeletal need statement.

HUMAN NEEDS AND NONHUMAN ANIMAL NEEDS

Modern need theorists generally focus their attention on human needs, and so designate 'A' as human in contradistinction to nonhuman animals.[2] However, the increasing concern over the rights and suffering of nonhuman animals has led to an emphasis on the similarities, rather than the differences, between human and nonhuman animal needs.[3] Speciesism, the privileging of the interests of one species over another, has become increasingly questioned.[4] As Rachels appositely notes, 'after Darwin, we can no longer think of ourselves as occupying a special place in creation – instead, we must realize that we are products of the same evolutionary forces that shaped the rest of the animal kingdom'.[5] The human species is, therefore, simply 'one animal species among something like a million others'.[6] Moreover, humans share with nonhuman animals fundamental basic needs – such as the 'need to survive, to be healthy, to avoid harm, to function properly'.[7] What, then, can it mean to denote needs as 'human', distinct from nonhuman animal needs? A Cartesian dualism makes such a distinction possible by portraying nonhuman animals as determined in their actions, but depicting humans as thinking begins who can consciously direct their activity.[8] Within modern need theory, this type of distinction rests on understanding nonhuman animal needs as 'drives'.

It is ironic, therefore, that Abraham Maslow's seminal study does actually equate human needs with drives.[9] Maslow classifies needs into five types hierarchically.[10] The first he defines as physiological needs, such as the need to satisfy hunger or thirst. The satisfaction of these needs leads on to the second stage – the need for safety. This is the desire to live in an ordered world free from fear. The third level is what he calls the need for belongingness and love. The esteem needs are the fourth level which Maslow sees as essential because people desire respect and look to their own self-regard. These four levels of needs are not enough on their own, however, for there is still a need for self-actualisation. People must satisfy the need for self-fulfilment by doing what is true to their nature – a musician must write music or an artist paint, for instance. The hierarchical order of the needs arises from Maslow's 'principle of relative potency',[11] which states that the strongest needs are those that dominate an organism. He sees the physiological needs to satisfy thirst and hunger, therefore, as the most overriding. Such needs are the basic requirements humans have to satisfy in order to exist. Similarly, he depicts the need for safety as stronger than the need for love when both are being frustrated in some way. The lower needs of physiological and safety requirements are thus prerequisites for the higher cognitive needs of belongingness, self-esteem and self-actualisation. For Maslow, all these needs are so basic as to be universal or 'instinctoid', as he calls them, across the human race.[12]

Critics of Maslow's theory, however, question the coherence of his categories. Springborg, for instance, notes how Maslow's ordering of these needs is contradictory. She argues that esteem needs, for example, could come before safety needs if a person wants to gain respect by performing a particularly courageous but dangerous act.[13] Despite these problems, Maslow's sociobiological[14] approach to needs does appear to have a degree of credibility on an intuitive level at least. It seems obvious that humans have basic needs just as nonhuman animals do. Midgley, for example, observes how wolves are very similar to humans in their behaviour patterns: they pair for life, show affection to one another, are loyal to the pack, kill to eat and, like all social animals, have a variety of ceremonies in which to achieve co-operation and friendship, and strengthen social cohesion.[15] Are humans no different from wolves?

Many of these characteristics would indeed fit into Maslow's hierarchical needs schema. So the overcoming of the Cartesian dualism is conceivable, but only by understanding basic needs as drives. Yet the problem with equating needs with drives is that it may suggest humans are indistinguishable from nonhuman animals. Just as animals are driven to pursue particular courses of action so too are humans. Any real notion of human autonomy therefore diminishes as humans become slaves to their drives.

As Doyal and Gough argue, however, recognising similarities between humans and nonhuman animals does not imply that humans are the same as nonhuman animals in terms of biologically driven needs. For Doyal and Gough, sociobiological arguments ignore the fact that humans, unlike nonhuman animals, can choose to override their 'biological "needs"'.[16] Doyal and Gough argue, for example, that if there is a conflict between a mother's natural need to care for her child and the need for her to go out to work, then the woman can choose which to do. Her biological make-up does not force her to stay at home and care for the infant.[17] So Doyal and Gough certainly recognise the importance of biological needs as a background factor in our deliberations, but they are keen to stress that biological considerations do not determine the way we, as human beings, make choices about our lives. Consequently, they retain the Cartesian dualism to demarcate the human from the nonhuman animal, even though they wish to challenge such a dichotomy.[18]

There are two particular problems with Doyal's and Gough's argument here. First, it may be that nonhuman animals can and do overcome these biological needs themselves. They may not be as 'driven' as is supposed. This was, of course, suggested by Darwin himself, who observed that the:

> orang in the Eastern islands, and the chimpanzee in Africa, build platforms on which they sleep; and as both species follow the same habit, it might be argued that this was due to instinct, but we cannot feel sure that it is not the result of both animals having similar wants and possessing similar powers of reasoning.[19]

Nonhuman animals may look as though they are acting from instinct, but we cannot be certain that this is actually the case. Indeed, more recent research suggests that nonhuman animals do reason about things, although not in the same way as humans.[20]

Second, Doyal and Gough contradict their desire to keep needs distinct from drives. They approvingly quote[21] Thompson's contention[22] that a drive to require something does not necessarily mean one needs it. For instance, a person may have a drive to consume more food but does not need to because he has already taken the necessary amount in terms of nutrition, vitamins, etc. The concept of 'drive' also explains behaviour or action whereas 'need' justifies it.[23] On this basis it is then possible to make distinctions between the drive of hunger and thirst, and the need for food and water. The former explains why we strive after food and water, while the latter is an attempt to justify such behaviour, according to Thompson and, by implication, also to Doyal and Gough. Yet unlike Thompson, Doyal and Gough accept that humans have 'biological "needs"', which implies, therefore, that humans also have drives – the internal motivation to satisfy hunger, for instance.[24] All they are really saying is that drives are not deterministic because we can choose to override them. Nevertheless, this is not the same as denying that drives can be needs. It does seem that in endorsing Thompson's arguments, therefore, they in fact contradict their own position when trying to distinguish needs from drives.

What this discussion suggests, however, is that constituting the distinctly 'human need' against the 'nonhuman animal need' requires careful consideration. This will be particularly relevant when examining the arguments of Hegel and Marx in future chapters. Both allude to a human/nonhuman animal distinction in terms of need. They argue that humans have spiritual needs which they can only satisfy properly beyond the realm of natural necessity. In contrast, they interpret the needs of nonhuman animals as remaining firmly within this realm. Both, therefore, certainly exaggerate the limitations of need-satisfaction of nonhuman animals. Nevertheless, they see the emphasis on humans' spirituality as crucial for ensuring that they can be truly free. For Hegel and Marx, only by overcoming natural necessity can humans properly achieve spiritual freedom.

In terms of the need/drive distinction, however, they would oppose the type of demarcation Thompson attempts. Instead, they emphasise how drives can actually take the form of needs which themselves take further need-forms. Hegel's and Marx's concern, therefore, is to highlight the inner connections between concepts. Need can then be understood in its movement and transition, rather than as a static concept distinct from other related concepts. In this way, we can better capture the different manifestations of need and their satisfaction through the self-activity of human beings. For now, we can take the subject, 'A', of the need statement, 'A needs X in order to Y', to refer to the human animal. An examination of what this term 'human' actually means will take place later in the discussion of needs and ends. Concerning the relationship between needs and drives, however, Doyal and Gough do seem to equate the two. In contrast, Thompson rejects using the term 'need' in any way that links it to a 'drive', other than by distinguishing justification from explanation.

NEEDS AND WANTS

The biological aspects of the subject, 'A', now give way to the consideration of how the statement 'A needs X in order to Y' differs from the statement 'A wants X in order to Y'; that is, how is a need distinguishable from a want? Some modern need theorists make this distinction by identifying needs as objective, and thereby understandable in relation to some universal standard, but wants as subjective and therefore dependent on relative human perceptions.[25] Designating wants as subjective means that these theorists interpret them as being psychological rather than physiological. One way they highlight this fact is by suggesting that we can need what we do not want, and want what we do not need. The diabetic who may not want insulin does actually need it. Alternatively, an Imelda Marcos figure may want new shoes, but as she possesses hundreds of pairs already it is difficult to see a need for them. 'A needs X' and 'A wants X', although syntactically similar, differ in that what 'A' wants depends on her beliefs, but what she needs depends on objective criteria available to everyone. The diabetic, for instance, may want sugar but what she really needs is insulin. The want is subjective whereas the need is objective, because people can accept that diabetics need insulin to avoid illness. The word 'need' also carries with it a sense of 'urgency'[26] – a trait that is important in distinguishing it from the less 'urgent' want.

A further and more rigorous way in which to differentiate between a need and a want is as follows.[27] To say, for example, that 'A' needs a rump steak means that 'A' actually needs that object or something that is identical with it. To say that 'A' wants a rump steak, however, depends on 'A's' belief about the attributes of that steak. 'A' does not want that steak if it contains BSE, for instance. In the case of needs, though, it really has to be a rump steak and not a rump steak that contains BSE. The truth or falsity of a want statement depends, therefore, on how a person subjectively thinks or believes. A need statement, however, can only be true objectively, on how things actually are rather than how we think they are. Wants relate, therefore, to a person's psychological state whereas needs do not.[28] The psychological basis to wants enables theorists to argue that statements about wants are intentional and referentially opaque.[29] Intentionality and referential opacity relate to the fact that terms which refer to the same thing in a sentence are not interchangeable because they will alter the truth-value of that statement. In contrast, a need statement is referentially transparent because the substitution of terms with the same meaning does not alter the truth-value of the statement.[30] For example, if I want to kill X and X is my wife, then that does not entail that I want to kill my wife. If I need to kill X, however, and X is my wife, then I need to kill my wife. The substitution of the term 'wife' for 'X' changes the truth-value of the want statement. That I want to kill X does not mean that I want to kill my wife. The fact that I need to kill X, however, means that I need to kill whoever X is, even if it is my wife. The truth-value of the need statement therefore remains. The objective nature of needs that demarcates them from the subjectivity of wants, however, is not as pronounced as these examples would suggest. This becomes readily apparent when considering the relation between needs and their ends.

NEEDS AND ENDS

Brian Barry argues that a need cannot be normatively independent of its end because the case for meeting a need must always derive from the achievement of its end state.[31] This raises the issue of what 'Y' is in our original need statement. For many need theorists, 'Y' refers to the avoidance of serious harm. This is particularly the case for Thompson, who states: 'to say that A has a fundamental need for X is to assert that so long as A is without X he must suffer serious harm'.[32] This implies that needs are parasitic on ends and thus require the avoidance of harm, or some other end, to be included to make the statement normative. We will discuss the relationship between needs and harm more fully in a moment. First, it is necessary to be clear about the importance of ends or goals in this context.

Barry indicates that ends themselves have to be justifiable, that is, they must appear desirable or worthy to pursue. The problem is that people can differ in their justification of ends. A welfare liberal, for instance, may justify the end of social justice by emphasising the need for a minimum wage. A libertarian, however, would argue that this end is not justifiable because a minimum wage interferes with the need of an individual to offer or hire labour at the market price. The problem of relativism arises. We cannot define needs because to understand needs we have to understand the ends to which those needs relate; but the normative evaluation of ends can find no consensus in society. If there is no consensus on the value of ends then there is no consensus on needs. The contention that needs are objective in comparison to wants begins, therefore, to look questionable. It is here that the basic problem of theorising about needs becomes prominent.

Need theories are now being seen as dividing into two types: 'thick' and 'thin'.[33] A 'thin' theory of need aims at universalising need without reference to cultural content and subjectivity. A 'thick' theory, on the other hand, focuses on how people experience their needs either in a culture, or individually, and is therefore particular. It is the 'thin' theory that is attempting to see needs as objective, whereas the 'thick' is stressing the importance of subjectivity. The previous section indicated how certain theorists give short shrift to the suggestion that a need can be subjective. They argue that once subjectivity enters, wants rather than needs are at issue. The 'thick' and 'thin' distinction, however, treats the subjective aspect not as a want but as a need. On the terms of this debate, a need can be either objective ('thin') or subjective ('thick'). Those adhering to the latter inevitably stress the culturally relative or subjective nature of needs, and reject the imposition of universal, objective needs on people. As Kate Soper notes, it does seem on one level that 'thick' theorists are 'on the side of the angels', because they are focusing on what people think are their needs, rather than dictating to them what has been decided they need.[34] 'Thin' conceptions of need endorse, therefore, the practice of 'cultural imperialism' because they are not sensitive to the needs of particular cultures or individual subjects. Western conceptions of universal needs become a dominant imposition over and against the needs of particular individuals and cultures.[35] Against this tendency, certain writers argue for a 'thicker' conception of need. Stephen Marglin, for instance, suggests that practices, and needs themselves, only make sense 'in context, as part of a cultural whole'.[36] A correct understanding of needs, therefore, locates them within the 'power of belief' that operates inside a particular culture.[37] One example he offers is the perceived need for the circumcision of females in many African cultures. Marglin argues that people's own beliefs are paramount in judging this practice, rather than some westernised notion of what is good or bad. Indeed, he suggests that situating such a need within the operations and practices of a particular way of life gives it a clear credibility. He even proposes that denying the need to circumcise females in this culture could actually have a very damaging effect on the lives of these women. He argues, for example, that 'if parents, uncles, aunts, grandparents – not to mention the larger society – believe that the offspring of uncircumcised women are inferior, these unfortunate children may be reared in just the fashion that confirms their inferiority'.[38] For Marglin, then, there seems little benefit in trying to refute the need for female circumcision when such a powerful belief system so clearly supports it.

Marglin's emphasis on respecting the rights of particular cultures to assert their own needs is certainly commendable. However, major problems can arise in seeing needs in this way. First, the needs of different cultures may come into conflict with each other. If so, then some form of dialogue about an objective understanding of needs is necessary to ensure a degree of harmony. Simply emphasising particular needs against universal needs misses the potential for mediating need across cultures and overcoming such conflict. It is ironic, therefore, that Marglin justifies his own argument on what is evidently a universal need to avoid serious harm. He thinks that the power of the belief system operating in the African culture will make everyone see the offspring of uncircumcised women as inferior; thus causing these women serious harm. Overemphasising the particular makes him ignore even the slightest possibility of universal mediation that may be present through a notion such as serious harm.

Second, Marglin seems to adopt a very homogeneous understanding of cultural groups. On his view, adopting the perspective and rationale of the African culture means that there is a need for circumcising women. Marglin is assuming, however, that such a 'power of belief' is dominant in that culture; but this may not necessarily be the case. Many cultures are far more differentiated than people assume them to be.[39] It is quite possible that certain females themselves may reject such a belief and regard circumcisions as a violation of their own bodies. This may result in the inferior treatment of these females in their own culture but perhaps it is a price they feel worth paying. Women who fought for the need for birth control, for instance, suffered many forms of disapprobation for their beliefs and actions. If they had accepted the dominant (male) belief system in society, however, then the improvements in women's health and the increase in freedom birth control allowed would have been impossible.

Finally, Marglin is quite hostile to universal conceptions of needs. Instead, he prefers the particular needs of a culture that are present within a certain belief system. However, the tyrannical aspect he deduces for universal needs re-emerges in his preference for the particular needs of the culture. The particular need for female circumcision is actually a universal need within those African cultures that engage in such practices. These cultures are imposing their collective needs onto the individual needs of subjects – the women involved – who may be too young or too afraid to speak out against such a practice. Protecting the needs of a 'culture' over the particular needs of some of its members can therefore result in tyranny – the very tyranny that Marglin suggests is intrinsic to universal notions of need. Not surprisingly, then, the 'thick' and 'thin' debate results in the key issue in modern need theory, namely, 'how to chart basic need-satisfaction or objective welfare without either embracing relativism or working at such a level of generality that the relevance of our theory for specific social problems is lost'.[40] Certain theorists attempt to overcome this problem by identifying aspects that 'A', in the 'A needs X in order to Y' statement, has universally in common with all humans.

HUMANS AND BASIC NEEDS

Martha Nussbaum is one of the most prominent theorists who adopt this type of approach. Her concern is to dispel the arguments of the cultural relativists by positing Aristotelian essentialist virtues of what it means to be human universally and across cultures. She calls this the 'thick vague theory of the good',[41] which leads into a long list that includes the need for food, drink, shelter, sexual desire and many more basic needs.[42] Nussbaum accepts that cultural differences do exist, but insists that ultimately there is a conception of a universal common humanity that crosses all societies. She maintains that universal needs can emerge on the basis of this common humanity, which itself is so overpowering that people recognise each other as human even when they may not want to do so. Drawing on research by Raul Hilberg, for instance, she stresses how Nazis recognised Jews as human when it was impossible for them not to do otherwise (such as in personal conversations).[43] The universality of the term 'human', therefore, offers a foundation on which to build universal conceptions of need. There are, however, problems with this type of argument. For instance, in the recurring cases of atrocities throughout history, the perpetrators do see their victims as nonhuman. Odd personal conversations of 'human' recognition can hardly outweigh such occurrences. For theorists such as Richard Rorty, therefore, appeals to the idea of humanness are essentially meaningless.[44] To suggest, for instance, that deep down the Bosnian Serb sees his Muslim victim as human means little as he actually kills or rapes the Muslim. Rorty's point is that using the idea of humanness has absolutely no moral effect on the perpetrator of an atrocity. Rorty's own solution is to say to the perpetrator: 'This could be your son/father/mother'; but this also looks weak. The response is likely to be: 'Well, it is not my son/father/mother, it is a Muslim/Jew etc., and I have no qualms about killing him/her.' So using the notion of 'human' as a basis for universal needs presents as much difficulty as the rejection of such a basis.

Despite such problems, theorists do attempt to posit needs that are basic to everybody, and which people can universally accept regardless of their cultural location. Doyal and Gough do this by expressing the basic need statement as: 'A needs physical survival/health and autonomy in order to avoid serious harm.'[45] Aware of the danger of relativism, Doyal and Gough propose a universal notion of serious harm, which they define as 'dramatically impaired participation in a form of life'.[46] They argue that physical health and autonomy, therefore, are *the* basic needs to satisfy if an individual is to engage in social participation and thereby avoid serious harm. On this view, it is common sense that all people need to be healthy and have a degree of autonomy if they are to pursue their particular life plans. Doyal and Gough realise that the satisfaction of these universal needs of health and autonomy depends upon everyone having access to the gratification of what they term 'intermediate needs'.[47] The latter refer to 'those properties of goods, services, activities and relationships that enhance physical health and human autonomy'.[48] They offer a specific list of these 'intermediate needs', ranging from nutritional food and clean water to safe birth control and child-bearing, which they derive from 'scientific sources'.[49] The only criterion for inclusion in the list is a positive and universal contribution to physical health and autonomy.[50] So the 'intermediate need' for nutritional food, for instance, is universal to all cultures, and has a positive effect on the basic needs of health and autonomy. All humans need proper nutritional food to be healthy and to have the capacity to follow their life plans. Both basic and 'intermediate needs' are therefore universal. However, Doyal and Gough recognise that the ways in which individuals satisfy these 'intermediate needs' will be relative.[51] The satisfaction of the universal need for nutritional food, for instance, will vary in and between many different cultures. Thus, Doyal and Gough seem to have overcome the 'thick' and 'thin' dichotomy of relativism on the one hand, and too much generality on the other.

The sensitivity Doyal and Gough display regarding the needs of individuals within particular cultures is an obvious advantage for any need theory. They seem to assuage the worries of relativists because the basic and 'intermediate needs' Doyal and Gough posit appear sensible and open to universal agreement.[52] Moreover, that they recognise their list of 'intermediate needs' to be in some sense 'arbitrary' gives an added awareness to the diversity of needs within and between cultures.[53] Universal conceptions of need are therefore being linked with the particular. Uniting the universal with the particular is obviously important, but one of the ways in which Doyal and Gough do this requires a caveat. They make a clear distinction between a need as objective and a want as subjective.[54] The basic needs and the 'intermediate needs' they posit are objective. Subjective wants arise beyond what they refer to as the 'minimum optimorum' or 'minopt' level of intermediate need-satisfaction.[55] This 'minopt' level is *'the minimum quantity of intermediate need-satisfaction required to produce the optimum level of basic need-satisfaction* in terms of the physical health and autonomy of individuals'.[56] The 'intermediate need' for nutritional food, for instance, is a need for the minimum level of food that yields the optimum level of health and autonomy in a particular society. Doyal and Gough use the 'minopt' level as a standard, therefore, to judge the satisfaction of needs in any nation state.[57]

It is in a response to criticism from Kate Soper that Doyal's and Gough's emphasis on distinguishing needs from wants, through the use of this 'minopt' level, runs into difficulty.[58] Soper criticises them for neglecting the importance of the wants of individual subjects in terms of human flourishing.[59] She argues that a greater consideration of 'spiritual' wants in relation to basic needs could give a better comprehensiveness to their theory.[60] In his reply, Doyal equates the term 'want' with desire, and suggests that such wants or desires are not as distinct from needs as Soper supposes.[61] He states, for instance, that, 'the satisfaction of need can, and often does, completely overlap with the satisfaction of desire'.[62] 'Desire' used euphemistically as a 'want', however, undermines their search for universal, objective basic needs distinct from the subjective wants that was the bedrock of their theory in the first place. They posited their 'intermediate needs' as distinct from wants so such needs could apply to all cultures. Now Doyal seems to be saying needs and wants can overlap, which weakens the very universality of their original theory. It seems that their preoccupation with universal needs leads them to neglect the relationship between such needs and wants – a one-sidedness which Doyal does admit to.[63] So while they do attempt to overcome relativism, it may be at the cost of undertheorising the relationship between needs and wants. This will be of importance later when considering how such arguments apply to the concept of need in the writings of Hegel and Marx. As I intimated at the outset, their emphasis on analysing forms means that they do not understand universal and particular notions of need as distinct and separate. On the contrary, comprehending these moments of need means grasping them as a contradictory unity. Deducing their inner connection, in terms of their universal and particular form, can then offer the possibility of overcoming the dichotomy that besets modern need theory. That both Hegel and Marx do this will become clear throughout the rest of this book.

CONCLUSION

This overview of some of the main issues in modern need theory will serve as a useful reference point for our analysis of Hegel's and Marx's understanding of needs in the forthcoming chapters. Debates around the human/nonhuman animal distinction for needs, along with the more crucial relationship between needs and wants and the issue of relativism, will all reappear in the forthcoming examination of Hegel's and Marx's writings. Indeed, I have already given some general indications of how Hegel's and Marx's understanding of needs can make a cogent contribution to the major problems that beset modern need theory. This will become abundantly clear in the forthcoming chapters. To begin with, however, it is essential to examine the methods of Hegel and Marx. A major argument of this study is that it is their own method of analysis which we can usefully employ to deduce a proper understanding of the concept of need from their writings. The next chapter offers an explication, therefore, of how Hegel and Marx analyse concepts and conduct their own inquiries. Analysing forms is the key to this procedure, and its efficacy will become clear in the examination of the concept of need in their works.

NOTES

1. K. Soper, *Troubled Pleasures* (Verso, London and New York, 1990), p. 72.
2. Some of the principal works have been: R. Fitzgerald (ed.) *Human Needs and Politics* (Pergamon, Ruschcutters Bay NSW, 1977); K. Lederer, *Human Needs* (Oelgeschlager, Gunn and Hain, Cambridge MA, 1980); K. Soper, *On Human Needs: Open and Closed Theories in a Marxist Perspective* (Harvester Press, Brighton, 1981); P. Springborg, *The Problem of Human Needs and the Critique of Civilisation* (Allen and Unwin, London, 1981); G. Thompson, *Needs* (Routledge and Kegan Paul, London, 1987); D. Braybrooke, *Meeting Needs* (Princeton University Press, Princeton NJ, 1987); L. Doyal and I. Gough, *A Theory of Human Need* (Macmillan, London, 1991).
3. See P. Singer, *Animal Liberation* (Jonathan Cape, London, 1976), Ch. 2. This is not to deny that the term 'human' does not contain further problems. Some feminists, for instance, argue that philosophers conceive the term 'human' as applying only to men. See, for example, S. M. Okin, *Women in Western Political Thought* (Princeton University Press, Princeton NJ, 1979), p. 7.
4. Singer, *Animal Liberation*, pp. 9–10.
5. J. Rachels, 'Darwin, Species and Morality', *Monist*, 1, 70, 1987, p. 98.
6. R. J. Halliday, 'Human Nature and Comparison', *Australian Journal of Politics and History*, 36, 3, 1990, p. 347.
7. J. Griffin, *Well-Being: Its Meaning, Measurement and Moral Importance* (Clarendon Press, Oxford, 1988), p. 42.
8. R. Descartes, 'Discourse on Method', in R. Descartes, *Discourse on Method and Other Writings*, trans. A. Wollaston (Penguin, Harmondsworth, 1966), pp. 78–82.
9. A. Maslow, *Motivation and Personality* (Harper and Row, New York, Evanston and London, 2nd edition, 1970).
10. Maslow, *Motivation and Personality*, pp. 35–46.
11. Maslow, *Motivation and Personality*, p. 97.
12. See Maslow, *Motivation and Personality*, Ch. 6.
13. Springborg, *Problem of Human Needs*, pp. 184–90.
14. The term 'sociobiology' was developed by E. O. Wilson in his *Sociobiology: The New Synthesis* (Harvard University Press, Cambridge, MA, 1975), and *On Human Nature* (Harvard University Press, Cambridge, MA, 1978). It basically refers to the explanation of the social activities of all social animals in terms of biological factors. For an overview of the issues this raises see A. L. Caplan, *The Sociobiology Debate: Readings on Ethical and Scientific Issues* (Harper and Row, New York, 1978); P. Kitcher, *Vaulting Ambition: Sociobiology and the Quest for Human Nature* (MIT Press, Cambridge MA, 1985).

15. M. Midgley, *Beast and Man* (Methuen, London, 1978), pp. 25–6.

16. Doyal and Gough, *Theory of Human Need*, p. 38.

17. Doyal and Gough, *Theory of Human Need*, p. 38.

18. Doyal and Gough, *Theory of Human Need*, p. 37.

19. Quoted in Rachels, 'Darwin, Species and Morality', p. 101.

20. See S. Walker, *Animal Thought* (Routledge and Kegan Paul, London, 1985).

21. Doyal and Gough, *Theory of Human Need*, p. 36.

22. Thompson, *Needs*, pp. 13–15.

23. Thompson, *Needs*, p. 13.

24. Doyal and Gough, *Theory of Human Need*, p. 38.

25. A. White, *Modal Thinking* (Blackwell Oxford), 1971, p. 114; Doyal and Gough, *Theory of Human Need*, p. 39; D. Wiggins, *Needs, Values, Truth* (Blackwell, Oxford and Cambridge MA, 2nd edition, 1991), p. 6; D. Miller, *Social Justice* (Clarendon Press, Oxford, 1976), p. 129.

26. On this see T. M. Scanlon, 'Preference and Urgency', *Journal of Philosophy*, 72, 1975. Cited in B. Barry, *Political Argument* (Harvester Wheatsheaf, Hemel Hempstead, 1990), p. lxix.

27. Doyal and Gough, *Theory of Human Need*, pp. 41–2; Wiggins, *Needs, Values, Truth*, p. 6; White, *Modal Thinking*, p. 114.

28. Miller, *Social Justice*, p. 129.

29. Doyal and Gough, *Theory of Human Need*, p. 42. R. Plant, *Modern Political Thought* (Blackwell, Oxford and Cambridge MA, 1991), pp. 190–1, drawing on White, *Modal Thinking*, p. 112.

30. On the terms 'intentionality/extensionality' and 'referentially opaque/transparent' see S. Blackburn, *The Oxford Dictionary of Philosophy* (Oxford University Press, Oxford, 1994), pp. 132–3, 196, 323.

31. Barry, *Political Argument*, pp. lxv–lxvi.

32. Thompson, *Needs*, p. 9; Doyal and Gough, *Theory of Human Need*, p. 39.

33. See N. Fraser, *Unruly Practices: Power, Discourse and Gender in Contemporary Social Theory* (Polity Press, Cambridge, 1989), p. 163.

34. K. Soper, 'A Theory of Human Need', *New Left Review*, 197, January/February, 1993, p. 116.

35. For a selection of these types of argument see the essays in F. Apffel Marglin and S. A. Marglin (eds) *Dominating Knowledge: Development, Culture and Resistance* (Clarendon Press, Oxford, 1990).

36. S. A. Marglin, 'Towards the Decolonization of the Mind', in Apffel Marglin and Marglin (eds) *Dominating Knowledge*, p. 12.

37. Marglin, 'Towards the Decolonization of the Mind', p. 14.

38. Marglin, 'Towards the Decolonization of the Mind', p. 14.

39. For a more open and diverse understanding of cultural membership see J. Waldron, 'Minority Cultures and the Cosmopolitan Alternative', in W. Kymlicka (ed.) *The Rights of Minority Cultures* (Oxford University Press, Oxford, 1995). As a clear example that belief systems in a culture are not total, Gutman offers the case of the conflicting understanding of kinship within the supposedly homogenous cult of Mormonism. A. Gutman, 'The Challenge of Multiculturalism in Political Ethics', *Philosophy and Public Affairs*, 22, 3, 1993, as discussed in S. Mendus, 'Human Rights in Political Theory', *Political Studies*, 43, Special Issue, 1995, p. 12, Alternatively, Russell Jacoby stresses the increasing homogeneity of cultural identity. He suggests, for instance, that the reputedly multicultural society of America is in fact one culture. As he states: 'America's multiple "cultures" exist

within a single consumer society . . . Chicanos, like Chinese Americans, want to hold good jobs, live in the suburbs, and drive well-engineered cars. This is fine – so does almost everyone – but how do these activities compose unique cultures?' R. Jacoby, 'The Myth of Multiculturalism', *New Left Review*, 208, November/December, 1994, p. 123

40. Soper, 'Theory of Human Need', p. 114.

41. M. Nussbaum, 'Human Functioning and Social Justice: In Defence of Aristotelian Essentialism', *Political Theory*, 20, 2, May, 1992, p. 214.

42. Nussbaum, 'Human Functioning' pp. 216–23.

43. Nussbaum, 'Human Functioning', p. 226.

44. See R. Rorty, 'Human Rights, Rationally and Sentimentality', in S. Shute and S. Hurley (eds) *On Human Rights: The Oxford Amnesty Lectures* (Basic Books, New York, 1993).

45. Doyal and Gough, *Theory of Human Need*, pp. 39–42, 50–5. This has been explained more concisely by Len Doyal in his response to Soper's criticism of their book. See L. Doyal, 'Thinking About Human Need', *New Left Review*, 201, September/October, 1993, pp. 114–15.

46. Doyal and Gough, *Theory of Human Need*, p. 55.

47. Doyal and Gough, *Theory of Human Need*, p. 157.

48. Doyal and Gough, *Theory of Human Need*, p. 157.

49. Doyal and Gough, *Theory of Human Need*, pp. 157–8. The full list is: nutritional food and clean water; protective housing; a non-hazardous work environment; a non-hazardous physical environment; appropriate health care; security in childhood; significant primary relationships; physical security; economic security; appropriate education; safe birth control and child-bearing.

50. Doyal and Gough, *Theory of Human Need*, p. 158.

51. Doyal and Gough, *Theory of Human Need*, p. 157.

52. It should be noted, however, that extreme relativists see even the preference of life over death as a particularly western conception. So they would be forced to argue that health is not a basic need. See F. Apffel Marglin, 'Smallpox in Two Systems of Knowledge', in Apffel Marglin and Marglin (eds) *Dominating Knowledge*. See also Nussbaum's discussion of this issue, 'Human Functioning', pp. 203–4.

53. Doyal and Gough, *Theory of Human Need*, p. 159.

54. Doyal and Gough, *Theory of Human Need*, pp. 39–42.

55. Doyal and Gough, *Theory of Human Need*, pp. 162–3. Doyal, 'Thinking About Human Need', p. 125.

56. Doyal and Gough, *Theory of Human Need*, pp. 162–3.

57. Doyal and Gough, *Theory of Human Need*, p. 169.

58. Doyal, 'Thinking About Human Need', p. 125.

59. Soper, 'Theory of Human Need', pp. 127–8.

60. Soper, 'Theory of Human Need', pp. 127.

61. Doyal, 'Thinking About Human Need', pp. 127–8.

62. Doyal, 'Thinking About Human Need', p. 127.

63. Doyal, 'Thinking About Human Need', p. 128.

2

HEGEL, MARX, DIALECTIC
AND FORM

How should we understand Marx's relation to Hegel in terms of his dialectic? Marx was in no doubt about this when he declared: 'My dialectical method is, in its foundation, not only different from the Hegelian, but exactly opposite to it.'[1] In the introduction, however, we noted how the Hegel–Marx relationship depicted in this book would be one of general agreement rather than opposition. Yet here is Marx saying quite explicitly that he opposes Hegel on the issue of the dialectic. How can this be?

Marx's gripe, of course, was that Hegel's idealistic philosophy shrouded the dialectic in mysticism. Consequently, this led many Marxists after Marx either to expunge or materialistically appropriate Hegel's dialectic to make it fit for a Marxist discourse untainted by idealism.[2] What this chapter intends to show, however, is that Marx and subsequent Marxist expungers and appropriators are wrong. I emphasise how Hegel's *and* Marx's dialectic are the same because they are both concerned to analyse forms to discover their inner connection. Hegel operates with a dialectic of universal and particular concept that is analogous to Marx's use of general and determinate abstraction. Only by misreading Hegel, as Marx and later Marxists have, does the need to expunge or materialistically appropriate his dialectic arise.

To accomplish this task, I begin by clearly outlining Hegel's dialectic and contrasting it with previous modes of thought, mainly, though not exclusively, through his *Logic*. Such an analysis reveals the materialist basis to Hegel's dialectic, highlighting the crucial role played by the movement of the Will. After explicating Marx's 'own' dialectic, drawing, in particular, on his comments in the *Grundrisse*, the final section examines his misplaced criticisms of Hegel's dialectic and thereby displays the similarities between the approaches of both thinkers in terms of analysing forms. The efficacy of this approach for understanding the concept of need will become clear in future chapters.

The emphasis on the *Logic* and the *Grundrisse* is important because

Marx explicitly referred to Hegel's *Logic* as being of 'great service' to him when formulating his 'own' method.[3] An understanding of Hegel's method in the *Logic* is therefore crucial for comprehending Marx's discussion of method in the *Grundrisse*. The *Logic/Grundrisse* interconnection is not, of course, the only route for exploring the Hegel–Marx relation. Some Marxists, following Kojeve[4] and French Hegelianism in general, have instead profitably explored the links between Hegel's *Phenomenology of Spirit* and Marx's early writings.[5] Marxists in this tradition, though, have tended to see the *Logic* and, in particular, the *Philosophy of Right* as essentially conservative texts in comparison to the radical nature of the *Phenomenology*.[6] So a further benefit of my discussion is to highlight the very radical implications of Hegel's thought even in his mature works. The *Logic* is my starting point as it was for those Marxists who were fully aware of the potency of this text for understanding the unity between theory and practice. 'There is no concrete problem that I meet daily', declared Raya Dunayevskaya, 'no matter how minor, that doesn't send me scurrying to the *Logic*.'[7] We too, now, must 'scurry' to this work to grasp the dialectical movement of the subject in and against the very world it has created.

HEGEL AND SPECULATIVE DIALECTICS

Hegel explains his dialectic through what he terms his 'Speculative Logic'.[8] The latter 'contains all previous Logic and Metaphysics: it preserves the same forms of thought, the same laws and objects – while at the same time remodelling and expanding them with wider categories'.[9] So speculative logic builds on previous philosophy by taking over its concepts and subjecting them to a careful critique. Hegel encapsulates this development through the three moments of this logic: the understanding, the dialectic and the speculative.[10]

Thought at the level of the understanding holds determinations in a fixed manner, and sees them as being abstract and distinct from one another.[11] Hegel refers to this phase of philosophical development as the 'Pre-Kantian Metaphysic'. Its weakness was that it remained in the realm of abstract identities and was unable, therefore, to advance from these universal abstractions to their particular manifestations in reality.

In contrast, empiricism, a further moment of the understanding, did move away from abstractions and concentrated on the 'actual world'.[12] This was an important contribution to philosophical thought because it suggested that the external world was a repository for truth.[13] Even so, the data or assumptions empiricism used were 'neither accounted for nor deducted'.[14] It treated phenomena in the world in a 'style utterly thoughtless and uncritical'.[15] Moreover, empiricism failed to relate universal and particular aspects of phenomena to each other, apprehending them only as opposed and distinct entities.[16]

The dialectic is the recognition of the movement between these fixed determinations which 'supersede themselves, and pass into their opposites'.[17] At this stage 'reason is negative . . . because it resolves the determinations of the understanding into nothing'.[18] It is Kant whom Hegel credits with restoring the dialectic to its 'post of honour'[19] through his antinomies or contradictions of reason.[20] Whereas the old metaphysical philosophy of the understanding believed that the existence of contradictions resulted from an accidental mistake in argument, Kant, in contrast, realised that thought necessarily brings in contradictions or antinomies. For him, these antinomies were concrete evidence that we had mistakenly tried to know something that was beyond our experience. He argued that this necessarily resulted in contradictions leading to a *'dialectic of illusion'*.[21] The aim of Kant's critique of pure reason is, therefore, 'only negative', its purpose being 'not to extend, but only to clarify our reason, and keep it free from errors'.[22]

Kant's limitation, according to Hegel, was in not realising the 'true and positive meaning of the Antinomies', which was 'that every actual thing involves a coexistence of opposed elements. Accordingly, to know, or in other words, to comprehend an object is equivalent to being conscious of it as a concrete unity of opposed determinations.'[23] Only with the final speculative stage does 'Positive Reason' emerge as we conceive the determinations, not as fixed or simply opposites, but as a 'unity . . . in their opposition'[24], or as the 'positive in the negative'.[25] The speculative stage for Hegel goes beyond the merely negative stage of reason in Kant. Speculative philosophy:

> rises above such oppositions as that between subjective and objective, which the understanding cannot get over, and absorbing them in itself, evinces its own concrete and all embracing nature . . . [Hence] in reality the subjective and objective are not merely identical but also distinct.[26]

Speculative philosophy goes beyond Kant in asserting that we can know the 'essential nature' of things through discerning the emanation of the positive in and out of the negative.

To try to get a clear understanding of this process, we can consider Hegel's discussion of being and nothing in the *Logic*. Hegel's aim in the latter is to 'begin with the subject matter itself, without preliminary reflections'.[27] Subjective thought must not take anything for granted or assume any concepts or principles of philosophical investigation. The problem with the understanding is that it does not contain this critical dimension and takes concepts like being and nothing as static and separate. However, if we begin by abstracting from all presuppositions and enter indeterminacy, then thought becomes '*being, pure being*, without any further determination'.[28] The only thing that thought can be in this state is nothing because it is 'pure indeterminateness and emptiness'.[29] So being, which, from the perspective of the understanding, seemed distinct from nothing, actually contained nothing within it. Similarly, nothing is not simply nothing. To think of nothing is to think of something (that is, nothing), and in thinking of nothing we are thinking of the indeterminate. So 'nothing is, therefore, the same determination or rather absence of determination, and thus altogether the same as, pure *being*'.[30]

An identity has occurred which equates pure being with pure nothing. The dialectical stage sees these categories as superseding themselves and turning into their opposites. It seems, though, that this identity between being and nothing leaves thought trapped and unable to escape from either being or nothing. However, it is the movement between the two that Hegel wants to capture. The moment pure being is thought, it thinks not only of itself but of what it is to become, its opposite, which is nothing. Nothing is similarly going to become being, which implies that 'their truth is, therefore, this movement of the immediate vanishing of the one in the other: *becoming*, a movement in which both are distinguished, but by a difference which has immediately resolved itself'.[31] This 'becoming', the movement out of dialectical opposition into something new, is the speculative stage of 'positive reason'.

It is on the basis of this discussion that we can begin to discern the crucial role of the concept for Hegel. He argues that the dialectic, the negative stage of reason, is the 'moving principle of the concept'.[32] The concept itself is 'genuine thought' about a thing rather than mere opinion.[33] For Hegel, 'philosophy is a knowledge through concepts'.[34] Whereas the understanding sees concepts as 'dead, empty and abstract', Hegel sees them as the 'principle of all life', which possess a 'character of thorough concreteness'.[35] It is through the concept that philosophers can discover scientific truth.

Hegel indicates that the concept has three moments: the universal, the particular and the individual.[36] He stresses that we are to comprehend these moments, not as distinct or separate, but as 'simply one and the same concept'.[37] The universal concept, for instance, is not the same as the 'abstract generality' used by the understanding. The latter wrongly sees the universal concept as simply those features that are common to specific phenomena, whilst the 'particular . . . enjoys an existence of its own'.[38] The understanding abstracts from the particular, holding it distinct and separate. The universal concept, however, contains the particular and universal within itself.[39] To separate these moments – as the understanding does – is to operate with 'hollow and empty concepts' that are 'mere phantoms and shadows'.[40] Instead, the universal concept is 'self-particularising or self-specifying, and with undimmed clearness finds itself at home in its antithesis'.[41] To understand fully the concept of man, for example, requires a uniting of man as an abstraction with man in his mode of existence within the world.

So the universal, particular and individual are all interrelated, and when we concentrate on one we do so in the knowledge that we include the other moments also. We have to understand them as contradictions in a unity, otherwise we fall into the trap of positing empty abstractions, as in the old metaphysic, or, at the other extreme, remaining simply within the concrete sphere, as in empiricism.

The universal concept contains these moments and must also pass through them. Take Marxism as an example. As a universal concept, as an abstraction, it contains many general characteristics. In its particular manifestation it takes many forms. Stalinism was one such form. The particular manifestation of Marxism emerges in an individual, Stalin. Universal moves through the particular and the individual. Yet this is not a one-way process. There is a back-and-forth movement between these moments. The individual existence of Marxism in Stalin itself becomes a universal, or at least it did in terms of the former east European states. This reflects back into the universal concept of Marxism, which, conveniently, becomes indistinguishable from its Stalinist mode of existence. Universal, particular and individual are therefore distinct but also in a unity. The universal concept contains these moments and actualises itself through them.

Having indicated the important moments of the universal concept, Hegel continues to trace the dialectical development of the concept right up to the Idea. The definition of the latter is the concept and its actualisation.[42] What Hegel means by this is that the universal concept manifests itself into society. We comprehend the concept of property, for instance, not just as a concept – that is, the universal term 'property' – but as that concept becomes manifest in the real world as laws of property.[43] When the objective reality of property corresponds with the universal concept of property, then the Idea of property achieves reason and truth.[44] When they are not in correspondence, then the result is untruth or 'mere *Appearance*'.[45]

This relationship between the concept and its actualisation is crucial. Its misinterpretation can easily lead to a depiction of Hegel as a 'mystical idealist' in contrast to the materialist Marx. For instance, Paul Mattick Jr asserts that Hegel's preoccupation is with the 'self-development of

concepts', whereas Marx has a greater concern to explain 'the development of concepts by the "real individuals" whose activity constitutes the
history of society'.[46] Similarly, Tony Smith, despite making a decisive
contribution to showing the similarities between the dialectics of Hegel
and Marx, states that Hegel's 'idealistic theory of verification . . . never
leaves the sphere of ideas'.[47] In contrast, he contends, Marx emphasises
the importance of realising such theory in practice.[48] These writers
rebuke Hegel, therefore, for remaining at the level of theory, distinct
from practice, and for ignoring human self-activity in creating the world.
However, we can refute such criticisms in two important ways.

First, if Hegel remained at the level of ideas, in theory as distinct from
practice, then he would actually be contradicting what is distinctive about
his own method compared to the pre-Kantian metaphysic. The latter, as
we have seen, remained in the realm of abstraction and understood the
universal as distinct from the particular. Hegel, in contrast, wants to
understand the universal and particular not as separate, not as distinct
phenomena, but in a contradictory unity. He wants to unite theory and
practice by understanding the dialectical relationship between the concept, not just as an abstraction, but in its actualisation.

Second, the concepts themselves cannot be abstract propositions
thought up by Hegel separate from reality. This would suggest that
we could presuppose concepts and magically conjure them up from thin
air. Hegel is adamant that this is not a legitimate method of inquiry. This
is why he stresses the importance of beginning an inquiry without any
presuppositions. Instead, he argues that we must see these concepts as
arising from reality itself – from human beings in their interaction with
each other in the world. Concepts do not 'self-develop' because they are
tied to the development of what Hegel calls the Will, which as we shall
now see, represents the very 'real individuals' that critics such as Mattick
speak of.

Hegel indicates that the Will contains two moments, the universal and
the particular. The Will is universal when it is in a pure state of
indeterminacy,[49] and particular when it becomes concrete.[50] By abstracting from the 'real' world the Will can make itself universal. In its moment of
particularity, however, no such abstraction takes place, so the Will has to
posit itself in this 'real' world. As a particular Will, it looks after the
interests of itself, not of others. However, a two-way process takes place.
The individual Will interacts with other Wills to create institutions, which
themselves act to universalise the individual Will. It is through such
institutions that the particular Will develops into a universal one. The Will,
which in its immediate stage achieves universality by abstracting from the
particular, becomes particular as it actualises itself in the real world. The

universal, which embodies the rational aspect of this real world, eventually negates this particularity, resulting in an individual Will.[51]

Hegel refers to this Will as 'the activity of man in the widest sense'[52] and suggests that:

> it is only by this activity that the Idea as well as abstract characteristics generally, are realized, actualized; for of themselves they are powerless. The motive power that puts them in operation, and gives them determinate existence, is the need, instinct, inclination, and passion of man.[53]

Human beings give the reality to the concepts. On their own, simply as abstractions, such concepts are meaningless. Hence, for Hegel, just as for Marx, theory must be in a unity with practice. As C. L. R. James rightly argued nearly fifty years ago:

> *we will forget . . . at our peril*, that [for Hegel] categories, the forms of logic, are in Desire, Will, etc., *human feelings and actions.* We abstract them to think about them. But they come from there . . . [Hence] the key to the Hegelian dialectic and therefore to marxist thinking . . . [is that t]hought is not an instrument you apply to a content. The content moves, develops, changes and creates new categories of thought, and gives them direction.[54]

Whereas 'intelligence merely proposes to take the world as it is, Will takes steps to make the world what it ought to be'.[55] The Will does this by 'cancelling the contradiction between subjectivity and objectivity and in translating its ends from their subjective determination into an objective one'.[56] Just in case we are in any doubt, Hegel affirms how 'this activity is the *essential development* of the substantial content of the Idea, a development in which the concept determines the *Idea*, which is *itself* at first *abstract*, to [produce] the totality of its system'.[57] The Will moves out of abstraction, into society, and creates that society itself through 'its activity and labour', thereby realising the Idea.[58] Concepts do not 'self-develop' in the realm of thought separate from practice. Certainly, the ambiguity of Hegel's comments may at times suggest otherwise, but to argue as such would be to commit the same errors as the pre-Kantian metaphysic. The latter, as we have seen, stayed simply within the realm of thought, separating the abstract from the concrete. Hegel, however, explicitly repudiates such a dichotomy and instead roots his analysis in the concrete activity of real human beings, uniting abstract and concrete in a contradictory unity.

The dialectic, then, is the 'moving principle of the concept'. The concept is the Will. So the dialectic is the moving principle of the Will in and between its particular and universal aspects. Hegel argues that the driving force of the dialectic, and ultimately the concept or Will itself,

comes from the positive overcoming the negative.[59] The speculative stage
of 'positive reason' emerges out of this dialectical movement of the Will.
Out of the opposition of particular and universal in and against each
other, reason begins to manifest itself. It is in this sense that 'what is
rational is actual; and what is actual is rational'.[60] This does not mean that
what currently exists is rational in its observable form and that Hegel is
therefore justifying existing institutions and conditions. On the contrary,
it means that the rational is present even within an imperfect world, and
the speculative philosopher's task is to comprehend this rationality.[61]
Such comprehension has to take place amidst an observable disunity
between the particular and universal aspects of the Will. Yet it is through
such a division that a speculative philosophy can discern reason. Out of
the dislocations between the particular and universal, the very 'slaughter
bench'[62] of historical development, a 'positive content' emerges. It is the
'positive in the negative' that speculative philosophy is attempting to
grasp. Analysing the non-identity of the particular and universal can
reveal the identity between them.[63] This identity is the Idea itself and
occurs when the concept corresponds with its actuality; when universality
and particularity are in a unity. When the concept does not correspond to
actuality then the latter is 'mere *Appearance*' and untruth.[64] What is
rational in 'external existence . . . emerges in an infinite wealth of forms,
appearances and shapes . . . which only the concept can penetrate in order
to find the inner pulse, and detect its continued beat'.[65] The rational takes
these forms because there are contradictions between the concept and
actualisation through the movement of the Will. If we take the example of
labour, for instance, there is an obvious dislocation between the concept
of labour and its actualisation in society. Hegel sees labour as liberating,
but it is not liberating for all people in the form it takes within society.
This is because there is a disjunction between the universal and
particular. The mediation between the Will and the organisation of
society has taken an alien shape contrary to the fulfilling nature of
labour. Speculative philosophy's task is to unearth the rational aspect
of this non-identity, to make labour liberating and therefore congruent
with its concept.

   The notion of form, therefore, is crucial to a proper understanding of
Hegel's dialectic. Consequently, it is important to be aware of the ways in
which Hegel uses the term. At times, he seems to use form (*Form*) in
contrast to the word 'shape' (*Gestalt*). For instance, he notes how 'the
shape (*Gestaltung*) which the concept assumes in its actualisation . . . is
different from its *form* (*Form*) of being purely as a concept'.[66] However,
the distinction being made here is between 'form of being' and 'shape'.
'Form of being' is the universal concept, and 'shape' is the form that the

concept takes in its actualisation.[67] Hegel makes this much clearer when he refers to the concept as taking a 'specific form' as it becomes determinate.[68] This contrasts with 'form as totality' which relates to the concept as 'universal', and the 'immeasurable abbreviation of the multitudes of particular things'.[69] So the concept has a universal form, and a particular form, which Hegel, at times, also refers to as a 'shape' (*Gestalt*).

Hegel's discussion of essence and appearance emphasises further the importance he attaches to the notion of form. He declares that 'essence *has* a form and determinations of the form'.[70] So essence has a universal form and, in its determination, a particular form. For Hegel, the particular form essence assumes is appearance.[71] However, he takes care to note that essence in this form 'is not something beyond or behind appearance, but just because it is the essence which exists – the existence is *Appearance*'.[72] Appearance is therefore the mode of existence or form of essence. Essence is not something 'beyond' or 'behind' appearance and therefore unknowable – as Kant suggested – but appearance itself.[73] In contrast to Kant, Hegel argues that we can know what essence is because it becomes manifest, and exists in, the form of appearance. As we have seen, this is typical of all Hegel's categories. Being and nothing, for instance, are modes of existence of each other. His quantity/quality distinction is another classic example, in that 'quality is implicitly quality . . . and quantity is implicitly quality' and in their dialectical development they 'pass into each other'.[74] Quality's mode of existence is quantity and quantity's mode of existence is quality. Phenomena, then, can be the mode of existence of each other and thereby take particular forms in their existence. Being can exist as nothing, quantity as quality, universal as particular and so on. Speculative philosophy's task is to analyse these forms to discover their 'innermost nature . . . and their necessary connection'.[75]

The preceding analysis discovered a number of crucial aspects to Hegel's dialectic, and we will soon see how Marx replicates them in his 'own' dialectic. Hegel's concern is to examine the forms of particular phenomena, establish their connections with each other, and highlight the positive moments in the negative. These very forms arise from the conflicts between the universal and particular moments of the Will. We grasp this dialectical movement through speculative philosophy. We begin with the form, the complex concrete, and subject it to careful critique. We note the distinction between the universal aspect of the phenomenon under question and its determinate, particular mode of existence. This distinction is that not of the understanding, of keeping universal and particular separate, but of recognising them in a contradictory unity. We comprehend them not as *either* abstract *or* concrete, but as a back-and-forth movement between the two. Consequently, 'Hegel's categories are saturated with reality' and 'the Idea itself is real, *lives, moves, transforms reality*'.[76]

The portrayal of Hegel as a 'mystical idealist' is only possible, therefore, by ignoring the distinctiveness of his dialectic to previous thought, and by neglecting the role of the Will. Consequently, the criticisms of Marxists such as Mattick and Smith are as unfounded as Marx's – as the final section of this chapter will show. Next, however, we need to explicate Marx's 'own' dialectic.

CATEGORIES AND METHOD IN MARX

In the *Grundrisse*, which contains Marx's clearest attempt to outline his method, he makes a distinction between general and determinate abstractions. General abstraction refers to the abstraction from concrete social circumstances, which then allows attention to focus on a common element amongst phenomena.[77] An example of this, for Marx, is 'production in general', which is an abstraction from the differences that arise in production in particular social periods.

Determinate abstraction is a movement from the general to the particular or concrete. For Marx the 'scientifically correct method' is the ascent from 'the simple relations, such as labour, division of labour, need, exchange value, to the level of the state, exchange between nations and the world market'.[78] Hence, determinate abstraction involves understanding the concrete as a 'concentration of many determinations'.[79] The world market is thus a concentration of determinate abstractions that go all the way back to labour.

It is on this basis that Marx distinguishes his method from the method of classical political economy. Marx praised all the classical economists since the time of William Petty for investigating 'the real internal framework of bourgeois relations of production', in contrast to the:

> 'vulgar economists who only flounder around within the apparent framework of those relations . . . proclaiming for everlasting truths, the banal and complacent notions held by the bourgeois agents of production about their own world, which is to them the best possible one.'[80]

Previous classical political economy made a real contribution because it did try to analyse the internal framework of phenomena. Its 'best representatives', Smith and Ricardo, did attempt to analyse capital scientifically by investigating the commodity and its value.[81] Their chief failing, however, was in not asking the important question: 'Why this content has assumed that particular form.'[82]

Vulgar and classical political economists, however, do share a common weakness. Both confuse determinate with general abstractions. They posit what is particular to capitalist society as true for all societies. Inevitably, then, bourgeois political economists are unaware that their categories are ahistorical and have 'grown in the soil of capitalist society'; they have become 'imprisoned in the modes of thought created by capitalism'.[83] They see the forms labour or production takes in capital as always being this way – an 'everlasting truth' – and thus fail to realise that such forms are specific to the mode of production that prevails in a particular historical period. In this sense, political economy stopped being a scientific inquiry and simply became an apology for capital itself.[84]

Smith and Ricardo, for instance, make the mistake of having a concept of an individual as a general abstraction – the 'isolated hunter and fisherman' – which they then 'project into the past' as a 'natural individual'.[85] They make the general abstraction of the individual into the determinate abstraction, not as an individual necessarily was in that particular historical circumstance, but as Ricardo and Smith suppose the individual to be from their own 'notion of human nature'.[86] Recognising these abstractions as distinct and in a unity, however, can avoid such mistakes, whilst also exposing some of the uncritical assumptions of bourgeois thought.

For Marx, it is through tracing the internal relation between phenomena that we can discover the antagonistic relationship between capital and labour. This antagonistic relationship always expresses itself in forms, such as the state-form, value-form, etc. Penetrating these forms can unearth the very social relation they deny; so a relation that appears to be between things can in fact be revealed as a social relation between people. Why, though, do these social relations take fetishised forms? A key comment from Marx should help elucidate:

> The specific economic form in which unpaid surplus labour is pumped out of the direct producers determines the relationship of domination and servitude, as this grows directly out of production itself and reacts back on it in turn as a determinant. On this is based the entire configuration of the economic community arising from the actual relations of production, and hence also its specific political form.[87]

A basic antagonism exists at the heart of society which involves the exploitation of one group by another. Class struggle – the struggle over the extraction of this surplus[88] – is the basis of this conflict on which forms are realised. Capitalism operates in a way that denies workers control over what they produce, which means that commodities them-

selves begin to take on forms that seem devoid of social content. Hence, a
'definite social relation between men . . . assumes . . . the fantastic form
of a relation between things'.[89] The social relations of production – the
conflict over the extraction of the surplus – exist *'in the mode of being
denied'*.[90] Capitalism *appears* as the 'realm of Freedom, Equality, Property
and Bentham',[91] but it is really a realm of exploitation and conflict. As
Holloway notes, capitalism 'is a fragmented world, in which the interconnections between people are hidden from sight'.[92] Determinate
abstraction – the understanding of concrete forms as a contradictory
unity, which we analyse to discover their inner connection – can expose
this social basis.

For Marx, just as for Hegel, however, these forms are not appearances
that we penetrate to discover 'true reality'. They are instead mediations or
modes of existence of the class antagonism within capitalist society. This
is evident in Marx's comment that for producers, 'the social relations
between their private labours appear as what they are, i.e. they do not
appear as direct social relations between persons in their work, but rather
as material relations between persons and social relations between
things'.[93] This comment is only intelligible by understanding appearance
as a mediation of the social relation of these producers, otherwise Marx
would be endorsing a fetishised perspective and contradicting his whole
argument.[94] Moreover, the importance of recognising forms in this way
also rules out any dualistic understanding of phenomena. If the latter exist
as modes of existence of each other, then we must comprehend them as
contradictions in a unity and not as distinct and separate.

The foregoing analyses of both Hegel's and Marx's dialectics can now
serve as a basis for undermining Marx's criticisms of Hegel. The points of
contact between the approaches of the two thinkers already indicate this
possibility. Both share a concern to analyse forms in society to discover
their inner connection. Both understand phenomena, not separately or as
distinct, but as contradictions in a unity. Both operate their inquiries with
similar abstractions. Hegel's universal concept is Marx's general abstraction; Marx's determinate abstraction is Hegel's concept in its particularity
through the manifestation in society of the Will. On this basis, it is very
difficult to see how Marx can distinguish his own dialectic from Hegel's;
just how difficult will now become clear as we put Marx's quibbles to the
test.

MARX'S MISPLACED CRITICISMS

On most, if not all, the occasions Marx refers to Hegel, it is to praise him
on the one hand while bemoaning his deficiencies on the other. A typical

example is Marx's critique of Hegel's *Philosophy of Right*, written in 1843, in which he asserts that mysticism envelops Hegel's method, trapping it within the realms of thought. As Marx argues:

> The family and civil society are real parts of the state, real spiritual manifestations of will, they are the state's forms of existence; the family and civil society make *themselves* into the state. They are the driving force . . . [Hence] the state evolves from the mass existing as members of families and civil society; speculative philosophy, [however], explains this fact as the act of the Idea, not as the Idea of the mass, but as the act of a subjective Idea.[95]

Marx is suggesting that Hegel's speculative philosophy understands the formation of the state only theoretically, abstractly, not practically. As we have seen, however, Hegel makes no such contention. For Hegel, the 'Idea of mass' *is* in fact the Will actualising itself in the world – the very 'real spiritual manifestation' that Marx is so keen on. Hegel's point is precisely that it is human beings, the mass, that create the state, and this is how the concept of state becomes actualised. Marx is interpreting Hegel's Idea as something mental, but it is in fact the very 'Idea of mass' that Marx himself is eager to support.

Marx commits further misinterpretations of Hegel's dialectic in the *Grundrisse*, where, as we have seen, Marx has most clearly set out his 'own' dialectical method. He argues that Hegel 'fell into the illusion of conceiving the real as the product of thought concentrating itself, probing its own depths, and unfolding itself out of itself, by itself'.[96] He suggests that Hegel errs in supposing that thinking itself can cause changes in the 'real'.[97]

Again, this is a clear misinterpretation of Hegel's argument. We have seen him say that thought is 'powerless'[98] without the Will to actualise it. Thought arises from, and is actualised by, the 'real' in a dialectical unity – the unity of theory and practice. Thought does not unfold itself out of itself but is manifest in the dialectical movement of the Will as the 'activity and labour' of real human beings.

Even ten years before his death, Marx was still trying to divorce his own dialectical method from the 'mystical' dialectic of Hegel. This is in response to a review of *Capital* by the Russian economist I. I. Kaufmann. The latter criticises Marx for having a philosophically 'idealist' method of presentation, and a 'realistic' method of inquiry.[99] Marx attempts to use the actual review by Kaufmann to refute such a contention.

Kaufmann notes how Marx's concern is to find the laws of phenomena that have a 'definite form and mutual connection within a given historical period'.[100] Even more importantly, he realises that Marx wants to understand phenomena in 'their transition from one form into another; from one series of connections into a different one'.[101] Immediately, Kaufmann presents us with the importance of form and dialectical transition, recognising that phenomena have inner connections with each other – contradictions in a unity. 'What else', asks Marx, 'is [Kaufmann] depicting but the dialectical method?'[102] What else, of course! However, Marx neither recognises nor acknowledges that such a method of analysing forms is the same as Hegel's.

Marx still has to respond to Kaufmann's criticism concerning the idealistic presentation and the realistic form of inquiry. In so doing, he again unwittingly displays the similarity of his own dialectical method to Hegel's. Marx argues that presentation and inquiry must indeed differ. The method of inquiry 'has to appropriate the material in detail, to analyse its different forms of development and to track down their inner connection'.[103] The method of inquiry is, therefore, nothing other than the analysing of forms. The phenomena under consideration are subject to a critique which attempts to find their inner relation. These phenomena are forms, modes of existence, which are not distinct and separate from one another, but intrinsically linked in a dialectical unity – unity in difference. Only at the end of this inquiry is the 'real movement' presented as the 'life of the subject matter is reflected back into the ideas'. Marx realises that this can give the impression of an '*a priori* construction', and this is what Kaufmann has mistakenly taken for the 'idealistic' method of presentation.[104]

What Marx is saying here is that when we carry out any particular investigation of phenomena, we begin by a concrete analysis of these phenomena understood as forms. When this inquiry is complete, its presentation begins not with the concrete but with the abstract. The method of inquiry moves from concrete to abstract, but the method of presentation moves from abstract to concrete. As Marx pointed out in the *Grundrisse*:

> The concrete is concrete because it is the concentration of many determinations, hence unity of the diverse. It appears in the process of thinking, therefore, as a process of concentration as a result, not as a point of departure, even though it is the point of departure in reality and hence also the point of departure for observation and conception.[105]

Any investigation of phenomena confronts the concrete, which itself is complex. If we were to examine the concept of money, for instance, we would see that it takes many different forms in society. In its concrete manifestation it is a complex phenomenon. To thought, this concrete appears as a 'result', an end point, not a starting point: 'This is money. This is how money manifests itself in society'. Money *appears* to thought in this way, yet in reality this appearance is not an end point but the 'point of departure'. For 'observation and conception', we actually begin with the result – the concrete form money takes in society. The method of inquiry must therefore begin with the forms phenomena take in society and subject them to a critique to find their inner connection. Once accomplished, the method of presentation is then from the abstract to the concrete; from general to determinate abstraction. Marx, just like Hegel, realises that anyone beginning an inquiry with a general abstraction presupposes what he has yet to prove. Instead, a dialectical approach must begin with phenomena as they appear in actuality. Hegel's own method mirrors the approach of Marx.

The reflection of Marx's general abstraction is Hegel's concept as universal. The particularisation takes place in the concrete through the movement of the Will in society. Thought, therefore, begins with the concrete appearance of the concept in the real world; that is, the form it takes in its manifestation within society. It is not changes in thought that change the 'real' for Hegel, as Marx implies, but the Will actualising itself in the world.

This similarity between Hegel and Marx becomes even clearer when Marx, in his discussion of the concept of labour, mentions how 'the abstraction of the category "labour"', "labour as such"', labour pure and simple, becomes true in practice'.[106] In capitalist society, labour as an abstraction in thought becomes determinate; that is, it manifests itself in concrete reality. The concept has become actualised and the form it takes in capitalist society is itself abstract.[107] The link with Hegel is clear: Marx is talking about the concept and its actualisation just as Hegel is, despite Marx's attempt to confine Hegel's dialectic to the realm of thought.

Notwithstanding Marx's assertions here, Carver suggests that he does not follow the edicts of his own method in *Capital*.[108] Carver argues that Marx's starting point with the commodity is not a matter of ascending from the abstract to the concrete or simple to complex. However, Carver does indicate that the overall structure of *Capital* conforms to such a method in the movement from the commodity to money to capital accumulation, circulation of capital and the 'process as a whole'.[109] In contrast to Carver, Murray argues that Marx does begin *Capital* by moving from the abstract to the concrete as set out in the *Grundrisse*. Murray points out that the general abstraction Marx makes here is the use value of the commodity, whereas the determinate abstraction is the exchange value of the commodity.[110] Both arguments, however, are very problematic. Murray, in arguing that use value is the general abstraction, and Carver, in arguing that Marx starts with the concrete

commodity, have both missed Marx's first move, which is not the
commodity, but the general abstraction of wealth. As Marx states:

> The wealth of societies in which the capitalist mode of production prevails appears
> as an 'immense collection of commodities'; the individual commodity appears as its
> elementary form. Our investigation begins therefore with the commodity.[111]

Wealth, the general abstraction, takes the 'form' of the commodity. The
commodity is itself a determinate abstraction, with further determinate
abstractions in terms of use value and exchange value. Marx analyses the
commodity because it is the 'elementary form' wealth takes in society.[112]
This process develops through further determinate abstractions as value
manifests itself in the circulatory sphere in the form of prices, interests,
etc. Eventually, we reach the contradictory unity of the concrete itself
with all the different forms wealth can take. So Marx is moving from the
abstract to the concrete, simple to complex, in *Capital*, contrary to
Carver's assertion, and from the general abstraction of wealth not use
value, contrary to Murray's. Ironically, Murray does eventually identify
wealth as a general abstraction.[113] How this general abstraction relates to
his supposed general abstraction of use value, however, is unclear.

Further support for such an argument is evident in the *Grundrisse*
itself. In his foreword to this work, Nicolaus correctly notes how, in the
last page of the seventh notebook on value, Marx employs almost the same
opening sentence that he will use for Volume 1 of *Capital*.[114] Marx
himself says that 'this section is to be brought forward'.[115] So at the end of
the *Grundrisse*, which is, after all, Marx's method in action, he reaches a
conclusion that must be *presented* at the beginning. The method is
therefore concrete to abstract, but the presentation has to be abstract
to concrete, which confirms what we have just outlined. This becomes
even clearer in Marx's 'Notes on Adolph Wagner' where he states:

> I do not start out from 'concepts', hence I do not start out from 'the concept of
> value', and do not have 'to divide' these in any way. What I start out from is the
> simplest social form in which the labour-product is presented in contemporary
> society, and this is the 'commodity'. I analyse it, and right from the beginning, in
> the *form in which it appears*.[116]

Although Nicolaus recognises this fact, he falls into the same trap as
Carver in seeing the commodity as Marx's 'concrete' starting point in
Capital. Yet as the above quotation suggests, Marx is obviously referring
to his method of inquiry, beginning with the form, rather than the method
of presentation.

Marx's method of inquiry, concrete to abstract, and presentation, abstract to concrete, find a direct correspondence in Hegel's own approach. In terms of the method of inquiry, Hegel begins with forms, appearances in the complex concrete that arise through the dialectical development of the Will. To understand these forms properly we abstract from them in terms of a universal concept. We then examine and identify the positive and negative moments between the universal concept and its particular manifestation, tracing the dialectical movement between these universal and particular, abstract and concrete, moments. When we present this, the starting point is the abstract universal and not the complex forms of the concrete. Hegel's *Philosophy of Right*, for instance, moves from abstract right to morality to ethical life, following the development of the Will. His method of inquiry, however, begins with '*what is*' – the complex concrete of 'forms, appearances and shapes'.[117] The investigation of these forms through the universal concept can uncover their positive moments, their interconnections and their 'innermost nature'.[118]

It should be clear, then, that Marx's method of inquiry of analysing forms finds a direct correspondence in Hegel's own method. Both thinkers move from the concrete forms to the abstract, particular to universal. In their method of presentation they move from the abstract to the concrete, universal to particular.

This discussion should make us sceptical, therefore, concerning Marx's most famous, or rather infamous, comment on the relationship of Hegel's dialectic with his own. Marx argues that, for Hegel, the dialectic 'is standing on its head' so 'it must be inverted, in order to discover the rational kernel within the mystical shell'.[119] In trying to account for this statement, Carver has noted how 'Hegelian and Marxian definitions of the dialectic are couched in strikingly similar terms' in that they both involve an 'account which specifie[s] the contradictory – e.g., positive *and* negative – aspects of whatever [i]s under scrutiny'.[120] Carver interprets the latter as being the 'rational kernel' Marx refers to. The 'mystical shell' relates to 'Hegel's confusion between what Marx called . . . "the conceived world" (or "the movement of categories") and actuality'.[121]

Carver may be giving an adequate account of the way Marx thought he was superseding Hegel's dialectic, but that does not mean Marx was correct. Indeed, our preceding argument shows the fallacy of Marx's argument here. Hegel's dialectic does not need inverting because he does not encase it in a mystical shell. Hegel does not confuse the movement of categories with movement in the world because the activity of the Will makes the categories real. As MacGregor has rightly noted, in misinterpreting Hegel in this way Marx 'helped create the myth of Hegel the idealist who had everything upside down'.[122] Yet the only thing that was upside down was Marx's reading of Hegel itself. Consequently, much of

Marxist scholarship in this area has been far too content to see Hegel through Marx's eyes instead of subjecting Marx's own comments to a careful critique – a typically unmarxist approach to take.[123]

CONCLUSION

Marx's criticisms of Hegel serve only to reveal the basic similarities in their dialectical method. Marx operates with general and determinate abstractions. For Hegel, the general abstraction is the universal concept whilst the determinate abstraction is the actualisation of the concept in its particularity. Both thinkers understand the determinate abstraction and the particularisation to be forms – the mode of existence of the general abstraction or universal concept in society. In their method of inquiry both begin by analysing these forms to discover their inner connection. In terms of presentation both begin with the abstract and move to the concrete.

Marx's method emphasises the importance of understanding the forms class struggle takes in capital. Consequently, the very categories Marx uses are 'categories of antagonism' – 'fundamental forms in which the antagonistic social relations present themselves'.[124] This is why the concept of 'becoming', inherited from Hegel's discussion of being and nothing in the *Logic*, is so important. Marx mistakenly interprets Hegel as simply seeing concepts 'move' outside the real movement of history,[125] but as I have shown this is not the case. Hegel actually perceives concepts as being involved in a process of 'becoming', a process of motion. The concept and its actualisation, the movement of the concept through the movement of the Will in and between its universal and particular moments, are the forms that have to be subject to scrutiny for Hegel. Hegel *and* Marx are at one, therefore, on the importance of analysing forms to discover their inner connection. They both focus on the contradictory movement of human beings, real subjects, in the shaping and making of their world.

It follows, then, that a materialist appropriation or rejection of Hegel's dialectic is unnecessary for Marxists. On the contrary, Hegel 'is the most rigid of materialists', who 'practised and taught a very materialistic form of dialectic'.[126] Marx may not have seen this, but his 'own' dialectic clearly parallels that of Hegel's. General abstraction is universal concept; determinate abstraction is particular concept; the dialectic of Hegel *is* the dialectic of Marx.

It is on the basis of this method that we can now examine the concept of need in the writings of Hegel and Marx. I contend that attention to form is essential for a correct understanding of Hegel's and Marx's need theory.

Why do needs take the forms they do in capital? How do these forms relate to the social relations of production? These are the questions that we will consider when examining Marx's understanding of needs. Similarly, for Hegel, we have to comprehend the form the concept of need takes in society through the dialectical development of the Will – real human beings who make and shape their world on the basis of 'need, instinct, inclination and passion'.[127] To this end, the next three chapters consider the concept of need in three of Hegel's writings: *System of Ethical Life*; *Philosophy of Right*; and *Aesthetics*. An examination of each of these works will reveal the cogency of Hegel's need theory based on analysing needs as forms and deducing their inner connections.

NOTES

1. K. Marx, *Capital*, Volume 1, trans. B. Fowkes (Penguin, Harmondsworth, 1988), p. 102.
2. See above, p. 1.
3. K. Marx and F. Engels, *Selected Correspondence* (Progress Publishers, Moscow, 1975), p. 93.
4. A. Kojeve, *Introduction to the Reading of Hegel* (Basic Books, New York, 1969).
5. V. Descombes, *Modern French Philosophy* (Cambridge University Press, Cambridge, 1980).
6. R. Gunn, ' "Recognition" in Hegel's *Phenomenology of Spirit*', *Common Sense*, 4, 1988, p. 40.
7. R. Dunayevskaya, *The Philosophic Moment of Marxist Humanism* (News and Letters, Chicago, 1989), p. 23.
8. G. W. F. Hegel, *The Logic of Hegel*, trans. W. Wallace (Clarendon Press, Oxford, 1892), para 9; Cf. para 13.
9. Hegel, *Logic of Hegel*, para 9.
10. G. W. F. Hegel, *The Science of Logic*, trans. A. V. Miller (Allen and Unwin, London, 1969), p. 29; Hegel, *Logic of Hegel*, para 79.
11. Hegel, *Science of Logic*, p. 29; and *Logic of Hegel*, para 79.
12. Hegel, *Logic of Hegel*, para 38.
13. Hegel, *Logic of Hegel*, para 38R.
14. Hegel, *Logic of Hegel*, paras 9 and 38R.
15. Hegel, *Logic of Hegel*, para 38.
16. Hegel, *Logic of Hegel*, para 9.
17. Hegel, *Logic of Hegel*, para 81.
18. Hegel, *Science of Logic*, p. 28.
19. Hegel, *Logic of Hegel*, para 81A.
20. I. Kant, *Critique of Pure Reason*, trans. N. Kemp Smith (Macmillan, London, 1992), A406/B433–A460/B488 (I use the standard A and B references throughout.) Plato is seen by Hegel as the 'inventor of dialectic' (*Logic of Hegel*, para 81A) but it is the 'deep thinking' Heraclitus that he particularly praises for overcoming the merely negative dialectic of the Eleatic philosophers Melissus, Parmenides and Zeno. See Hegel, *Science of Logic*, p. 83; Hegel *Logic of Hegel*, para 89A. For the importance of Heraclitus for Hegel's dialectic see H. Williams, *Hegel, Heraclitus and Marx's Dialectic* (Harvester Wheatsheaf, Hemel Hempstead, 1989).

21. Kant, *Critique of Pure Reason*, A293/B350.
22. Kant, *Critique of Pure Reason*, A12/B25.
23. Hegel, *Logic of Hegel*, para 48A.
24. Hegel, *Logic of Hegel*, para 82.
25. Hegel, *Science of Logic*, p. 56.
26. Hegel, *Logic of Hegel*, para 82A.
27. Hegel, *Science of Logic*, p. 43.
28. Hegel, *Science of Logic*, p. 82.
29. Hegel, *Science of Logic*, p. 82.
30. Hegel, *Science of Logic*, p. 82.
31. Hegel, *Science of Logic*, p. 83.
32. G. W. F. Hegel, *Elements of the Philosophy of Right*, trans. H. B. Nisbet (Cambridge University Press, Cambridge, 1991), para 31R, hereafter cited as PR.
33. Hegel, PR, p. 14.
34. Hegel, *Logic of Hegel*, para 160A. For ease of understanding I will be using the word 'concept' for '*Begriff*' rather than the term 'notion'.
35. Hegel, *Science of Logic*, p. 83.
36. Hegel, *Science of Logic*, pp. 600–1; Hegel, *Logic of Hegel*, paras 163–5.
37. Hegel, *Science of Logic*, p. 613.
38. Hegel, *Logic of Hegel*, para 163A.
39. Hegel, *Logic of Hegel*, para 164.
40. Hegel, *Logic of Hegel*, para 163A.
41. Hegel, *Logic of Hegel*, para 163A.
42. Hegel, PR, para 1; Hegel, *Logic of Hegel*, para 213; Hegel, *Science of Logic*, pp. 755–6.
43. Hegel, *Logic of Hegel*, para 160A; cf. M. Westphal, 'Hegel's Theory of the Concept', in W. E. Steinkraus and K. I. Schmitz (eds) *Art and Logic in Hegel's Philosophy* (Harvester, Brighton 1980).
44. Hegel, *Science of Logic*, p. 757.
45. Hegel, *Science of Logic*, p. 756.
46. P. Mattick Jr, 'Marx's Dialectic', in F. Moseley (ed.) *Marx's Method in Capital: A Reexamination* (Humanities Press, Atlantic Highlands NJ, 1993), p. 132.
47. T. Smith, *The Logic of Marx's Capital: Replies to Hegelian Criticisms* (State University of New York Press, Albany NY, 1990), p. 40.
48. Smith, *Logic of Marx's Capital*, p. 40.
49. Hegel, PR, para 5.
50. Hegel, PR, para 6.
51. Hegel, PR, para 24.
52. G. W. F. Hegel, *The Philosophy of History*, trans. J. Sibree (Dover, New York, 1956), p. 22.
53. Hegel, *Philosophy of History*, p. 22.
54. C. L. R. James, *Notes on Dialectics* (Allison and Busby, London, 1980), pp. 29, 15.
55. Hegel, *Logic of Hegel*, para 234A.
56. Hegel, PR, para 28.
57. Hegel, PR, para 28. Term in square brackets in the original translation.
58. Hegel, *Philosophy of History*, p. 22.
59. Hegel, PR, para, 1R.
60. Hegel, PR, p. 20.
61. Cf. S. Sayers, 'The Actual and the Rational', in D. Lamb (ed.) *Hegel and Modern Philosophy* (Croom Helm, London, 1987).
62. Hegel, *Philosophy of History*, p. 21.

63. G. Rose, *Hegel Contra Sociology* (Athlone, London, 1981), p. 49.

64. Hegel, *Science of Logic*, p. 756.

65. Hegel, PR, p. 21.

66. Hegel, PR, para 1R; G. W. F. Hegel, *Werke*, Volume VII (Suhrkamp Verlag, Frankfurt, 1970), p. 29.

67. As Inwood indicates in his discussion of these terms, '*Form*' can be both universal and particular, whereas '*Gestalt*' usually refers to a particular form. See M. Inwood, *A Hegel Dictionary* (Blackwell, Oxford, 1992), pp. 107–8.

68. Hegel, *Science of Logic*, p. 39.

69. Hegel, *Science of Logic*, p. 39.

70. Hegel, *Science of Logic*, p. 448.

71. Hegel, *Logic of Hegel*, para 131.

72. Hegel, *Logic of Hegel*, para 131.

73. Hegel, *Logic of Hegel*, para 131A; Kant, *Critique of Pure Reason*, A30/B45.

74. Hegel, *Logic of Hegel*, para 111A.

75. G. W. F. Hegel, *Philosophy of Spirit*, trans. W. Wallace and A. V. Miller (Oxford University Press, Oxford, 1971), p. 50.

76. R. Dunayevskaya, *Philosophy and Revolution* (Columbia University Press, New York, 1989), p. 43.

77. K. Marx, *Grundrisse*, trans. M. Nicolaus (Pelican, London, 1973), p. 85.

78. Marx, *Grundrisse*, pp. 100–1.

79. Marx, *Grundrisse*, p. 101.

80. Marx, *Capital*, Vol. 1, pp. 175–6, n. 34.

81. Marx, *Capital*, Vol. 1, p. 174, n. 34.

82. Marx, *Capital*, Vol. 1, p. 174. As Ollman correctly asserts: 'What is called "Marxism" is largely an investigation of the different forms human productive activity takes in capitalist society, the changes these forms undergo, how such changes are misunderstood, and the power acquired by these changed and misunderstood forms over the very people whose productive capacity brought them into existence in the first place.' B. Ollman, *Dialectical Investigations* (Routledge, London and New York, 1993), p. 43.

83. G. Lukács, *History and Class Consciousness*, (Merlin, London, 1990), p. 8.

84. Marx, *Capital*, Vol. 1, p. 97.

85. Marx, *Grundrisse*, p. 83.

86. Marx, *Grundrisse*, p. 83.

87. K. Marx, *Capital*, Volume 3, trans. D. Fernbach (Penguin, Harmondsworth, 1991), p. 927.

88. G. E. M. de Ste Croix, *The Class Struggle in the Ancient Greek World* (Duckworth, London, 1983), Ch. 2.

89. Marx, *Capital*, Vol. 1, p. 165.

90. R. Gunn, 'Against Historical Materialism: Marxism as a First-Order Discourse', in W. Bonefeld, R. Gunn and K. Psychopedis (eds) *Open Marxism. Volume II: Theory and Practice* (Pluto, London, 1992), p. 14.

91. Marx, *Capital*, Vol. 1, p. 280.

92. J. Holloway, 'Crisis, Fetishism, Class Composition', in Bonefeld, Gunn and Psychopedis (eds) *Open Marxism. Volume II*, p. 152.

93. Marx, *Capital*, Vol. 1, p. 166.

94. R. Gunn, 'Marxism and Mediation', *Common Sense*, 2, 1987.

95. K. Marx, 'Critique of Hegel's Doctrine of the State', in K. Marx, *Early Writings*, trans. R. Livingstone and G. Benton (Penguin, Harmondsworth, 1992), pp. 62–3.

96. Marx, *Grundrisse*, p. 101.

97. Similar sentiments can be found in Marx's critique of Proudhon in 1847. See K. Marx and F. Engels, *Collected Works*, Volume 6 (Lawrence and Wishart, London, 1976), particularly pp. 161–5.

98. Hegel, *Philosophy of History*, p. 22.

99. Marx, *Capital*, Vol. 1, p. 100.

100. Marx, *Capital*, Vol. 1, p. 100.

101. Marx, *Capital*, Vol. 1, p. 100.

102. Marx, *Capital*, Vol. 1, p. 102.

103. Marx, *Capital*, Vol. 1, p. 102.

104. Marx, *Capital*, Vol. 1, p. 102.

105. Marx, *Grundrisse*, p. 101.

106. Marx, *Grundrisse*, p. 105.

107. Marx, *Grundrisse*, p. 104.

108. T. Carver, 'Commentary', in K. Marx, *Texts on Method*, (trans. and ed.) T. Carver (Blackwell, Oxford, 1975), p. 135.

109. Carver, 'Commentary', p. 135.

110. P. Murray, *Marx's Theory of Scientific Knowledge* (Humanities Press, London, 1990), p. 141.

111. Marx, *Capital*, Vol. 1, p. 125.

112. As Cleaver suggests, this seemingly innocuous starting point is steeped in the basically antagonistic nature of the capitalist system itself. It is through the commodity form that capital forces people to labour to survive and to receive part of the social wealth they have created. See H. Cleaver, *Reading Capital Politically* (Harvester, Brighton, 1979), pp. 71–2.

113. Murray, *Marx's Theory of Scientific Knowledge*, p. 147.

114. M. Nicolaus, 'Foreword', in Marx *Grundrisse* p. 37.

115. Marx, *Grundrisse*, p. 881.

116. Marx, *Texts on Method*, p. 198.

117. Hegel, PR, p. 21.

118. Hegel, *Philosophy of Spirit*, p. 50.

119. Marx, *Capital*, Vol. 1, p. 103.

120. T. Carver, 'Marx – and Hegel's *Logic*', *Political Studies*, XXIV, 1, 1976, p. 66.

121. Carver, 'Marx – and Hegel's *Logic*', p. 67.

122. D. MacGregor, *The Communist Ideal in Hegel and Marx* (George Allen and Unwin, London and Sydney, 1984), p. 3. See also A. Shamsavari, *Dialectics and Social Theory: The Logic of Capital* (Merlin Books, Braunton, 1991), Ch. 4.

123. A tendency which is clearly present in Boger's discussion of the 'Afterword' to *Capital*. See G. Boger, 'On the Materialist Appropriation of Hegel's Dialectical Method', *Science and Society*, 55, 1, Spring, 1991, pp. 47–8.

124. Holloway, 'Crisis, Fetishism, Class Composition', p. 151.

125. Carver, 'Marx – and Hegel's *Logic*', p. 67.

126. James, *Notes on Dialectics*, p. 57.

127. Hegel, *Philosophy of History*, p. 22.

3

NEEDS IN HEGEL'S *SYSTEM OF ETHICAL LIFE*

Hegel wrote the *System of Ethical Life* between 1802 and 1803, well before he had fully worked out his speculative philosophical method, which I outlined in the previous chapter. This may cast doubt on being able to utilise Hegel's emphasis on form for discussing the concept of need in relation to this text. However, as H. S. Harris has suggested, the *System of Ethical Life* does offer the 'best example' of Hegel's 'method in its early form'.[1] J. E. Toews has also emphasised how it was during Hegel's Jena years that his speculative logic was born.[2] So the *System of Ethical Life* presents Hegel's method embryonically and can thus serve as a useful foundation for analysing Hegel's understanding of the concept of need through analysing forms.

As we saw in the previous chapter, speculative philosophy supersedes whilst preserving all previous thought, and one example of this was Hegel's transcendence of Kant's critical philosophy. In this early work, Hegel uses Kant's contrast between 'concept' and 'intuition' to chart the development of an individual consciousness through various levels or stages (*Potenzen*).[3] Hegel posits a persistent opposition between nature (concept) and spirit or ethical life (intuition) as the individual passes through these levels or stages.[4] In contrast to Kant and critical philosophy in general, however, Hegel understands these phenomena as 'oppositions in a unity', and not simply unmediated 'oppositions'.[5] Hegel, therefore, grasps the 'transition from propositions of identity to speculative propositions'.[6] Hence, the concept (nature) has to be subsumed under intuition (life), and intuition (life) has to be subsumed under the concept (nature) through relations of identity and non–identity. As Hegel states: 'each must be posited over against the other, now under the *form* of particularity, again under the *form* of universality'.[7] When the concept and intuition establish a 'perfect adequacy' between themselves, an individual attains 'knowledge of the Idea of the absolute ethical order' and thereby becomes fully rational.[8]

Right at the outset, then, in one of Hegel's earliest works, he refers to the importance of form for his overall framework of analysis. Both concept and intuition take the form of universal and particular. The dialectical movement of the unity and diversity between the two terms eventually reaches its 'absolute' in the totality that has the 'absolute people' as intuition, and the 'absolute oneness' of individuals as concept – the realm of ethical life proper where consciousness reaches its full development.[9]

The whole of the *System of Ethical Life* therefore represents movements between the subsumption of intuition under concept, and that of concept under intuition, which themselves take universal and particular forms. Moreover, the opposition Hegel posits between spirit and nature is one which recurs in his later writings and emphasises his concern for humans to overcome the tyranny of natural necessity. We can now see how Hegel highlights this opposition by focusing on how humans attempt to satisfy their needs at the most primitive level of ethical life.

NEEDS IN THE FIRST LEVEL OF ETHICAL LIFE

For Hegel, a moment of ethical life is present initially as a 'drive' (*Trieb*) within an individual consciousness even when the individual is in his or her most natural state.[10] 'Driven on, as impulse (*Trieb*) or striving (*Streben*)', the individual attempts to unite particularity with universality.[11] The subsumption of the concept under intuition begins this process at what Hegel calls the 'first level', the level of '*practice*', or the most 'natural' form of ethical life – 'nature proper'.[12] Here, ethical life is in a state of 'complete undifferentiatedness' as intuition wholly immerses itself in the singularity of '*feeling*' (*Gefühl*).[13] The supersession of feeling as 'singular and particular' is possible through the 'negation of the separation into subject and object'.[14] For Hegel, this 'feeling of separation is *need* (*Bedürfnis*)', whereas the supersession of the feeling of separation, through the mediation of labour, is 'enjoyment' (*Grenuß*).[15]

Feeling, itself, has two aspects, namely, feeling as subsuming the concept and feeling as subsumed under the concept.[16] When feeling is subsuming the concept this is 'the formal concept of feeling', which contains the moments of need, labour and enjoyment.[17] Humans are asserting a moment of spirit or the ethical as they begin to subordinate nature to the satisfaction of their needs. For example, if we have a need for a table it is initially an image in our heads. In this sense, there is a separation between the subject and the object. Labour is the mediation which overcomes this separation as we now actually construct a table. Once we realise our initial ideal determination and also use the table, we overcome the feeling of separation, or need, and therefore experience enjoyment. We have reached 'unity arising out of difference', the difference between the separation of subject and object.[18]

Hegel refers to feeling subsumed under the concept as 'the concept of practical feeling unfolded in all its dimensions'.[19] The preoccupation here is only with the nullification of the object. Hence, need in this moment is 'a feeling restricting itself to the subject and belonging entirely to nature'.[20] These are basic needs and concerned mainly with eating and drinking.[21] Achieving enjoyment in this aspect of feeling is 'purely sensuous' and 'negative', as it remains particular and tied to the individual's subjectivity.[22] Life or spirit is now being dominated by nature, but the very fact that it begins from a difference – the feeling of separation between need (for food) and object (bread) – does mean that the individual has some consciousness of ethical life, albeit very limited.

So when feeling is subsumed under the concept the following moments are present: need, at a basic or simple level 'belonging entirely to nature'; and enjoyment.[23] In the Jena lectures of 1805–6, Hegel captures these basic needs more precisely with the term 'natural needs' (*natürlichen Bedürfnissen*).[24] Although he does not explicitly use this term in the *System of Ethical Life*, 'natural need' does play a crucial role in his need theory. For as we shall now see, the further mediations of need-satisfaction are the forms in which these very 'natural needs' become satisfied.

Hegel suggests that 'feeling in the form of difference or of the subsumption of intuition under the concept' has to be comprehended as a totality.[25] This totality involves feeling as labour, product and tool.[26] Labour, as the mediation between need and enjoyment, works on and transforms an object, rather than simply nullifies it. Hegel replaces need with desire here when he asserts that 'in labour the difference between desire (*Begierde*) and enjoyment (*Genusses*) is posited; the enjoyment is obstructed or deferred'[27] – I may desire to live in a house, say, but I first have to build it. Labour therefore introduces the moment of deferred enjoyment. Through this aspect of labour there emerges the following development: desiring to take possession; labour; and possession of the product. An individual desires an object and wants to take possession of it. This is an 'ideal [moment]' or the 'moment of rest'.[28] The second moment is labour – the 'reality or movement'.[29] The individual or subject is subsuming the reality of the object by actually working upon it. The third moment, which Hegel calls the 'synthesis, is the possession, preservation and saving of the object'.[30] It is a synthesis because the third moment contains the first moment – the ideal that it desired – but now as actual reality; through the second moment of labour it has now taken the form which the individual originally wanted. Either possession can take the form of annihilation of the product (enjoyment in eating) or, through human labour, the object can take a new form which could lead to deferred, rather than immediate, enjoyment.

So at this first level of ethical life we have feeling as subsuming the concept which contains the moments of need, labour and enjoyment. We also have feeling subsumed under the concept which contains the moments of need and enjoyment. Finally we have subsumption of intuition under the concept which consists of the moments of desire (taking possession), labour, and possession (enjoyment or labour).

When feeling is subsumed under the concept, the main concern is with the satisfaction of 'natural needs' in an immediate form. When feeling subsumes the concept, labour is being performed to satisfy a 'natural need' less immediately, thereby deferring satisfaction. When feeling takes the form of intuition being subsumed under the concept, this leads to the possibility of labour not being used for immediate enjoyment. Instead, labour becomes a means for the making of a tool for use in further labour and eventual enjoyment. Hegel is quick to grasp the significance of this development, indicating that 'in the tool the subjectivity of labour is raised to something universal. Anyone can make a similar tool and work with it. To this extent the tool is the persistent norm of labour.'[31] For Hegel, the tool itself is higher than the labour and the end of that labour. This is because the tool is a means through which we can overcome natural necessity and why 'all peoples living on the natural level have honoured the tool'.[32] Hegel is therefore offering a developmental theory of need which progresses through certain stages[33] as follows:

1st stage   (Need → Enjoyment)
             Need immediately satisfied.
2nd stage   (Need → Labour → Enjoyment)
             Need-satisfaction deferred. Humans labour before satisfaction.
3rd stage   (Need → Labour → Tool → Labour → Enjoyment)
             Need-satisfaction deferred. Humans labour to make a
             tool which indirectly, that is, through use, will
             eventually satisfy a need.

Hegel delineates three clear stages of need-satisfaction at this primitive level of ethical life. The stages develop from the initial 'drive' towards ethical life proper that is present in an individual. The important point to note, however, is Hegel's attempt to understand needs in their movement, beginning with the subjective satisfaction of individual needs. He is recognising the subjective needs of individuals as a form in which they satisfy their 'natural needs' – the need to eat and drink being prime examples.[34] This is the most basic or simple level of need-satisfaction. As

Hegel indicates, this level 'is not the place for comprehending the manifold and systematic character of this feeling [of need]'; that must come later in human development through the mediations of labour and the tool.[35] In his Jena lectures of 1805–6, Hegel makes this quite clear when he states that 'in the element of being as such, the existence and range of natural needs (*natürlichen Bedürfnisse*) is a multitude of needs (*Menge von Bedürfnissen*). The things serving to satisfy those needs are worked up, their universal inner possibility posited [expressed] as outer possibility, as form.'[36] 'Natural needs' exist in the form or mode of existence of a 'multitude of needs'. One form is the subjective needs of individuals. The emphasis could not be clearer. The movement is from 'natural needs', satisfied in an immediate form, through various mediations to the form of a 'multitude of needs'. At this primitive level, the mediations are labour and the tool, but as we shall see in the next section, further mediations appear as society develops.

Labour does not seem to appear at the first stage, even though the satisfaction of the 'natural needs' of eating and drinking must involve labour of some sort.[37] After all, hunters still have to catch their food even if we assume they eat it raw. So some form of labour must be present, unless Hegel is excluding hunting as labour. H. S. Harris suggests that this is indeed the case.[38] He argues that labour – unlike hunting and gathering – produces objects in order for them to be retained – such as consumable goods and tools. Yet, as Harris himself admits, even the most primitive societies have tools.[39] However, he suggests that only in an 'agricultural society' do Hegel's two 'crucial points' come into play, namely, 'the reduction of territory to a possession, and labouring to make tools'.[40] The crucial difference is this reduction of territory to a possession, but Hegel does not talk about possession in this manner. Possession consists in either consuming the product or working on the product, whereas taking possession is 'the ideal determination of the object by desire'.[41] In the first stage of immediate satisfaction of needs, taking possession and possession exist 'purely as a moment; or rather neither of them is a real moment; they are not fixed or kept distinct from one another'.[42] So what distinguishes the second stage of need from the first is this conflation between the two aspects of possession. For individuals to demarcate their desire from the consumption of the object is not possible. For example, taking possession and possession of a deer for the hunter are not distinct; they are at a rudimentary stage of development. Hunters do not look at the deer and ideally determine it (taking possession) as a cooked piece of meat and a coat, then labour and then consume it (possession). The fact that hunters hunt to live and live to hunt means that they are merely acting on instinct. Taking possession and possession are present, but they are not 'real' because hunters do not reflect on them in this way. They are, however, latent moments that they will realise in the progression to higher levels of development. This suggests that humans in the first stage are savage, or at the level of nonhuman animals, when satisfying their 'natural need' for food and drink. At such a level there is no reflection, according to Hegel, only action.[43]

Hegel is not explicit about why humans do not remain at the nonhuman animal level. The implication is that humans' interaction with nature makes them realise that they constantly have to satisfy their 'natural needs'. The development of the tool speeds up labour, or at least makes labour easier, and consequently lessens the time expended in satisfying 'natural needs'. As we shall see later, Hegel attaches particular importance to limiting the realm of natural necessity (nature) in order to allow humans a greater degree of freedom (spirit).

Before we consider the next level of ethical life, we first have to examine some of the implications of Hegel's account. One aspect centres on his starting point of a 'drive' towards ethical life that is present within an individual consciousness. Some commentators on this text have actually suggested that 'needs' and not drives are the starting point. Cullen, for instance, argues that humans begin with 'unthinking needs and desires' which they must satisfy.[44] Dickey reports that, for Hegel, 'man had been forced out of his presocial condition by need'.[45] Dallmayr gets a little closer to the true starting point by recognising that it begins with 'feeling'.[46] Even this is not close enough, however, because humans begin with drives that manifest themselves in feelings that take the form of needs. Attention to the importance of form is therefore essential to grasp concepts in their movement and transition. Drives become needs. Needs take further forms as humans manifest themselves in the world and interact with nature and, eventually, with other humans.

Harris actually recognises the role of drives at the outset of Hegel's argument, but again, not in a completely correct manner. Harris suggests that 'the negative moment that brings natural consciousness to birth is . . . the *drive* of need'.[47] This is misleading because it wrongly suggests that the need is 'driving' the 'drive', so to speak. In contrast, Hegel is depicting humans with a 'drive' towards absolute ethical life that begins by taking the form of a feeling of separation which is a need. Encouragingly, Avineri recognises 'impulse' or drive as the starting point for human progression to ethical life proper.[48] However, he argues that this impulse is to 'overcome' human 'separateness from nature'.[49] This is incorrect. The 'drive' humans have is a drive towards ethical life. At this immediate level of existence Hegel states quite clearly that 'ethical life is a drive'.[50] The form this drive takes is need as a 'feeling of separation'. The human attempt to overcome the natural environment then leads to further forms of need and their satisfaction. The starting point, however, is a drive towards the ethical and a higher level of freedom. The overcoming of nature is one form this drive takes, but the drive initially is towards ethical life. Attention to form is therefore crucial for a proper under-standing of needs in Hegel's theory. This attention highlights the way in which drives exist in the form of needs. Moreover, focusing on forms reveals Hegel's emphasis on humans' continual search to satisfy their need to be free.

Another implication of Hegel's argument is that he might be equating drives with needs. As we saw in Chapter 1, Abraham Maslow's study of human motivation was subject to this criticism.[51] Certainly, there seems to be some similarity with Maslow's first type of physiological need that acts as a drive to overcome hunger or thirst. Modern need theorists, such as Thompson, are, of course, very critical of those who confuse 'drives' with 'needs'. For Thompson, 'drives' entail a lack of some sort whereas needs may not. Drives also explain human behaviour whereas needs are an attempt to justify it. On this argument, Hegel could be committing the same errors as Maslow.

For Hegel, however, the emphasis on form means that such a demarcation fails to capture concepts in their movement and transi-tion. For Thompson, a drive can never be a need. For Hegel, a drive can take the form of a need. Hegel's approach based on analysing forms offers a greater sensitivity to the way in which subjects manifest their drives through their needs.[52] Hegel then follows the forms needs take as humans interacts with nature and other humans. Hegel is attempting to grasp the subject positing himself or herself particularly and universally through his or her needs. Initially, the subject's needs are subjective, particular and related only to himself or herself. As the subject moves into the next realm of ethical life, however, he or she will soon realise that his or her own particular need is inseparable from the universal needs of other people.

Hegel's definition of need as the feeling of separation between subject and object would also raise problems for modern need theorists. In Chapter 1, I discussed how these theorists try to make a clear distinction between needs and wants.[53] They would therefore see 'feeling' as indicative of a want rather than a need. The interpretation of need as a feeling of separation might commit Hegel to saying that whenever humans experience this feeling then they must have a need. This can quickly lead into anything being considered a need simply because anyone says so. From the perspective of modern need theory, such subjective claims signal that wants, and not needs, are being dealt with. For instance, if 'A' says 'I need gold bath taps', and feels the separation between himself and the bath taps, then Hegel would have to construe this as a need. Yet to discover whether it really was a need, modern need theorists would ask 'A' particular questions: 'Why do you need bath taps? Why do you need them to be gold?' etc. Only after answering these questions would they determine whether it was really a need or not. So modern need theorists would conclude that Hegel's definition of need as a feeling of separation confuses needs with wants. As we have already seen in the discussion of Hegel's method of analysing forms, however, he would reject the attempt to hold needs and wants so rigidly apart. To do so would be committing the errors of the understanding. Instead, Hegel is trying to comprehend the form 'natural needs' take, beginning with the subjective or particular satisfaction of individuals. This allows Hegel to grasp the concept of need in its movement and transition from universal to particular forms and *vice versa*. To keep needs separate from the forms they assume can only result in a limited understanding of needs.

Hegel's introduction of desire as a substitute for needs could also be problematic. Many modern need theorists argue that need and desire are distinct. Diabetics may desire sugar, for instance, but what they really need is insulin. What one desires and what one needs are two different things. If Hegel is using the term 'desire' in this way, then it could lead him into the mistaken assumption that whatever a person desires is what a person needs. For instance, I may desire a sports car, but this may not mean that I need a sports car. Querying what I desire is not possible because desire is subjective, whereas questioning what I need is possible because need is objective and open to discussion. Again, Hegel would be wary of making these rigid distinctions because they fail to comprehend concepts in their movement, transition and inner connection. He does, however, contrast need with desire. Need, as we have seen, is the feeling of separation between subject and object. Desire, on the other hand, relates to the 'nullification of the subjective and the objective . . . [through] effort and *labour*'.[54] Desire distinguishes itself from need because it is part of the overcoming of the separation between subject and object through labour. Enjoyment itself is the unity of need and desire.[55] An individual begins with a 'natural need' that she or he has to satisfy. This 'natural need' takes the form of a feeling of separation. Overcoming that separation through labour is a desire because it is the 'ideal determination of the object'.[56] For example, if I need some shelter, this may cause me to picture a hut or a house in my mind. This image is my desire, the 'ideal determination', for the hut or house that I begin to build through my labour. Once constructed, the need for shelter and the desire to build a house or hut both become satisfied. Even so, need is

evidently linked with desire because desire is one form of the manifestation of a person's need. Hegel is suggesting, therefore, that desire is an
important aspect of a person's need. Modern need theorists fail to capture
the movement between these concepts. They therefore treat the very
preferences and desires of the subject as almost unimportant compared to
the more urgent concept of need.

Hegel's emphasis on the subjective formation of a person's need, and its
interaction with desire, would therefore find an echo in modern need
theorists who operate with a 'thick' and 'thin' understanding of need.
However, the tendency amongst these theorists is either to emphasise the
'thick' whilst neglecting the 'thin' or *vice versa*. In contrast, Hegel is
understanding the two aspects of need as a contradictory unity. He has a
'thin' conception of 'natural need' which refers to the universal needs that
all individuals have to satisfy to exist – such as eating and drinking. He
then captures the movement of this concept by concentrating on the form
such needs and their satisfactions assume in the individual's progression
towards absolute ethical life. This is the 'thick' form such needs take. As
we have just seen, at the first level of ethical life the satisfaction of 'natural
needs' take a simple and immediate form. Such satisfaction becomes more
complex with the mediations of labour and the tool as humans defer their
gratification. Hegel is therefore understanding 'thick' and 'thin' conceptions of need not one-sidedly, not in terms of privileging one over the
other, but in relation to their movement and transition. From the analysis
of Hegel's method in Chapter 1, therefore, 'natural need' is the universal
concept of need. The various forms 'natural needs' can take are the
actualisation of this concept. This will become even clearer as we now
consider the further forms needs and their satisfactions assume when an
individual moves into the second, higher level of ethical life.

NEEDS IN THE SECOND LEVEL OF ETHICAL LIFE

Hegel continues with the movements between the subsumption of
concept under intuition and intuition under the concept. In the first
level, the singular individual was dominant, but at the second level it is
the universal that prevails.[57] Even so, such universality is still only
'formal' because it is not fully manifest.[58] The potential development
of the universal depends upon the further mediations that will occur at
this level of ethical life.

The first manifestation of universality occurs under the subsumption
of the concept under intuition, and in the form of a division of labour. In
contrast to the first level, where one person satisfied his or her own needs,
now many people become involved. Consequently, their labour 'applied

to the object as an entirety, is partitioned'.[59] Humans thus increase
productivity and in doing so are not as tied to necessity as at the first level
of ethical life. The individual in the division of labour produces not
simply for himself or herself, but for others, and his or her particularity
takes on a more universal aspect. However, the division of labour also has
the negative effect of making the individual's labour 'mechanical' and
'deadening'.[60] Despite this, a positive outcome is that humans create a
surplus that goes beyond the satisfaction of a particular person's need.[61]
The production of a surplus leads to the process of exchange as intuition
is now subsumed under the concept. The performance of surplus labour
means that the link between an individual and part of what he or she has
produced becomes broken. The individual has worked on the object not
for his or her own need and own use, but for the need of someone else.
Whereas at the first level of ethical life the individual had a 'oneness with
the object through [his or her] own labour', now we get 'real difference' or
'the cancellation of the identity of subject and object'.[62] A 'legal, and
formally ethical, enjoyment and possession' occurs.[63] Legal relations
develop to decide who has a right to what goods. This issue did not
arise at the first level because the individual worked only for himself or
herself and controlled his or her own production methods. With the
development of the division of labour, and the interdependence this
creates between individuals, such control is no longer possible. Greater
contact with the universal means, therefore, that consciousness is making
its progression along the path to absolute ethical life.

The emergence of exchange leads Hegel to distinguish between the
value and price of an object. He refers to value as 'equality as abstraction'
or 'the ideal measure [of things]'.[64] Price, on the other hand, is the
'empirical measure' of the object; that is, the value given to the object on
the market. Individuals who exchange goods are 'concerned with both a
surplus and an unsatisfied need at the same time'.[65] Hegel means by this
that an individual creates a surplus object to use in exchange for another,
different object in order to satisfy a need. Exchange itself can take 'two
forms':[66] the direct exchange of goods; or exchange over a longer period,
which necessitates the importance of a contract.[67]

The two preceding subsumptions of concept under intuition, and
intuition under concept, now come together as 'indifference' or the
'totality' of exchange and possession.[68] Individuals work to satisfy their
own needs and create a surplus to satisfy the needs of others. The form in
which they satisfy these needs is money. As Hegel states: 'labour, which
leads to a surplus, leads also, when mechanically uniform, to the
possibility of universal exchange and the acquisition of all necessities
. . . [M]oney is the universal, and the abstraction of these, and mediates

them all'.[69] This produces trade, which is money 'posited as activity, where surplus is exchanged for surplus'.[70] Labouring to satisfy needs in an exchange economy leads to the form of money because the worker does not directly receive the surplus she or he has created. The surplus transforms into money, which the worker receives and then spends to achieve a level of enjoyment. Consequently, we can discern a fourth stage of need here as:

Need → Labour → Surplus → Money → Enjoyment.

The first stage of need is one of immediacy where humans, like nonhuman animals, eat to live and live to eat. They spend the majority of their time satisfying their 'natural needs' in an immediate form. This also seems to apply in the second stage even though humans are now engaging in labour. Once an exchange economy develops, humans are no longer in control of the product that they make. What they get back for what they put in depends on the redistribution process in society. We will develop this point shortly when considering the 'system of needs'. For now, we need to note an important consequence of the loss of workers' control over their own production.

Hegel argues that the movement from labour to surplus to money leads to the domination of one person over another in the form of master and servant.[71] The singular individual of the first level now exists among a 'plurality of individuals'.[72] The 'difference of power and might' between these individuals leads to the relation of master and servant.[73] Hegel argues that:

> the master is in possession of a surplus, of what is physically necessary; the servant lacks it, and indeed in such a way that the surplus and the lack of it are not single [accidental] aspects but the indifference of necessary needs (*notwendigen Bedürfnisse*).[74]

Hegel recognises that in an exchange economy some will dominate and force others to work for them through sheer power and control over the surplus produced. The servant's lack of the surplus is not 'accidental', but instead arises from the 'indifference of necessary needs'. These 'necessary needs' are what we have previously referred to as 'natural needs'. Satisfying such needs is 'physically necessary' for a person to carry on existing. The 'indifference' or totality of these 'necessary needs' is both the surplus *and* the lack of surplus. For the master and the servant these two aspects take a particular manifestation: the 'form of indifference' for the master (the surplus), and the form of 'difference' in the servant (lack of the surplus).[75]

It is the institution of the family that temporarily overcomes the 'difference' between master and servant.[76] In the family 'the surplus, labour and property are absolutely common to all'.[77] Each member of the family engages in the labour she or he has an aptitude for, but what each produces is 'common property'.[78] There is no transferral of the surplus produced through exchange, because it is already 'inherently' communal. In contrast, the master/servant relation resulted in the 'antithesis of person to person' because of the master's power and control of the surplus.[79] The family overcomes this antithesis through the 'identity of external needs (*äußeren Bedürfnisse*)'.[80] Needs that were in opposition, or 'externally' related to each other, in the master/servant relation, now find an identity in their opposition. The particular needs of individuals transform into the 'universal' needs of the family.[81] All family members labour to satisfy their particular needs, but the surplus produced is for the family as a whole. So universal and particular, in opposition for the master and servant, now achieve an identity even in their externality. This external opposition means that even the family has 'singularity as its principle'.[82] Individuals must overcome such 'singularity', however, if they are to attain a rational consciousness. The child, the expression of the 'rationality' of the family relationship, attempts to accomplish this when entering the realm of ethical life proper.

ETHICAL LIFE AND NEEDS

Hegel argues that at this level of ethical life universal and particular are internally related. There is now a cancellation of the 'individual's subjectivity' but her or his very 'essence', as a 'subject', is 'allowed to persist'.[83] Universal and particular exist, therefore, in a contradictory unity – the universal cancels subjectivity, but the particularity of the subject still continues. In this way, Hegel conceives that 'the living individual, as life, is equal with the absolute concept and that its empirical consciousness is one with the absolute consciousness'.[84] At this level, 'the universal, the spirit, is in each man and for the apprehension of each man, even so far as he is a single individual'.[85] The individual moves into ethical life and unites her or his particularity with the universal. Consequently, Hegel contends that at this level of ethical life all 'connection with need and destruction is superseded, and the sphere of practice which began with the destruction of the object has passed over into its counterpart, into the destruction of what is subjective, so that what is objective is the absolute identity of both'.[86] The stage of human development that simply 'destroyed' the object – by either consumption or reshaping through labour to satisfy a 'natural need' – now becomes sublated. The subjective satisfaction of this need unites with the objective satisfaction of all needs, bringing them into a contradictory unity. Individuals are thereby mediating their particularity with moments of the universal.

Hegel introduces the mediating institution of the 'estate' (*Stand*) so individuals can try and achieve contact with the universal.[87] Commentators often translate the term 'estate' (*Stand*) simply as 'class' (*Klasse*),[88] but, as Allen Wood suggests, Hegel does make a distinction between these two terms.[89] Historically, estates represented 'constituted bodies of various kinds' that existed in feudal and early absolutist societies.[90] Such estates offered people 'social positions and economic roles' in society.[91] 'Class', in contrast, is seen by Hegel as referring to '*inequalities* in wealth, upbringing and education'.[92] When Hegel uses the term '*Stand*', therefore, we must interpret it as 'estate' and not as 'class' (*Klasse*). Consequently, different classes can exist within the same estate, the significance of which will shortly be revealed.

Hegel refers to three main estates: the absolute estate; the estate of honesty; and the estate of peasants.[93] The absolute estate, or military nobility, has 'absolute pure ethical life as its principle', and its concern, therefore, is only with the universal.[94] It cannot provide for its own needs because this would involve a moment of particularity. Accordingly, this estate has to rely on other estates to provide and satisfy its needs.

The preoccupation of the 'estate of honesty'[95] is with 'work for needs, in possessions, gain, and property'.[96] This estate is not as purely universal as the absolute estate because it engages in the particular activity of possession. Some contact with the universal arises through exchange and trade, which contains a 'universal system of all needs'.[97] Such a development within the estate of honesty leads to the commercial estate, 'which adjusts particular need (*besondere Bedürfnis*) to a particular surplus' through the exchange of money, which represents the 'universality of labour'.[98] The estate of honesty fulfils its most important function by contributing to the needs of the first estate, and giving aid to the needy. So this estate engages in universal and particular activities respectively.[99]

The estate of peasants involves itself in 'physical needs' (*physische Bedürfnis*), and 'its labour and gain forms a greater and more comprehensive totality'.[100] The labour it engages in 'is more of a means, affecting the soil or an animal, something living' rather than wholly intellectual labour or labour involved in the preparation of something to meet a need.[101] Hegel argues that in this estate the peasant's labour masters the living thing, but the living thing 'produces itself by itself'.[102] We can understand the type of distinction Hegel is making here by contrasting the work of a peasant with the work of a carpenter. If a carpenter has a piece of wood and does nothing to it, then it remains a piece of wood. It cannot 'produce itself by itself'. Alternatively, a seed planted by a peasant can, to some extent, 'produce itself', given the right weather. So the peasant is only assisting in that development. In contrast, the carpenter is more actively changing the piece of wood when he or she works on it. So Hegel is suggesting that the labour which shapes the objects of the external world is a higher form of activity.

Some commentators question the capacity of these estates to mediate the particularity of individuals properly with some aspect of the universal. One major criticism is the exclusion of workers that are 'directly involved in production' from these mediating institutions.[103] According to this view, Hegel brilliantly captures the alienating existence of these workers tied to mechanical and factory production without incorporating them into the system of estates.[104] We should remember, however, that Hegel is writing in 1802, when the industrial working class was very small.[105] Hegel was, of course, a keen observer of Britain, the first nation to industrialise. He avidly read British newspapers,[106] and studied the works of the Scottish political economists, most notably Adam Smith and Sir James Steuart.[107] However, the industrial working class in Britain was not preponderant during Hegel's lifetime. Indeed, by 1850, nearly twenty years after Hegel's death, agriculture was still the dominant provider of employment in British society.[108] So the creation of an industrial working class was an incipient tendency within Britain during Hegel's time of writing. Hegel is therefore grasping this very tendency as an antagonistic presence within the system of estates. Avineri, however, argues that the working class involved in factory labour, '*Fabrikarbeit*', are missing from Hegel's discussion.[109] Yet Hegel does mention the presence of 'mechanical and factory labour (*Fabriksarbeit*)' in what he later refers to as the business estate.[110] In a strange statement, however, he raises the possibility of sacrificing part of the business estate to the 'barbarism' of such labour for the greater good of society.[111] Harris has quite rightly suggested how this comment sits oddly with Hegel's persistent concern about the negative aspects of mechanisation and work in factories.[112] Indeed, in the lectures of 1805–6, Hegel explains how 'man' is 'alienated', and 'no longer counts' as an individual.[113] Instead, society measures humans only by their money. Such 'harshness of spirit' or 'complete mercilessness' is symptomatic of the way 'factories, manufacturing, base their subsistence on the misery of one class (*Klasse*)'.[114] Factory and mechanical labour, as a representation of an embryonic working class, are therefore present antagonistically within Hegel's system of estates and are not 'left out' as Avineri suggests.[115] The point is that the estates do not fully mediate the particularity of all individuals with the universal.

Needs play a crucial role, therefore, in the progression of an individual consciousness towards absolute ethical life. Nevertheless, the very presence of these needs also means that contradictions between the universal and particular abound. The system of production actually produces a class whose 'misery' exists within the supposedly 'mediating' estates themselves. This leads to the development of a government to try to overcome these contradictions.

UNIVERSAL GOVERNMENT AND THE SYSTEM OF NEEDS

Hegel suggests that a universal government 'provides for the need which is universal, and provides for it in a universal way'.[116] The concern of universal government is with the provision of universal or 'natural needs' of society as a whole. It does not actively involve itself in the production of goods to satisfy universal needs, but instead ensures that society can satisfy these needs. The production of the goods to satisfy universal needs occurs in the first system of government, which is the system of need. Hegel defines the system of need as 'a system of universal physical dependence on one another'.[117] Individuals can no longer satisfy the totality of their needs on their own, but have to depend on others. This links back to the fourth stage of need, where individual contributions to need-satisfaction take the form of a surplus and then money. As Hegel suggests, the value of the surplus produced by an individual 'is independent of him and alterable'.[118] It depends on how the surplus created relates to the needs of society. 'Thus in this system what rules appears as the unconscious and blind entirety of needs and the modes of their satisfaction. But the universal must be able to master this unconscious and blind fate and become a government.'[119]

So here we have a society where need-satisfaction takes the form of a surplus. A government then has to distribute this surplus, making it equal the total need of society. The free market as an 'alien power' over individuals is unfit to carry out this task.[120] Consequently, Hegel seems to be suggesting the requirement of some form of economic planning. He says that 'the whole [i.e., the surplus] does not lie beyond the possibility of cognition . . . [and] it is possible to know how the surplus stands in relation to need [which] must be determined by intuition'.[121] Assessing the climatic conditions of the country to try to predict the level of harvest is one of the ways to achieve this. Additionally, it also involves assessing a basic minimum for society as a whole 'by taking the average of what in a [given] people is regarded as necessary for existence'.[122] Imbalances between the surplus produced and the needs of society can occur through poor harvests, or because particular areas have higher productivity levels, allowing the production of cheaper goods. For Hegel, the government then needs to intervene to stabilise prices and restore equilibrium.

At this level of ethical life, needs become 'empirically endless' along with enjoyment itself. 'Civilized enjoyment volatilizes the crudity of need and therefore must seek or arrange what is noblest, and the more different its impulses, the greater the labour they necessitate.'[123] Hegel is recognising the capacity for people's needs to multiply. He realises, in an almost ecological vein, that this may not necessarily be beneficial. For instance, he notes how the expansion of needs and enjoyment manifests itself in luxuries. Production of these luxuries occurs domestically, but such is their expansion that imports are necessary from abroad. The development of needs to the point of luxury, therefore, 'makes charges on the whole earth'.[124] Needs grow and expand to such a level that the whole of the world is merely a resource for their satisfaction.

Other problems arise from the operation of the market system. Inequalities in wealth lead to the reappearance of the master/servant relation.[125] This transpires particularly acutely in the business estate, where, as we saw earlier, Hegel has discerned the formation of an industrial working class. The master is now 'tremendously wealthy [and] becomes a might' over the servant.[126] So, on one side of this inequality is wealth, which belongs to the master; and on the other side is poverty, which is the preserve of the servant. Any bond or 'ethical principle' that held people together has now 'vanished' leaving a 'bestiality of contempt for all higher things'.[127] Hegel suggests that the government should do everything it can to overcome this inequality between rich and poor. One way is to stop people making so much wealth. He argues that 'the wealthy man is directly compelled to modify his relation of mastery, and even [others'] distrust for it, by permitting a more general participation in it',[128] The rest of society must therefore have a greater involvement in the power of the wealthy man. Consequently, 'the urge to amass wealth indefinitely is itself eradicated'.[129] The task of government, therefore, is to ensure the satisfaction of the universal needs of all society by 'taking directly into its possession without work the ripe fruits [of industry] or in . . . working and acquiring'.[130] Taxation achieves this for the former, and possession and the leasing of this possession for the latter. Hegel sees taxation as the '[best] external means for restricting gain' in society, and also as a means for allowing the government to influence the expansion and restrictions of different parts of the economy.[131] Hegel realises the disincentive effect taxation can have on individuals, and how it can result in 'less [being] needed',[132] Even so, he still regards it as a positive factor in meeting universal needs.

The contradictions present in the 'system of needs' lead to a second system of government, namely, the 'system of justice'.[133] The latter attempts to offer 'pure justice' in determining a person's right, 'possession and gain',[134] This in turn leads to the third and final system of government – the 'system of discipline'.[135] The latter has the 'universal as Absolute', and attempts to inculcate universality in individuals through education, training and discipline.[136]

HEGEL'S STAGES OF NEED

The various ways in which needs figure in the *System of Ethical Life* are as follows:

First stage

Need → Enjoyment

Second stage

Need → Labour → Enjoyment

Third stage

Need → Labour → Tool → Labour → Enjoyment

Fourth stage

Need → Labour → Surplus → Money → Enjoyment

In the fourth stage, 'labour' will obviously include the 'tool' as an accessory in the production process, and may take the form of machinery. So the interpretation of the second moment of labour could be: means of production, labour and machinery. So the fourth stage would actually be:

Need → Labour/Machinery → Surplus → Money → Enjoyment

Hegel's stages of need trace the forms needs take in their satisfaction. At the first stage, humans are in a condition of natural immediacy. Their concern is only with immediate satisfaction of their 'natural needs'. As human consciousness develops, they labour on the object before satisfying their need. By the next stage, humans have learnt to make tools to ease them in this task. When humans reach the fourth stage of a developed exchange economy, using machinery and the division of labour, productivity is so great that they, jointly, produce a surplus. The people who create this surplus do not directly receive it because it then takes the *form* of money. Money is the final mediation that leads to 'enjoyment' and the satisfaction of people's needs. Yet, as Hegel realises, the power of the master in society can inhibit such satisfaction. Perhaps this is why a year later, in his *First Philosophy of Spirit*, he could call this movement of need and labour into the universality of money 'a monstrous system of community, . . . a life of the dead body, that moves itself within itself, one which ebbs and flows in its motion blindly, like the elements, and which requires continual strict dominance and taming like a wild beast'.[137] Not surprisingly, then, Hegel sees the 'activity of labouring and need' growing into 'the movement of the living dead'.[138] From his initial starting point of need as a feeling of separation in an individual, the result is a huge, overbearing system of need-satisfaction mediated through labour, machinery and money. Hegel is tracing the form needs and their satisfactions take through the dialectical interaction between their universal and particular moments. The contradictions that beset the movement of needs in a complex society require some form of regulation. This leads Hegel to mention some measures to overcome these contradictions. Consequently, he will allow the government to take 'possession' of property and to ensure the provision of the universal needs for all.

Again and again, Hegel presents a constant movement back and forth between universal and particular moments of human progression. He persistently depicts movements of mediation that turn into opposites. The immediate satisfaction of 'natural needs' becomes deferred through the mediations of labour, the tool, machinery and money. The very needs individuals begin with return to haunt them like a monstrous beast which they themselves have created. It is a little strange, therefore, that Lukács can criticise Hegel for ignoring the fact that crises of the economic system are due to contradictions within the system itself.[139] Hegel discerns the very contradictions Lukács speaks of from humans' initial attempt to satisfy their 'natural needs'. All individuals have to satisfy these 'natural needs' to continue existing. The forms these needs take are particular and lead eventually to conflict through the relation of master and servant. The family partially overcomes this contradiction, but the latter soon reappears as the child leaves the family to enter a higher realm of ethical life. In the 'system of need', where an individual interacts with others, contradictions abound. The individual brings his or her own particular needs into some form of universality by having to satisfy the needs of others. The role of the system of estates is to ensure greater contact with the universal, but within it is a new breed of dehumanised workers – dehumanised by the 'system of needs' itself. Hegel leaves us, therefore, with a feeling of unmediated contradictions. Even the government looks an unlikely tamer of the monstrous system that has arisen. As Avineri rightly concludes, in the *System of Ethical Life* human beings become 'enslaved' by their own needs and 'the modes of satisfying them'.[140] However, Avineri considers Hegel to be 'quietistic' in trying to overcome this problem.[141] In contrast, I will argue later that Hegel's emphasis on technological developments offers a way to overcome the contradictory nature of needs and their satisfaction. Through the saving of labour, humans can escape the constant burden of having to work to satisfy their 'natural needs'. As we shall now see, this is a crucial theme in the *Philosophy of Right* that attention to form elucidates.

NOTES

1. H. S. Harris, 'Hegel's Intellectual Development to 1807', in F. C. Beiser (ed.) *The Cambridge Companion to Hegel* (Cambridge University Press, Cambridge, 1993), pp. 36–7.
2. J. E. Toews, *Hegelianism: The Path Toward Dialectical Humanism 1805–1841* (Cambridge University Press, Cambridge, 1990), pp. 51–4.
3. G. W. F. Hegel, *System of Ethical Life and First Philosophy of Spirit*, trans. H. S. Harris and T. M. Knox (State University of New York Press, Albany NY, 1979), pp. 99–100; H. S. Harris, *Hegel's Development: Night Thoughts (Jena 1801–1806)* (Clarendon Press, Oxford, 1983), p. 106; G. Rose, *Hegel Contra Sociology* (Athlone, London, 1981), pp. 60–3.
4. H. S. Harris, 'Hegel's *System of Ethical Life*. An Interpretation', in Hegel, *System of Ethical Life and First Philosophy of Spirit*, p. 19.
5. Toews, *Hegelianism*, p. 52.
6. Rose, *Hegel Contra Sociology*, p. 60.
7. Hegel, *System of Ethical Life*, p. 100. Emphasis added.
8. Hegel, *System of Ethical Life*, p. 99.
9. Hegel, *System of Ethical Life*, p. 101.
10. Hegel, *System of Ethical Life*, p. 102; G. W. F. Hegel, 'System der Sittlichkeit,' in *Sämtliche Werke VII: Schriften zur Politik und Rechtsphilosophie*, (ed.) G. Lasson (Felix Meiner Verlag, Leipzig, 1913), p. 421.
11. Hegel, *System of Ethical Life*, p. 102; 'System der Sittlichkeit', p. 420.
12. Hegel, *System of Ethical Life*, p. 103. Emphasis in the original translation.
13. Hegel, *System of Ethical Life*, p. 103; 'System der Sittlichkeit', p. 422.
14. Hegel, *System of Ethical Life*, p. 104.
15. Hegel, *System of Ethical Life*, p. 104; 'System der Sittlichkeit', p. 422.
16. Hegel, *System of Ethical Life*, p. 104.
17. Hegel, *System of Ethical Life*, p. 104.
18. Hegel, *System of Ethical Life*, p. 104.
19. Hegel, *System of Ethical Life*, p. 104.
20. Hegel, *System of Ethical Life*, p. 104–5.
21. Hegel, *System of Ethical Life*, p. 105.
22. Hegel, *System of Ethical Life*, p. 105.
23. Hegel, *System of Ethical Life*, p. 105.
24. G. W. F. Hegel, *Hegel and the Human Spirit*, trans. L. Rauch (Wayne State University Press, Detroit, 1983), p. 120; G. W. F. Hegel, *Gesammelte Werke 8: Jenaer Systementwürfe III*, (eds.) R.-P. Horstman with J. Henrich Trede (Felix Meiner Verlag, Hamburg, 1976), p. 224.
25. Hegel, *System of Ethical Life*, p. 105.
26. Hegel, *System of Ethical Life*, p. 106.
27. Hegel, *System of Ethical Life*, p. 106; 'System der Sittlichkeit', p. 425.
28. Hegel, *System of Ethical Life*, p. 107. Term in square brackets in the original translation.

29. Hegel, *System of Ethical Life*, p. 107.

30. Hegel, *System of Ethical Life*, p. 107.

31. Hegel, *System of Ethical Life*, p. 113.

32. Hegel, *System of Ethical Life*, p. 113.

33. The use of the term 'stage' should not, of course, be understood undialectically. These stages are 'moments' which can be conceptually distinct but also mediate dialectically with each other. For a comparison with Marx's comments on this matter see below, p. 139, n. 14.

34. Hegel, *System of Ethical Life*, p. 105.

35. Hegel, *System of Ethical Life*, p. 105. Term in square brackets in the original translation.

36. Hegel, *Hegel and the Human Spirit*, p. 120. Term in square brackets in the original translation, *Gasammelte Werke* 8, p. 224.

37. Later, in the *Philosophy of Right*, Hegel notes how, 'there are few immediate materials which do not need to be processed: even air has to be earned'. G. W. F. Hegel, *Elements of the Philosophy of Right*, trans. H. B. Nisbet (Cambridge University Press, Cambridge, 1991), para 196A. Hereafter cited as PR. Labour seems, therefore, to be present at even the most immediate level of need-satisfaction. Cf. A. Reeve, *Property* (Macmillan, London, 1986), p. 140.

38. Harris, *Hegel's Development*, p. 113.

39. Harris, *Hegel's Development*, p. 113, n. 1.

40. Harris, *Hegel's Development*, p. 113, n. 1.

41. Hegel, *System of Ethical Life*, p. 106.

42. Hegel, *System of Ethical Life*, p. 107.

43. Marx's example of the difference between the best of bees and the worst of architects is an illuminating one in this instance. The bee, unlike the architect, builds on instinct and does not have what it is to build as an ideal moment in its imagination. It is this type of distinction that I think Hegel is making in the early stages of need, which therefore casts doubt on Harris's interpretation. See K. Marx, *Capital*, Volume 1, trans. B. Fowkes (Penguin, Harmondsworth, 1988), p. 284.

44. B. Cullen, *Hegel's Social and Political Thought: An Introduction* (Gill and Macmillan, Dublin, 1979), p. 58.

45. L. Dickey, *Hegel: Religion, Economics and the Politics of Spirit, 1770–1807* (Cambridge University Press, Cambridge, 1987), p. 237.

46. F. R. Dallmayr, *G. W. F. Hegel: Modernity and Politics* (Sage, London, 1993), p. 50.

47. Harris, *Hegel's Development*, p. 109.

48. S. Avineri, *Hegel's Theory of the Modern State* (Cambridge University Press, Cambridge, 1972), p. 88.

49. Avineri, *Hegel's Theory of the Modern State*, p. 88.

50. Hegel, *System of Ethical Life*, p. 102.

51. See above, p. 11.

52. As we shall see in the next chapter, Hegel will actually later state that needs are 'derived' from 'drives'. Hegel, PR, para 11A.

53. See above, pp. 13–14.

54. Hegel, *System of Ethical Life*, p. 104.

55. Hegel, *System of Ethical Life*, p. 104.

56. Hegel, *System of Ethical Life*, p. 104.

57. Hegel, *System of Ethical Life*, p. 116.

58. Hegel, *System of Ethical Life*, p. 116.

59. Hegel, *System of Ethical Life*, p. 117.

60. Hegel, *System of Ethical Life*, p. 117.

61. Hegel, *System of Ethical Life*, p. 118.

62. Hegel, *System of Ethical Life*, p. 120.

63. Hegel, *System of Ethical Life*, p. 120.

64. Hegel, *System of Ethical Life*, p. 121. Terms in square brackets in the original translation.

65. Hegel, *System of Ethical Life*, p. 121.

66. Hegel, *System of Ethical Life*, p. 121.

67. Hegel, *System of Ethical Life*, pp. 121–2

68. Hegel, *System of Ethical Life*, pp. 123–4.

69. Hegel, *System of Ethical Life*, p. 124.

70. Hegel, *System of Ethical Life*, p. 124.

71. Hegel, *System of Ethical Life*, p. 125.

72. Hegel, *System of Ethical Life*, p. 125.

73. Hegel, *System of Ethical Life*, p. 125.

74. Hegel, *System of Ethical Life*, p. 126. Term in square brackets in the original translation. 'System der Sittlichkeit', p. 447.

75. Hegel, *System of Ethical Life*, p. 126.

76. Hegel, *System of Ethical Life*, p. 127.

77. Hegel, *System of Ethical Life*, p. 127.

78. Hegel, *System of Ethical Life*, p. 127.

79. Hegel, *System of Ethical Life*, p. 127.

80. Hegel, *System of Ethical Life*, p. 127; 'System der Sittlichkeit', p. 447.

81. Hegel, *System of Ethical Life*, p. 127.

82. Hegel, *System of Ethical Life*, p. 129.

83. Hegel, *System of Ethical Life*, p. 131.

84. Hegel, *System of Ethical Life*, p. 143.

85. Hegel, *System of Ethical Life*, p. 144.

86. Hegel, *System of Ethical Life*, p. 145.

87. Hegel, *System of Ethical Life*, p. 152; 'System der Sittlichkeit', p. 475. Translation modified.

88. Harris and Knox do this throughout their translation of the 'System der Sittlichkeit'. For greater accuracy I will use the term 'estate' for '*Stand*' and 'class' for '*Klasse*'.

89. A. W. Wood, 'Hegel and Marxism', in Beiser (ed.) *Cambridge Companion to Hegel*, p. 423. Avineri is therefore wrong to say that 'for Hegel, classes always remain *estates*'. Avineri, *Hegel's Theory of the Modern State*, p. 105.

90. G. Poggi, *The State, its Nature, Development and Prospects*, (Polity Press, Cambridge, 1990), pp. 40–1. For a more detailed examination of the concept of '*Stand*' see G. Poggi, *The Development of the Modern State: A Sociological Introduction*, (Hutchinson, London, 1978), pp. 42–51.

91. Wood, 'Hegel and Marxism', p. 423.

92. G. W. F. Hegel, *Werke*, Volume IV (Suhrkamp Verlag, Frankfurt, 1970), p. 63, as quoted in Wood, 'Hegel and Marxism', p. 423. Cf. M. Neocleous, *Administering Civil Society: Towards a Theory of State Power* (Macmillan, London, 1996), p. 8.

93. Hegel, *System of Ethical Life*, pp. 152–6.

94. Hegel, *System of Ethical Life*, p. 152.

95. Hegel, *System of Ethical Life*, p. 153.

96. Hegel, *System of Ethical Life*, p. 153.

97. Hegel, *System of Ethical Life*, p. 154.

98. Hegel, *System of Ethical Life*, p. 154; 'System der Sittlichkeit', p. 478.

99. Hegel, *System of Ethical Life*, p. 155.

100. Hegel, *System of Ethical Life*, p. 156.

101. Hegel, *System of Ethical Life*, p. 156; 'System der Sittlichkeit', p. 480.

102. Hegel, *System of Ethical Life*, p. 156.

103. Avineri, *Hegel's Theory of the Modern State*, p. 109.

104. Avineri, *Hegel's Theory of the Modern State*, p. 109.

105. E. J. Hobsbawm, *The Age of Revolution: Europe 1789–1848* (Weidenfeld and Nicolson, London, 1962), p. 168.

106. M. J. Petry, 'Hegel and the *Morning Chronicle*', *Hegel-Studien*, 11, 1976,

107. For discussions of the influence of Smith and Steuart on Hegel see R. Plant, 'Hegel and Political Economy I and II', *New Left Review*, 103 and 104, May/June and July/August, 1977; R. Plant, 'Hegel and the Political Economy', in W. Maker (ed.) *Hegel on Economics and Freedom* (Mercer University Press, Georgia, 1977); Dickey, *Hegel: Religion, Economics and the Politics of Spirit*, pp. 194–9; N. Waszek, *The Scottish Enlightenment and Hegel's Account of Civil Society* (Kluwer Academic, Boston, 1988).

108. P. Mathias, *The First Industrial Nation: An Economic History of Britain 1700–1914*, (Methuen, London and New York, 1983), p. 234.

109. Avineri, *Hegel's Theory of the Modern State*, p. 109.

110. Hegel, *System of Ethical Life*, p. 171; 'System der Sittlichkeit', p. 496. See below p. 60.

111. Hegel, *System of Ethical Life*, p. 171.

112. Harris, 'Hegel's *System of Ethical Life*', p. 75. For a less sympathetic account see G. Lukács, *The Young Hegel. Studies in the Relation Between Dialectics and Economics* (Merlin, London, 1975), p. 332.

113. Hegel, *Hegel and the Human Spirit*, p. 166.

114. Hegel, *Hegel and the Human Spirit*, p. 166; *Gesammelte Werke 8*, p. 270. Lukács, himself, is forced to admit Hegel's 'incredible' 'insight' here. Lukács, *The Young Hegel*, p. 331.

115. Avineri, *Hegel's Theory of the Modern State*, p. 109.

116. Hegel, *System of Ethical Life*, p. 164.

117. Hegel, *System of Ethical Life*, p. 167.

118. Hegel, *System of Ethical Life*, p. 167.

119. Hegel, *System of Ethical Life*, pp. 167–8.

120. Hegel, *System of Ethical Life*, p. 167.

121. Hegel, *System of Ethical Life*, p. 168.

122. Hegel, *System of Ethical Life*, p. 168. Term in square brackets in the original translation.

123. Hegel, *System of Ethical Life*, p. 170.

124. Hegel, *System of Ethical Life*, p. 170.

125. Hegel, *System of Ethical Life*, p. 170.

126. Hegel, *System of Ethical Life*, p. 170.

127. Hegel, *System of Ethical Life*, p. 170–1.

128. Hegel, *System of Ethical Life*, p. 171. Term in square brackets in the original translation.

129. Hegel, *System of Ethical Life*, p. 171.

130. Hegel, *System of Ethical Life*, p. 172. Terms in square brackets in the original translation.

131. Hegel, *System of Ethical Life*, p. 173. Term in square brackets in the original translation.

132. Hegel, *System of Ethical Life*, p. 173.
133. Hegel, *System of Ethical Life*, p. 173.
134. Hegel, *System of Ethical Life*, p. 174.
135. Hegel, *System of Ethical Life*, p. 176.
136. Hegel, *System of Ethical Life*, p. 176.
137. Hegel, *System of Ethical Life*, p. 249.
138. Hegel, *System of Ethical Life*, p. 249.
139. Lukács, *The Young Hegel*, p. 332.
140. Avineri, *Hegel's Theory of the Modern State*, p. 98.
141. Avineri, *Hegel's Theory of the Modern State*, p. 99.

4

NEEDS IN HEGEL'S
PHILOSOPHY OF RIGHT

The concerns at the heart of the early *System of Ethical Life* reappear nearly twenty years later in the *Philosophy of Right*. As Avineri has indicated, there is a 'remarkable continuity' between these texts in terms of Hegel's political thought.[1] Hegel replicates this 'continuity' in his analysis of needs and their forms. He deepens his understanding of needs in the *Philosophy of Right* and develops the important concept of 'spiritual need', which humans can only satisfy properly when they are free from the realm of necessity. In terms of method, however, Hegel discards the Kantian contrast between concept and intuition that appeared in his early writings. Instead, he focuses on the contradictory movement of the Will, tracing its dialectical progression from abstract right to morality and, finally, to ethical life.[2]

Abstract right and morality both abstract from the social reality of a fully established society, which Hegel deals with in ethical life. As Ilting has suggested, both abstract right and morality are, therefore, a 'methodological fiction' which attain their 'true meaning and validity' only when they reach the concrete realm of ethical life.[3] The Will is the crucial mediation that unites the abstract with the concrete as it passes through these moments. As we saw in Chapter 2, remaining in the realm of abstraction was a particular error of the pre-Kantian metaphysic. On the other hand, staying within the realm of reality was a weakness of empiricism. According to Hegel, therefore, to understand phenomena correctly the abstract must be united with the concrete.

I will focus on the role needs play in this development by tracing the universal concept of need in its various forms as the Will progresses from the abstract to concrete. However, we should remember that Hegel understands these moments in a contradictory unity. Hence, even in the realm of abstraction he will refer to concrete moments such as property and money. He is therefore emphasising the back-and-forth, dialectical movement between these moments through the Will's progression to freedom.

Hegel begins his discussion of needs in the introduction to the *Philosophy of Right*. He devotes this section to an overview of the Will's search for freedom and a consideration of the concept of right.[4] Hegel argues that the Will can make itself universal by abstracting from 'needs (*Bedürfnisse*), desires (*Begierden*) and drives (*Triebe*)'.[5] When it 'steps into existence' and becomes determinate, however, it is particular.[6] The Will, in this 'immediate' state, now finds itself 'naturally determined' by 'drives, desires and inclinations' and the 'needs derived from them'.[7] Hegel wants to focus on the '*objective* element' of these drives, and the 'shape (*gestaltet*) this element assumes in its truth' and 'existence'.[8] This 'arbitrary will' encounters the problem of balancing the satisfaction of these drives with each other.[9] As a '*dialectic* of drives (*Triebe*)',[10] 'man' therefore has to 'liberate himself' from this immediate form of existence.[11] His drives must become 'the rational system of the will's determination'.[12] He must not be the prisoner of his drives as a nonhuman animal is.[13] Instead, he must 'stand above his drives', and 'determine and posit them as his own'.[14] For Hegel, therefore, the Will, in its immediacy, must master its drives and needs in some way in order to be free.[15]

ABSTRACT RIGHT

When the Will emerges in abstract right the 'shape' these drives and needs take is particular.[16] This is important to recognise because, as we saw in the previous chapter, Hegel is understanding drives as taking the form of needs which themselves take further forms through the progression of the Will. Hegel begins his discussion with the complete abstraction from needs and drives. These very needs and drives then naturally determine the Will in its immediate form of existence. These natural determinations are common to everybody – a universal. The Will then externalises itself as a particular Will. The initial form this externalisation takes in the realm of abstract right is property.[17] Property is the 'first reality' of freedom and, as Hegel is quick to add, a 'poor kind of reality' at that.[18] The Will is in such an immediate and undeveloped state that this is the only form of existence it can have. However, Hegel makes an important statement here in relation to needs. He asserts that the 'rational aspect of property is to be found not in the satisfaction of needs, but in the superseding of mere subjectivity of personality'.[19] For Hegel, then, the Will has a need for property to externalise itself and achieve a degree of freedom. As he indicates: 'I make something my own out of natural need (*natürlichem Bedürfnisse*) . . . [and] drive (Triebe)'.[20] Humans have a 'natural need' to possess an external thing. In this sense, the possession of property 'appears as a means' to the satisfaction of needs.

However, Hegel suggests the 'true position' is that property is an end in itself – the 'first *existence*' of freedom.[21] The 'rational aspect' in relation to external things, therefore, is the possession of property. The '*particular* aspect', however, is the 'subjective ends' and 'needs'.[22] The universal or 'natural need' to possess an external object – to externalise oneself – takes the form of a particular need. The determination of the Will's freedom exists as a moment within this very process. This freedom relates to the externalisation of the Will in the object, and not simply in the need for that object. Hegel is immediately attempting to make an important distinction in relation to freedom and needs that will recur persistently in the *Philosophy of Right*: the realm of natural necessity, the realm of having to satisfy our 'natural needs', contains within it moments of freedom.

Hegel continues with the further development of the Will and the further forms needs take. He suggests that need propels the Will not only to possess property, but also to use it. Hence '*use* is the realization of my need through the alteration, destruction or consumption of the thing'.[23] The 'thing' is simply 'reduced to a means of satisfying' a particular 'need'.[24] However, Hegel realises that where an object requires 'repeated use' there is therefore 'a continuing need (*fortdauerndes Bedürfnis*)' for that very object.[25] The need continually to use the object means that simple possession and consumption, as particular, turn into a 'sign' which indicates a 'universal act of possession'.[26] Other Wills then bestow a form of universality on this activity by recognising the particular Will's repeated use of the object.

Hegel is grasping the movement of need from particular to universal through the moments of use and possession. However, he understands universal and particular not as distinct, but in a contradictory unity. For instance, he states that the use of an object relates to a 'specific need' (*spezifisches Bedürfnis*).[27] However, the utility of the object is '*comparable*' to other objects with the same utility, just as the 'specific need' it satisfies is comparable with '*need in general*', and therefore comparable with other needs.[28] I look to my own 'specific need' when using an object but the object itself also serves to satisfy the needs of others – 'need in general'. For example, I can use a pan to boil water for my own need, but pans used collectively can satisfy this need for all. My particular need relates to the universal needs of others just as the particular object relates to other objects through its utility. As Hegel states, need 'is a term which can encompass the most diverse things, and it is their common quality that makes them commensurable'.[29] The qualitative aspect of the object 'disappears' in the 'form of the quantitative'.[30] The specific use of the object, its quality, takes the form of a 'quantitative . . . *value*'.[31] 'Value' in its most abstract form is money.[32] The Will's initial need for externalisation, which took the form of possession and use, now exists only as a 'sign' in the 'abstract' form of money, which 'does not depict the need itself'.[33] The particular or 'specific needs' of the Will become manifest in the universal form of money.

Within the realm of abstract right, therefore, Hegel offers us a clear indication of how needs manifest themselves in different forms (see Figure 4.1). After the initial abstraction from all needs the Will, in its immediate state, has 'natural needs' which are universal. The 'natural need' to externalise itself takes the form of the possession of property. The possession of an object leads to its use, which can then satisfy a 'specific need'. The 'specific need' itself, as a particular, can take the more universal form of a 'continuing need' through the repeated use of the object. So 'natural need' as universal has moved to the form of a particular, 'specific need', which in turn can take the form of a universal, 'continuing need'. The 'specific' and 'continuing need' can then take the further universal form of 'need in general'. The 'continuing need' already attains a form of universality because my repeated use of the object makes others recognise it as *mine*. My 'specific need', satisfied through possession and use of the object, appears to relate only to me. In reality, however, other people are satisfying their 'specific needs' in very similar ways. Particular thus takes on the form of a universal – 'need in general'. The qualitative aspect of each individual object, which relates to particular or 'specific needs', now takes on a quantitative form as universal commensurability. Quality gives over to quantity and use transforms into value. Expressed in its most universal form, value is money, which itself is only a 'sign' of need rather than its full representation. Needs that began as an abstraction now appear to have taken on an abstract form again in the 'sign' of money.

Abstract right presents us with a clear example, therefore, of the importance of form for understanding the dialectical development of needs in the *Philosophy of Right*. The movement from 'natural' (universal) to 'specific' (particular) to 'general' (universal) captures needs in their motion and transition from one concept to the other. The Will's initial abstraction from needs leads eventually to the abstract existence of needs in the universal form of money.

MORALITY

In the realm of morality, the Will is no longer in a state of immediacy, but is now 'reflected into itself'.[34] The *'natural subjective existence'* of the subject are its 'needs, inclinations, passions, opinions, fancies'.[35] Hegel refers to the satisfaction of the latter as *'welfare or happiness'*, which is

Figure 4.1   Needs in abstract right

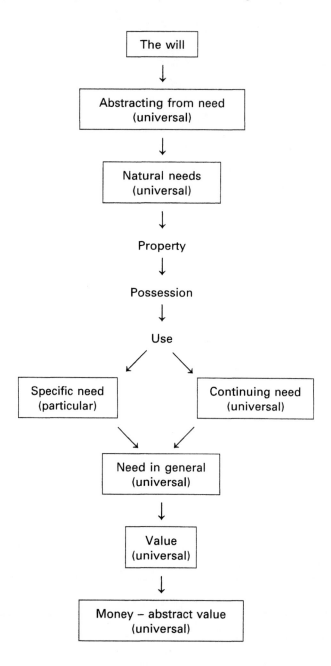

both particular and universal.[36] The subject 'man', as a 'living being', pursues his own welfare, making 'his needs his end'.[37] As the subject does not adopt the 'good' as an 'end in itself', he therefore remains within the realm of '*subjective freedom*'.[38] The universal 'welfare of *all*' is present only as a 'moment' within the subject's preoccupation with his own particular welfare.[39] Hegel refers to the satisfaction of the natural or most basic needs of an individual that ensure his existence as a '*right of necessity*'.[40] This right takes precedence over abstract right and an individual's right to his property. For instance, Hegel suggests that stealing a loaf to preserve one's life may infringe property rights, but it would be 'wrong' to refer to such an action as 'common theft'.[41] The necessity of the preservation of life is higher than any appeal to abstract right. As Hegel emphasises: 'no one should be sacrificed completely for the sake of right'.[42] So the satisfaction of basic human needs takes precedence over the formal rights of individuals. Consequently, abstract right is contingent upon the necessity of having to satisfy our basic needs in order to preserve an aspect of our freedom.[43] Hegel is asserting the Will's right of necessity in this realm of morality – a right that arises through the forms of need and their satisfaction (see Figure 4.2).

Figure 4.2   Needs in morality

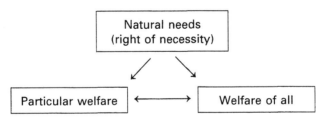

The Will begins by having to satisfy its 'natural needs' in order to exist. 'Natural needs' are so important, therefore, that they override any abstract rights – including the abstract right of property. Satisfying these needs ensures a person's welfare or happiness. The subjective nature of this satisfaction means that such welfare is particular to the individual. However, the universal welfare of all people exists as a moment within this very particularity. Even at this rudimentary stage of need-satisfaction, the universal lurks dialectically within the particular, linking our own welfare with the welfare of all. The further development of the Will through morality sees it attempting to acquire knowledge of the good and to develop a conscience.[44] However, the good and conscience at this level are still only abstract and subjective, and have not yet achieved an 'objective content'.[45] Subjective good and objective good must be in a unity and not simply distinct. The realm of ethical life is where such a reconciliation can take place.[46]

ETHICAL LIFE

The Will, which Hegel has considered in the realm of abstract right and morality as an abstraction, now turns outward into the real world. The universal concept of the Will unites with its 'existence' as a 'particular Will'.[47] Such a particular existence sees the Will objectify itself and come into contact with 'laws and institutions'. The latter are the 'fixed content' of the 'ethical powers' that govern the lives of individuals.[48] However, as the individuals themselves are the creators of these 'ethical powers', the latter are therefore not 'alien' to them.[49] The very particularity of individuals makes the ethical itself 'intensely actual'.[50] It is through the 'unity of the individual and the universal' that 'ethical substance' as 'spirit' becomes manifest.[51] This 'objectivization' of ethical spirit progresses through the 'form of its moments': the family, civil society, and the state.[52]

The family, as the 'immediate substantiality of spirit', arises out of the 'feeling' of love, which is itself 'ethical life in its natural form'.[53] Such a 'feeling' leads an individual to join with another person to receive, and give, recognition.[54] Marriage is the institution that accomplishes this ethical basis of mutual recognition.[55] However, Hegel is aware that the foundation of this movement towards another person is a 'natural drive' (natürliche Triebe) of passion, which must be 'extinguished' so that the 'ethical aspect of marriage' asserts itself.[56] Hegel argues that to achieve an 'ethical end' of 'love, trust, and the sharing of the whole of individual existence' within marriage, 'natural drive' must be 'made subordinate'.[57] Again, Hegel is stressing the importance of individuals not being slaves to their drives, but instead controlling and subordinating them to higher aims. This does not mean the rejection of passion and feeling within marriage; rather, it is the suggestion that a marriage based simply on such passion is prone to failure. As he indicates, marriage contains the 'moment of feeling' and in this very 'moment' its 'dissolution' becomes possible.[58] It is the controlling of this 'contingency of feeling' that can safeguard the ethical basis of the marriage relation.[59]

Hegel's emphasis on the role 'natural drive' plays in the formation of the family now leads to the 'need for possessions', which, as 'resources', allow the family to subsist.[60] The 'particular need' (besonderen Bedürfnisses) of the 'single individual' that existed in abstract right is 'transformed' into a more 'communal purpose' as the family satisfies its needs collectively rather than on an individual basis.[61] Even so, 'particularisation and contingency' are still present in some form because the family is still only an 'immediate' moment of spirit.[62]

The birth of children offers a further progression to a more substantial basis of the ethical by making the 'feeling' between man and wife 'objective'.[63] It is in the child that both man and wife 'see their love before them' in a 'spiritual form'.[64] In contrast, the 'unity' they achieve with each other in the sharing of resources is 'external'; that is, merely a means to an end rather than an end in itself. So Hegel is again contrasting the spiritual or ethical with the naturally necessary. The children lead, therefore, to the 'ethical dissolution' of the family as they become 'free personalities' and 'legal persons' in their own right.[65] They now pursue their own 'individual ends', or replace the family with a 'circle of friends', and eventually create their *own* families.[66] However, Hegel also indicates that one aspect behind the expansion of the family is 'interdependent needs (*verknüpfenden Bedürfnissen*) and their reciprocal satisfaction', which transform families into large communities or nations.[67] Spirit is therefore moving to its second moment – the '*world of appearance* of the ethical', namely, civil society.[68] It is in the realm of civil society and, in particular, the section on the 'system of needs' that Hegel's emphasis on the importance of the concept of need becomes even more evident.

Hegel argues that 'there are certain universal needs, such as food, drink, clothing, etc., and how these are satisfied depends entirely on contingent circumstances'.[69] 'Universal needs', therefore, are those needs an individual has to satisfy to exist – they are another term for 'natural needs'. The level to which individuals can satisfy these 'universal needs' is 'contingent' upon factors such as natural resources and labour productivity.[70] Such 'contingency' also arises, however, in terms of the needs of individuals. As Hegel notes, the 'concrete person' of civil society is a '*particular* person' who looks only to his or her own end.[71] As a 'totality of needs' this person is 'a mixture of natural necessity and arbitrariness'.[72] These needs are 'necessary' because a person has to satisfy them to live.[73] They are the aforementioned 'universal needs'. Hegel captures the 'arbitrary' aspect of a person's need with the term 'contingent need', which he links with 'subjective caprice' – the whims of an individual.[74] An individual as a particular being is therefore a combination of both 'natural needs' (universal) and 'contingent needs' (particular). The person shares the requirement of satisfying 'natural needs' with all other human beings. However, in his or her particularity, the person cares only for the satisfaction of his or her own particular or '*subjective need*', which is 'opposed to the universal will' of the rest of society.[75] Despite this, Hegel emphasises that the satisfaction of our own needs in civil society mediates with the satisfaction of the needs of others.[76] Such a mediation arises because in satisfying our own particular needs we receive the goods produced by other people. Similarly, through our own work we produce for others to consume. A moment of '*universality* asserts itself', therefore, out of the very particular satisfaction of our own needs.[77] It is through this dialectical movement between the particular needs of an individual, and the universal needs of society, that Hegel discerns the development in needs and their satisfaction. He attempts to explicate this development by formulating another sphere of needs in order to differentiate humans from nonhuman animals.[78]

Hegel argues that although both humans and nonhuman animals share 'natural needs' an important difference remains: nonhuman animals suffer from limitations both in the needs that they have, and in the manner in which they satisfy them. Human beings, on the other hand, are able to overcome such constraints. They display their 'universality' through the multiplication of their needs – the satisfying of needs in different ways – and by '*dividing* and *differentiating* the concrete need (*konkreten Bedürfnisses*) into individual parts and aspects which then become different needs, *particularized* and hence *more abstract*'.[79] Hegel regards humans as 'spiritual' beings with higher needs than those of nonhuman animals.[80] Humans display this spirituality by 'renouncing raw food, . . . making it fit to eat and destroying its natural immediacy'.[81] It may be the case that in certain circumstances, such as at the point of starvation, for example, people will eat food in any form and this aligns them with nonhuman animals; barring such extremities, however, it can generally be accepted that humans will work on the food in some way before eating it. As 'spiritual beings', humans are also 'able to entertain wishes and desires which arise from their own thought and imagination, rather than instinct'.[82] This is in contradistinction to nonhuman animals, which remain tied to the immediate satisfaction of their 'natural needs'. They cannot develop the higher or 'spiritual' needs of humans.[83] For Hegel, then, humans multiply their needs and the methods by which they satisfy them. In what sense, therefore, is the 'dividing and differentiating' of 'concrete needs' distinct from their multiplication? Taking Hegel's own example: humans transcend the 'natural need' for food by making it fit for consumption, rather than simply accepting it in its 'immediate' state.[84] The need for meat, for instance, soon becomes the need for steak, well done, in a brandy sauce. The needs and the way humans satisfy them have multiplied. Instead of eating the meat raw, they now cook it and also add extra ingredients. The needs and the means for satisfying those needs have therefore increased.

'Concrete' or 'social needs' divide and differentiate through education.[85] It is education that 'resolves the concrete into its particulars', and

makes 'concrete' or 'social needs' take the form of 'abstract needs'
(*abstrakte Bedürfnisse*).[86] These needs are abstract in the sense that
particular needs multiply to such a degree that they become relative
to the subjective whims and refinement of different individuals.[87] As
Hegel recognises, this can easily lead to a situation where a need can be
'created' by those 'who seek to profit from its emergence'.[88] The
multiplication of needs therefore allows the possibility of their manip-
ulation. For Hegel, then, 'taste and utility become criteria of judgement'
so that 'it is no longer need but opinion which has to be satisfied'.[89]

We can elucidate what Hegel is saying here by bringing in the steak
example again. The well-done steak in a brandy source is a development
from the 'natural need' for food, which takes the form of the need for
meat. Through 'taste and utility', people have come to cook the meat in a
particular way and add a brandy sauce to it. The 'concrete need' for meat
has, therefore, 'divided and differentiated' itself. The 'concrete' or 'social
need' for meat has become a particular and 'abstract need'.[90] People now
require their steaks in different ways in accordance with their 'taste and
utility'. The more educated or refined these people become then the more
their tastes differ.[91] So positing universal needs into society leads to them
taking the form of a particular. However, particular needs can then take
the form of universal needs; they can become '*recognized*' as universal
through the 'mutual relations between individuals'.[92]

Hegel now seems to understand the 'contingent needs' we spoke of
earlier as 'opinions'. The consequence of this is quite dramatic for Hegel's
theory of needs, due to his conclusion that it is 'opinions' and not needs
that are being satisfied.[93] The 'dividing and differentiating' of needs
eventually lead to a situation where 'natural needs' exist in the form of
'opinions'. This has important implications because we need to know how
'natural needs' become 'opinions'. How, for Hegel, does the need for food
become an 'opinion' about food? Obviously, a lot turns on what Hegel
actually means by 'opinions'. Inwood's analysis of the use of the term
'opinion' (*Meinung*) in Hegelian thought is very enlightening here. He
cites Hegel in the *Lectures on the Philosophy of History* as associating
Meinung (opinion) with *Mein* (mine) and consequently with idiosyncrasy.
He quotes Hegel as stating that opinion is 'a subjective REPRESENTA-
TION [*Vorstellung*], a random thought, a fancy', which would clearly link
it to Hegel's conception of 'contingent needs'.[94] So we could interpret
Hegel as making a distinction between the objectivity of needs and the
subjectivity of 'opinions'. 'Opinions' differ from person to person
depending on the particular beliefs people have. Some want steak with
a brandy sauce, others with white wine, and some do not want steak at all.
Accordingly, 'opinions' are the form 'contingent needs' take through the

multiplication of taste and levels of refinement. For Hegel, the 'universal need' for food, for instance, takes the form of a particular or 'contingent need' for meat. The latter comes, 'in the end', to be an 'opinion' for something because it has been subject to the influence of 'taste and utility', which is an expression of the individual's character as a 'spiritual being'.[95] As needs multiply in number and variety, people are not as dependent on any one of them – 'necessity', therefore, becomes 'less powerful'.[96] So we may be satisfying a 'universal need' for food, but this has developed to such a stage that the form it takes is an 'opinion' of steak, well done, in a brandy sauce. 'Opinions' themselves, as particular forms of need, can then take the form of a universal. Hegel himself illustrates this with the case of Diogenes and need-satisfaction in Athenian society.

Hegel argues that Diogenes' adoption of Cynicism, a simple satisfaction of needs, was a 'product' of the very 'luxury' prevalent in the 'social life of Athens' at this time.[97] Needs multiplied so much that luxury was the universal form of need-satisfaction. However, the reaction to this excessiveness produced a particular manifestation of need which emphasised a more simple level of need-satisfaction. So a particular took the form of a universal which itself produced a particular. As Hegel indicates, 'what determined' Diogenes 'was the opinion against which his entire way of life reacted'.[98] So 'opinion' that was subjective and particular became universal in Athenian society. However, its dialectical movement meant that it brought forth a particular which was a more rudimentary level of need-satisfaction and a rejection of luxury. Hegel is offering an understanding of needs, therefore, in their movement and transition, as Figure 4.3 illustrates.

The 'natural drive' towards the family results in a communal satisfaction of 'natural needs'. The dissolution of the family through the development of the child, and the interdependency created by need, lead to civil society. Natural necessity reappears as self-sufficient individuals have to satisfy their 'natural needs' in order to live. The satisfaction of these needs takes the particular form of 'contingent needs' that people satisfy in many different ways. This particular need-satisfaction results in a universal as people recognise the links between their own needs and the needs of others in the form of 'concrete' or 'social needs'. These 'concrete needs' divide and differentiate to such an extent that they take the form of 'abstract needs', which are so particular that they, in turn, take the form of 'opinions'. The particular, as an 'opinion', can, however, become a universal and again produce a particular. Hegel understands needs, therefore, in their movement and transition from universal to particular, and particular to universal. There is thus a fluidity in Hegel's conceptualisation of need which allows him to see the contingency of the

Figure 4.3 Needs in ethical life

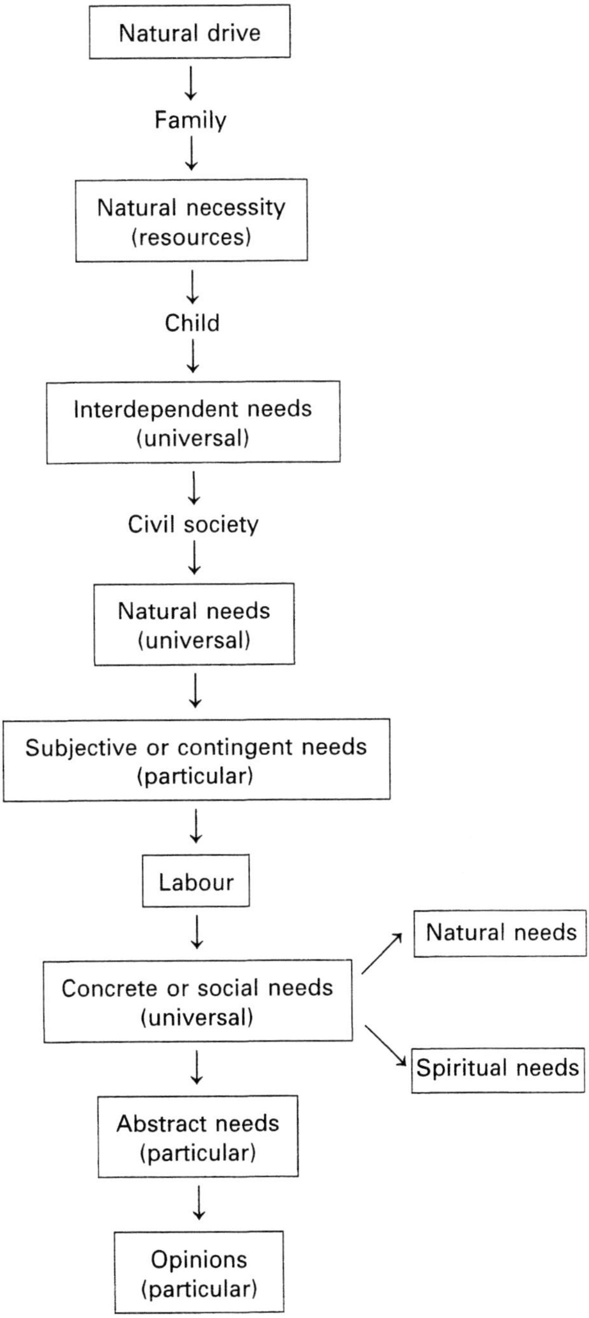

universal and particular. The universal contains the particular within itself just as the particular contains the universal. So we must understand needs in a contradictory unity to make proper sense of the way individuals formulate and satisfy their needs.

As we saw in the previous chapter, understanding needs in this way exposes Hegel to criticism from modern need theorists. Again, they would berate him for eliding 'need' with other concepts, such as a 'drive', which they see as being distinct. Moreover, they would also interpret Hegel's concepts of 'contingent need' and 'opinion' as 'wants' due to their subjective nature.[99] However, we can only stress again that Hegel's emphasis on analysing forms rejects such rigid distinctions. Instead, Hegel is attempting to grasp needs through the dialectical movement of the Will. Hegel is tracing the various modes of existence or forms of needs and trying to unearth their inner connection with each other. In doing so, he thinks we can better grasp the movements between universal and particular needs, as in the move from 'natural' to 'contingent' to 'concrete' to 'opinion', etc., in a constant process of motion and transition.

Hegel uses the reoccurring contrast between 'natural' and 'spiritual' needs to illustrate movements between the universal and particular further. To distinguish himself from the savage, from the nonhuman animal state, Hegel argues that humans must develop and satisfy their 'spiritual needs' (*geistigen Bedürfnisse*).[100] Yet 'man' can only accomplish this when he has overcome the 'strict natural necessity of need', and is instead under the control of 'a necessity imposed by himself alone'.[101] Humans can only begin to be truly free, therefore, when they have overcome the problem of satisfying the 'external necessity' of 'natural needs'.[102] Hegel sees nonhuman animals as being bound to the moment of particularity and limitation.[103] Humans, however, can transcend their particularity to take on aspects of the universal. Their particular needs take on a form that are common to everyone; that is, 'social'.[104] 'Social needs' (*gesellschaftlichen Bedürfnisse*) are a combination of 'natural' and 'spiritual needs' (see Figure 4.3).[105] Humans' requirement to satisfy their 'natural needs' coexists with their more spiritual concerns. For Hegel, it is the 'spiritual needs', as universal, that predominate.[106] Consequently, if it is the 'spiritual' needs that are universal, then only they can be truly free because they do not involve production for 'natural needs'.

Hegel is therefore scathing towards a Rousseauean state of nature that attempts to link freedom with 'natural needs of a simple kind'.[107] Satisfying 'natural needs' immediately in this realm is nothing more than a 'condition of savagery and unfreedom', because spirituality is 'immersed in nature'.[108] Real freedom, in contrast, 'consists solely in the reflection of the spiritual into itself [and] its distinction from the natural'.[109] 'Universality' asserts itself, therefore, at a higher level of production where people are truly free in the expression of themselves as human beings. Only at this level can 'spiritual needs' be fully satisfied outside the tyranny of natural necessity. Clearly, then, humans have to create a distinct realm to satisfy their 'spiritual needs' and thereby be free. Attention can now turn to how Hegel thought this could occur. One possibility appears to be through 'the moment of liberation which is present in work (*Arbeit*)'.[110] Famously, of course, it is in the master/slave section of the *Phenomenology of Spirit* that Hegel gives his clearest exposition of the importance of work for the development of human freedom.[111] Hegel argues that in working and shaping an object the slave expresses his or her own essence – the 'pure-being-for-self' – despite being under the domination of the master.[112] Initially, this seems promising, but there is a disappointing outcome. The slave does not attain freedom because the master does not recognise him or her as a free and independent self-consciousness.[113] Lack of recognition means that freedom is unattainable.[114]

Similarly, in the *Philosophy of Right*, freedom can only be possible where there is a distinction from nature and the immediate satisfaction of 'natural' needs. Yet this raises the issue of how Hegel can say that work is liberating when it involves the very satisfaction of these 'natural needs'. The indication is that by using the word 'moment' Hegel is suggesting that the liberation is not total but only part. This mirrors the example of the slave who, in working on the object, achieved only an aspect of freedom, but not total freedom. Dialectically, labour is the seed of freedom in the realm of unfreedom – natural necessity – which is why Hegel suggests that this liberation is only *'formal'*; that is, in form but not content.[115] Such a situation arises 'because the particularity of the ends remains the basic content'.[116] The universal is present in the moment of work, but particularity makes this work only a means to an end rather than an end in itself. Individuals *have* to satisfy the 'natural needs' of themselves and of others. Such an external pressure obviously curtails the individual's capacity to be free. This is the case even if the satisfaction of 'natural needs' multiplies infinitely into the indeterminacy of luxury consumption.[117] Work is still a means to an end and thus remains tied to particularity. So it follows that the creation of a distinct realm is essential to achieve a unity between the content and the form of liberation. To understand how this can happen, we have to consider the form that work takes through the Will's movement in civil society.

Hegel grasps the social basis to work in his declaration that 'it is by the sweat and labour of human beings that man obtains the means to satisfy his needs'.[118] When 'man' satisfies such needs it is 'human effort', embodied in 'human products', which he consumes.[119] Work allows the individual to develop important skills which enable him to produce objects as they 'ought to be', that is, in relation to universal require-ments.[120] Hegel notices how through this process 'the work of the individual becomes *simpler*, so that his skill at his abstract work becomes greater, as does the volume of his output'.[121] The limited nature of the task increases his skill but also extends his dependency on others – both in the workplace and in society. However, a further effect of the division of labour process is to make man's 'labour increasingly *mechanical*, so that the human being is eventually able to step aside and let a *machine* take his place'.[122] Labour, as the mediator between man's need and its satisfac-tion, results in man's expulsion from the labour process. Labour, which Hegel refers to as liberating, becomes 'mechanical' and severely limits man's capacity for freedom until he 'steps aside' from such a process.

Following this contradictory movement further, Hegel indicates that the interaction between the particular need-satisfaction of an individual and her or his link with the needs of others allows people to share in the resources of society.[123] Inequalities do arise, however, due to the assets a person already has, and the level of her or his own abilities and skills in acquiring such assets.[124] The particularity that ensues from this situation leads to the development of *'particular systems* of needs' which Hegel refers to as *'estates'* (*Stände*).[125] Estates mediate between particular individuals and the universal moment of the state.[126] They consist of the *'substantial* or immediate estate', the *'formal* estate', and the *'universal* estate'.[127]

The 'substantial estate' engages in agricultural production.[128] Due to the problem of seasonal fluctuations, the concern of this estate is with ensuring *'provision* for the future' and the 'lasting satisfaction of needs'.[129] Writing now in 1820, Hegel observes the increased mechanisation that has formed even in this section of the economy. He notes how agriculture is run 'like a factory' and as such resembles the second or 'formal estate'.[130] Even so, nature still dominates this level, and it immerses individuals in 'immediate feeling'.[131] Their concern is not with activities such as accruing wealth, but simply in immediately satisfying their needs.

The 'substantial estate' of agriculture takes natural products as they are. The second, 'formal estate' – the *'estate of trade and industry'* – focuses on *'giving form* to natural products' through the mediation of work and satisfying the needs of others.[132] This estate subdivides into three estates of *'craftsmanship'*, *'manufacturers'* and *'commerce'*.[133] The estate of craftsmanship arises in response to 'individual needs' (*einzelne Bed-ürfnisse*).[134] The estate of manufacturers also satisfies 'individual needs', but does so through the 'abstract work' of mass production, rather than the more specialised work of the craftsmanship estate.[135] Finally, the 'estate of commerce' engages in the exchange of commodities through the 'universal' form of money – a form that represents the 'abstract value' of all goods.[136]

Hegel sees the first estate of agriculture as being 'more inclined to subservience' than the second estate of trade and industry.[137] Individuals in the second estate have to rely on themselves and mediate raw materials instead of taking them as given. They are more independent, therefore, than members of the estate of agriculture, who show a 'willingness to accept whatever may befall [them] at the hands of other people'.[138] Consequently, Hegel sees the members of the estate of trade and industry as having a greater degree of freedom than their counterparts in agriculture.

The preoccupation of the third or 'universal estate' is with the '*universal interests* of society'.[139] This estate must be exempt from working for the direct satisfaction of its needs so that it is in complete contact with the universal and not the particular. This estate should thus have either private resources or some indemnity from the state to satisfy its needs.[140]

Hegel argues that although membership of an estate can depend on birth, the 'essential determinant' is '*subjective opinion* and the *particular arbitrary will*'.[141] People should therefore be free to choose their membership of an estate. They can then bring their arbitrary will into contact with the universal and develop a 'universal idea of *freedom*'.[142]

The liberation an individual experiences in an estate comes not from the specialised work undertaken, but from factors associated with the division of labour itself. One crucial factor is the 'recognition' from other 'estate' members that the individual is doing something useful for others.[143] For example, the fact that an individual masters the task of fitting hub caps to car wheels does not gain him or her recognition for the task itself. What people recognise instead is that in doing this task the individual is satisfying the needs of other people, and thereby displaying a moment of universality.

Such recognition is obviously important for human freedom, but the attempt to ground recognition as a fundamental right upon which to construct a community of ethical life[144] means little if humans remain tied to the realm of natural necessity. Only when humans overcome such a realm can they attain proper recognition and real freedom within an ethical community. The defeat of natural necessity is therefore a prerequisite for the development of the free individual and of ethical life. Consequently, a more potent moment of liberation than recognition has to be present in the division of labour to allow humans to escape this realm. I will disclose what exactly this 'potent moment' is shortly. For now, we must continue with the contradictory movement of the will as Hegel introduces the administration of justice.

Hegel argues that the system of needs contains the 'universality of *freedom*' only as an abstract right of property.[145] The administration of justice protects this right of property through law.[146] However, Hegel claims that this right 'comes into existence only because it is useful in relation to needs'.[147] It is therefore a practical measure which gives workers the right to protect the products of their labour. As Hegel states: 'only after human beings have invented numerous needs for themselves, and the acquisition of these needs has become entwined with their satisfaction, is it possible for laws to be made'.[148] So even laws themselves emanate from the individual satisfaction of needs. The right of the protection of property is not enough, however, as individuals also need their 'livelihood and welfare' to be '*secured*'.[149] To do this Hegel introduces the institutions of the 'Police' and the 'Corporation'.[150]

The police have a direct responsibly to interfere into the free operation of the market system to ensure the welfare of all individuals. The very 'multiplication' and 'interdependence' that arises from individuals' 'daily needs' leads to universal arrangements for their satisfaction.[151] Hence, Hegel perceives a need for public control over industries on which the whole community are dependent. The public authority therefore requires 'oversight' and 'advance provision' to ensure collective welfare.[152] Hegel includes a wide and extensive number of tasks that the police should undertake to counter the 'selfish ends' that are 'blindly' followed by supporters of free trade and commerce.[153] He argues that the police should settle disputes between producers and consumers, to ensure 'the public's right not to be cheated'.[154] He recognises that as many industries become dependent on international trade they need some form of guidance. Universal considerations might therefore have to predominate over the particular interests of each individual industry.[155] Hegel also identifies the need for carrying out major works projects publicly as opposed to privately, citing the building of the Egyptian pyramids as one historical example.[156]

Even more specifically, Hegel asserts that the police should also be responsible for providing 'street-lighting, bridge-building, the pricing of daily necessities and public health'.[157] Such intervention is crucial for Hegel, because civil society is an 'immense power' which 'tears' individuals away from the family, and makes them subject to 'contingency'.[158] The arbitrary nature of people's existence in the free market, based on inequalities in resources and skills, leads to the emergence of poverty.[159] Individuals reduced to poverty have the 'needs of civil society', but are

'deprived' of its advantages.[160] The contingency that arises out of
'*subjective* help' to alleviate this distress means that society has to try
to offer a more universal solution to the problem.[161] This proves very
difficult because of the dialectical operations of the free market. The
'unrestricted' development of civil society leads to the positive effect of
bringing people together 'through their needs' and the various ways in
which they satisfy them.[162] This also leads to the accumulation of wealth
and profit in society. The negative aspect of this process, however, is that
specialisation increases and the nature of work becomes more limited,
resulting in the 'dependence and distress (*Not*) of the class (*Klasse*) that is
tied to such work'.[163] This 'class' becomes unable to 'feel and enjoy the
wider freedoms' and 'spiritual advantages' of civil society.[164]

In the previous chapter, I indicated how Hegel distinguished between
'class' and 'estate'. Here again Hegel refers to workers tied to working in
the production process. The estate they belong to is the 'estate of
manufacturers' – a sub-estate of the 'estate of trade and industry' –
which performs the 'more abstract work of mass production'.[165] Within
this estate is a class of people who suffer particularly through the
expansion of civil society. They become a 'large mass of people' which
'sinks below the level of a certain standard of living'.[166] The 'certain
standard of living' is itself at a 'level necessary for a member of the society
in question'.[167] All members of society should at least be at this minimum
level. When people fall below this level they lose the 'feeling of right,
integrity, and honour' they gained through their work.[168] So there exists a
mass of people who descend into poverty due to the contradictions of civil
society. Within their midst arises a section of society who are at the
'lowest level of subsistence', which Hegel calls the 'rabble'.[169] Hegel
suggests that the minimum level of subsistence 'defines itself automati-
cally' as the minimum needed for an individual to live.[170] Constituted
socially in this way, it must therefore differ from society to society. The
poor, then, are people who are below a certain standard of living for a
society. Within the poor are the 'rabble', who live at the lowest level of
existence. As Hegel states: 'poverty in itself does not reduce people to a
rabble; a rabble is created only by the disposition associated with poverty,
by inward rebellion against the rich, against society, the government,
etc.'.[171] The 'hardship' associated with poverty is itself a 'wrong inflicted'
on this 'class' (*Klasse*).[172] Moreover, the tendency for 'disproportionate
wealth' to be 'concentrated in a few hands' further exacerbates such a
wrong.[173] The poor are in a dire situation because they cannot by
themselves use the mediation of work to satisfy their 'natural needs'.
Hegel notes how certain societies have attempted to address this problem.
One approach is simply to provide the poor with enough to maintain their

standard of living without work; but this seems to go against their own self-worth.[174] Another way is to make the poor work for money; but this only increases production, which is the very cause of their impoverished state in the first place.[175] Consequently, Hegel concludes that 'despite an *excess of wealth*, civil society is *not wealthy enough* . . . to prevent an excess of poverty and the formation of a rabble'.[176]

The natural operation of the market therefore produces poverty. Poverty is not some accident, but emerges from the natural working of the system itself through overproduction, necessitating a movement of goods to other economies to try to dissipate such a glut.[177] This allows the development of international trade and law, but also leads to the establishment of colonies.[178] The latter originate because of the 'emergence of a mass of people who cannot gain satisfaction for their needs by their work when production exceeds the needs of consumers'.[179] Overproduction and the onset of poverty, therefore, eventually lead to mass emigration.

So contradictions abound in civil society. As an 'immense power' it not only creates its own victims in the guise of the poor, but pushes itself beyond the boundaries of the nation state into the rest of the world. The mediating institutions of the estates seem ill-equipped to ensure the satisfaction of everyone's 'natural needs' beyond a meagre level. Similarly, the very expansion of the contradictions of civil society suggests that the police's attempt to provide some moment of universality could be far from successful. This leads to the development of a further mediating institution, the 'corporation', which contains the '*ethical*' as an 'immanent principle' within this realm of civil society.[180]

The corporation is 'specifically characteristic' of the 'estate of trade and industry' because the preoccupation of that estate is with the particular.[181] Individuals come together into a corporation through recognition of their particular trades and skills, and thereby come into contact with the universal.[182] The corporation therefore acts as a '*second* family' for its members by protecting them against contingency, ensuring a secure livelihood, and offering education to others to enable them to join.[183] Individuals now become conscious of the fact that they are providing for others.[184] The 'particularity of need and satisfaction' and 'abstract legal universality' are now 'inwardly united' within the corporation.[185] The welfare of individuals becomes a 'right' and actualises itself within this institution.[186] The achievement of greater universality, however, is possible only through the development of the state.[187] The state '*emerges*' from the 'ideal moments' of 'town and country'.[188] The country represents 'immediate ethical life', based on nature and the family, and the town represents the mediation of this 'immediate ethical life' through 'civil trade and industry'.[189]

The emergence of the state might suggest a solution to the destructive effects of natural necessity in civil society. Hegel, of course, refers to the latter very negatively as an '*external state*, the *state of necessity* (*Not*) *and of the understanding*'.[190] Civil society is an 'external state' because particularity and universality are still in contradiction with one another. People relate to each other 'externally' because they still see other people as a means to satisfy their own ends. However, aspects of interdependence and recognition emerge through people using each other in this way. Consequently, a universal element is present, but cannot assert itself fully until the state proper has been reached. This is because it is still the 'state of necessity' where humans satisfy their basic needs. The development of 'spiritual needs' is also taking place, but civil society still has the task of providing for everyone's basic needs. Humans can only be truly free, however, when they transcend the realm of necessity. Civil society is thus the realm where particularity and universality are still in contradiction with one another. People are pursuing their own ends and this activity contains a universal aspect. The particular and universal are only in a unity, however, when the individual is aware of such universality. Particularity and universality relate to one another externally in civil society because people comprehend them only as opposites.

The understanding is the level of cognition that dominates this realm. It conceives civil society as:

> an overly abstract and limited conception of the state which is unable to grasp the essential attributes of political life and instead focuses on certain 'external' aspects: the exchange of goods in a market, under the protection of a system of civil law, with certain welfare functions carried out by public and private agencies (the 'police' and the 'corporations').[191]

To understand universal and particular 'internally' and uncover the rational element present, we have to comprehend them in their totality, as contradictions within a unity. The selfish pursuit of my own ends in working for x hours a week to feed myself has the universal aspect of satisfying the needs of others through the products that I make. The particular moment of working to satisfy my own needs also contains within it the universal moment – my work in making goods for others. Only when I am conscious of this universality can true individuality and the rational element of freedom be achieved.

Elements of this consciousness do exist in civil society. The police, the corporation and work in general can offer mediation between universal and particular. Indeed, the importance of the mediating institutions in civil society has led writers such as Avineri to infer correctly that the role of Hegel's state is very minimalist. This is in contrast to interpretations, including Avineri's own previous views, which emphasised the more authoritarian aspect of the state.[192] Avineri argues that the state's relationship with civil society is not 'external'; the state does not impose its own sense of universality from outside, but is instead internally related to civil society. The universality or communitas, as Avineri describes it, 'grows organically within civil society itself'.[193] Yet this does not explain why Hegel should persist in calling civil society the 'external state'. I suggest that the main reason is that particularity and universality relate to one another externally and not internally within this realm. Within civil society particularity reaches its full development, and aspects of universality are present. However, individuals do not self-consciously work for and will those universal aspects. As Hegel points out, it is only in the state that individuals 'knowingly and willingly acknowledge this universal interest even as their own substantial spirit, and actively pursue it as their ultimate end'.[194] This does not mean that particularity has no role to play; on the contrary, the realisation of the universal is impossible without it. The difference is that 'individuals do not live as private persons merely for these particular interests without at the same time directing their will to a universal end and acting in conscious awareness of this end'.[195] The consciousness of universality, of actual willing, is what differentiates the individual in civil society from the individual in the 'ethical Idea' of the state.[196] Comprehending this distinction explains why Hegel referred to civil society as the 'external state' and why freedom is not 'actual' in that realm.

So the importance of humans overcoming the realm of natural necessity relates to their conscious willing of the universal, and the satisfaction of their 'spiritual needs'. How, though, can humans achieve this? Contradictions abound in civil society and even the state itself, as Avineri correctly notes, seems to have a minimal role in overcoming these difficulties. Moreover, the state is subordinate to 'world spirit', so it cannot be an end point for the Will's search for freedom.[197] I suggest that Hegel's comments concerning increased mechanisation and the expulsion of living labour from the production process can offer an answer to this problem (see Figure 4.4).

As we have already pointed out, Hegel is well aware that increased productivity allows the possibility of introducing automation in the production process. The fact that humans can 'step aside' from production and let a machine take their place is indicative of such a prospect.[198] Hegel expresses this most cogently and more fully in the early Jena lectures of 1805–6 in which, using Adam Smith's example of the pin factory, he states:

Figure 4.4   Freedom from necessity

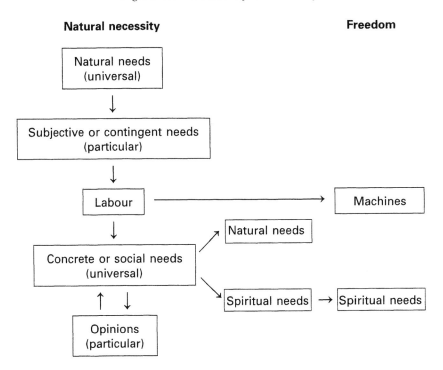

Universal labour . . . is division of labour, saving of labour. Ten men can make as
many pins as a hundred. Each individual, because he is an individual, labours for
one need. The content of his labour goes beyond his own need; he labours for the
needs of many, and so does everyone. Each person then satisfies the needs of many
and the satisfaction of his many particular needs is the labour of many others.[199]

Hegel is clearly equating the division of labour with the saving of labour
itself through increased productivity. The repetitive nature of the task is
not what is liberating; instead it is the increased productivity which
minimises the role of labour in the production process. Yet the irony is
that:

man only reduces labour for society as a whole, not for the individual; on the
contrary he increases it since the more mechanical the work is the less valuable it is
and so the more labour he must perform to make good the deficiency.[200]

The productivity and labour-saving aspects of the division of labour do
not free the individual from dull and repetitive work; instead they tie her
or him ever more firmly to such activity. The individual's 'dull labour
limits him to a single point and the work becomes more and more perfect
as it becomes more and more one-sided'.[201] It is 'one-sided' because

humans cannot truly express themselves through the creative power of labour, but instead find themselves reduced to a machine-like existence – the antithesis of their liberation. On this basis, Hegel clearly realised the degrading, stultifying nature of the tasks involved,[202] but he also noticed what was particularly valuable – the increased productivity which can reduce labour time in production and lead to a greater abundance of goods.

Interpreting Hegel in this way suggests that any production which is for immediate or 'natural needs' renders the individual non-universal and non-free. 'True' production can only take place after the initial satisfaction of 'natural needs'. When the individual engages in the production of 'natural needs' she or he is not universal. If the labour performed in the satisfaction of 'natural needs' is not universal then humans become indistinguishable from nonhuman animals, which, of course, satisfy only their immediate needs. As Hegel wants to distinguish humans from nonhuman animals the emphasis has to be on the satisfaction of humans' higher or 'spiritual needs', where creative work can then take place. The consequences of such an argument are deeply radical, because they suggest a need to minimise labour in the production of necessities in order to expand people's free time. Humans still have to satisfy their 'natural needs', of course, but the inference from Hegel seems to be that machines will increasingly do this, rather than people.[203] Hegel therefore overcomes the contradiction between 'nature' and 'spirit', necessity and freedom, that presented such a persistent and thorny problem throughout his writings.

IMPLICATIONS OF HEGEL'S NEED THEORY

We can now summarise the interpretation of Hegel's need theory suggested here by drawing on his analysis from the three moments of abstract right, morality and ethical life. As we indicated earlier, abstract right and morality are abstractions. The movement towards the realm of ethical life is therefore a movement from the abstract to the concrete. By drawing Hegel's analysis together from these moments, we can give an overview of the dialectical development of needs and their forms in the *Philosophy of Right* (see Figure 4.5).

Humans begin by having to satisfy their 'natural needs' in order to exist. Such needs are therefore universal, but the initial form they take is particular and relates to the 'subjective' or 'contingent need' of an individual. At a simple level of existence the satisfaction of these needs is immediate, but as society develops humans defer their gratification through the mediation of labour. The multiplication of their needs

Figure 4.5   Overview of needs in the Philosophy of Right

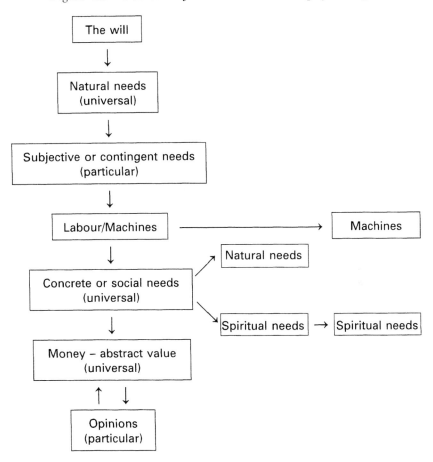

necessitates a division of labour and the introduction of machinery to produce a diversity of goods as productivity increases. Out of humans' necessity to satisfy their 'natural needs' arises an interdependent system of production, which results in 'social needs' that are universal. 'Natural needs', therefore, move from a universal form, to a particular form, and back to a universal. The introduction of money in a more developed economic system is a further universal form of need; but only symbolically. Money, as abstract value, is only a sign of need and not its full expression. Through the expenditure of money and changes in taste and utility, it seems that it is no longer needs that are being satisfied but 'opinions'. This suggests that society is at a high level of development because humans are not solely satisfying their 'natural needs' in a rudimentary manner. Although we still need water, for instance, we come to want mineral water from a particular spring.

There are tensions in this account of human development, which Hegel
is acutely aware of, however. As society develops, it reduces some people
to the appendages of a machine. The pursuit of need itself develops into
the pursuit of 'opinion' and luxury; at the same time, people fall into
depravity and destitution. There is, therefore, a dialectical conflict at the
heart of the development of the individual Will in the *Philosophy of Right*.
Some individuals will reach the level where they satisfy their 'opinions',
with their basic or 'natural needs' already secured. For others it will
simply be a matter of satisfying their 'natural needs' at a very simple level.
Some will overcome the level of the savage and reach the level of freedom,
while others will remain bound in the realm of unfreedom and immediacy. So although Hegel presents his 'system of needs' as the human
progression towards freedom, he also recognises the possibility of a
regression back to satisfying 'natural needs' in a very immediate manner. The 'spiritual needs' that are present as a moment in the realm of
natural necessity must become explicit and separate from this realm. The
implication I have drawn from Hegel's comments is that the introduction
of technology can overcome this separation by reducing the tyrannical
realm of natural necessity.

   The analysis of forms offers, therefore, a powerful understanding of
needs in Hegel's *Philosophy of Right*. Attention to form grasps needs
dialectically, in their movement and transition, from universal to particular and back again. Moreover, Hegel's emphasis on overcoming the
realm of natural necessity can itself be grasped as a moment within the
realm of unfreedom. 'Spiritual needs' exist as a moment within a realm
that seems to deny their very existence. Analysing the forms needs take
allows us to discern the dialectical movement of these moments so they
can receive full satisfaction in the spiritual realm of freedom.

NOTES

1. S. Avineri, *Hegel's Theory of the Modern State* (Cambridge University Press, Cambridge, 1972), p. 87; cf. B. Cullen, *Hegel's Social and Political Thought: An Introduction*
(Gill and Macmillan, Dublin, 1979), p. 58. The link between the *Philosophy of Right* and
the Jena writings suggests that Hegel's views did not become less radical in his later years.
The implicit nature of his comments in the *Philosophy of Right* had more to do with the
censorship prevailing at the time, not least in terms of the Carlsbad Decrees, than with any
reactionary turn in his thought. For the effect of censorship on Hegel's views see K.-H.
Ilting, 'Hegel's Concept of the State and Marx's Early Critique', in Z. A. Pelczynski (ed.)
The State and Civil Society: Studies in Hegel's Political Philosophy (Cambridge University
Press, Cambridge, 1984); S. Avineri, 'The Discovery of Hegel's Early Lectures on the
Philosophy of Right', *Owl of Minerva*, 16, Spring, 1985.
2. G. Rose, *Hegel Contra Sociology* (Athlone, London, 1981), p. 83.
3. K.-H. Ilting, 'The Structure of Hegel's *Philosophy of Right*', in Z. A. Pelczynski (ed.)

Hegel's Political Philosophy (Cambridge University Press, Cambridge, 1971), p. 99; cf. H. Brod, *Hegel's Philosophy of Politics: Idealism, Identity, and Modernity*, (Westview Press, Boulder co, San Francisco and Oxford, 1992), p. 20; A. W. Wood, *Hegel's Ethical Thought* (Cambridge University Press, Cambridge, 1990), pp. 21–2.

4. K. Westphal, 'The Basic Context and Structure of Hegel's *Philosophy of Right*', in F. C. Beiser (ed.) *The Cambridge Companion to Hegel* (Cambridge University Press, Cambridge, 1993), p. 246; Brod, *Hegel's Philosophy of Politics*, p. 36.

5. G. W. F. Hegel, *Elements of the Philosophy of Right*, trans. H. B. Nisbet (Cambridge University Press, Cambridge, 1991), para 5, hereafter cited as PR; G. W. F. Hegel, *Werke*, Volume VII (Suhrkamp Verlag, Frankfurt, 1970), p. 49.

6. Hegel, PR, para 6.

7. Hegel, PR, paras 11 and 11R.

8. Hegel, PR, para 11R; *Werke*, Vol. VII, p. 62.

9. Hegel, PR, paras 17 and 17A.

10. Hegel, PR, para 17; *Werke*, Vol. VII, p. 68.

11. Hegel, PR, para 18A.

12. Hegel, PR, para 19.

13. Hegel, PR, para 11A.

14. Hegel, PR, para 11A.

15. Hegel, PR, para 21.

16. Hegel, PR, para 37.

17. Hegel, PR, paras 41 and 41A.

18. Hegel, PR, para 41A.

19. Hegel, PR, para 41A.

20. Hegel, PR, para 45; *Werke*, Vol. VII, p. 107.

21. Hegel, PR, para 45R.

22. Hegel, PR, para 49.

23. Hegel, PR, para 59.

24. Hegel, PR, para 59A.

25. Hegel, PR, para 60; *Werke*, Vol. VII, p. 129.

26. Hegel, PR, para 60.

27. Hegel, PR, para 63; *Werke*, Vol. VII, p. 135.

28. Hegel, PR, para 63.

29. Hegel, PR, para 63A.

30. Hegel, PR, para 63A.

31. Hegel, PR, para 63A. Emphasis in the original translation.

32. Hegel, PR, para 63A.

33. Hegel, PR, para 63A.

34. Hegel, PR, para 123R.

35. Hegel, PR, para 123.

36. Hegel, PR, para 123.

37. Hegel, PR, para 123A.

38. Hegel, PR, para 124R.

39. Hegel, PR, para 125.

40. Hegel, PR, para 127.

41. Hegel, PR, para 127A.

42. Hegel, PR, para 127A.

43. Hegel, PR, para 127A and 128.

44. Hegel, PR, paras 129 and 136.

45. Hegel, PR, para 137A.
46. Hegel, PR, para 141A.
47. Hegel, PR, para 143.
48. Hegel, PR, paras 144 and 145.
49. Hegel, PR, para 147.
50. Hegel, PR, paras 154 and 156A.
51. Hegel, PR, paras 156A and 156.
52. Hegel, PR, para 157.
53. Hegel, PR, paras 158 and 158A.
54. Hegel, PR, para 158A.
55. Hegel, PR, paras 161 and 162.
56. Hegel, PR, para 163; *Werke*, Vol. VII, p. 313.
57. Hegel, PR, paras 163A and 163.
58. Hegel, PR, para 163A.
59. Hegel, PR, para 164R.
60. Hegel, PR, para 170.
61. Hegel, PR, paras 170 and 171.
62. Hegel, PR, para 171.
63. Hegel, PR, para 173A.
64. Hegel, PR, para 173A.
65. Hegel, PR, para 177.
66. Hegel, PR, paras 179 and 181.
67. Hegel, PR, para 181R; *Werke*, Vol. VII, p. 338.
68. Hegel, PR, para 181.
69. Hegel, PR, para 189A.
70. Hegel, PR, para 189A.
71. Hegel, PR, para 182.
72. Hegel, PR, para 182.
73. Hegel, PR, para 185.
74. Hegel, PR, para 185.
75. Hegel, PR, para 189.
76. Hegel, PR, para 182.
77. Hegel, PR, para 189.
78. Hegel, PR, para 190.
79. Hegel, PR, para 190; *Werke*, Vol. VII, p. 348.
80. Hegel, PR, para 190A.
81. Hegel, PR, para 190A.
82. S. Houlgate, *Freedom, Truth and History: An Introduction to Hegel's Philosophy* (Routledge, London, 1991), p. 107; see also Avineri, *Hegel's Theory of the Modern State*, p. 144; P Springborg, *The Problem of Human Needs and the Critique of Civilisation* (Allen and Unwin, London, 1981), p. 81.
83. As we saw in Chapter 1, the attempt to treat animals as determined by instinct is deeply problematic, as Darwin himself took care to indicate. See above, p. 11. Even the idea that nonhuman animals satisfy their 'natural needs' immediately also ignores the deferred gratification in some nonhuman animals, e.g. a squirrel hoarding nuts.
84. Hegel, PR, para 190.
85. Hegel, PR, paras 190, 190A, 192.
86. Hegel, PR, paras 190A, 191, 192; *Werke*, Vol. VII, p. 349.
87. Hegel, PR, para 191.

88. Hegel, PR, para 191A.
89. Hegel, PR, para 190A.
90. Hegel, PR, para 192.
91. Hegel, PR, para 191.
92. Hegel, PR, para 192.
93. Hegel, PR, para 190A.
94. M. Inwood, *A Hegel Dictionary* (Blackwell, Oxford, 1992), p. 48. Terms in square brackets in the original translation.
95. Hegel, PR, para 190A.
96. Hegel, PR, para 190A.
97. Hegel, PR, para 195A.
98. Hegel, PR, para 195A.
99. Cf. S. Benhabib, 'The "Logic" of Civil Society: A Reconsideration of Hegel and Marx', *Philosophy and Social Criticism*, 8, Summer, 1981, p. 157, who captures the movement from need to what she calls 'abstract want' but not in terms of the inner connections between different forms of need.
100. Hegel, PR, para 194; *Werke*, Vol. VII, p. 350.
101. Hegel, PR, para 194.
102. Hegel, PR, para 194.
103. Hegel, PR, para 190 and 190A.
104. Hegel, PR, para 192.
105. Hegel, PR, para 194; *Werke*, Vol. VII, p. 350.
106. Hegel, PR, para 194.
107. Hegel, PR, para 194R.
108. Hegel, PR, para 194R
109. Hegel, PR, para 194R
110. Hegel, PR, para 194R; *Werke*, Vol. VII, p. 350; cf. Avineri, *Hegel's Theory of the Modern State*, pp. 144–5. Hegel uses the term '*Arbeit*' throughout the *Philosophy of Right* and it is translated interchangeably as 'work' and 'labour' by both Nisbet and Knox. For the Knox translation see G. W. F. Hegel, *Philosophy of Right*, trans. T. M. Knox (Oxford University Press, Oxford, 1973).
111. G. W. F. Hegel, *Phenomenology of Spirit*, trans. A. V. Miller (Oxford University Press, Oxford, 1972), paras 178–96.
112. Hegel, *Phenomenology of Spirit*, para 196.
113. Hegel, *Phenomenology of Spirit*, paras 197–8; cf. R. Norman, *Hegel's Phenomenology: A Philosophical Introduction* (Sussex University Press, London, 1976), pp. 55–6.
114. For seminal contributions on the concept of recognition see A. Kojeve, *Introduction to the Reading of Hegel* (Basic Books, New York, 1969); G. A. Kelly, 'Notes on Hegel's "Lordship and Bondage"', in A. MacIntyre (ed.) *Hegel: A Collection of Critical Essays* (University of Notre Dame Press, London and Notre Dame, 1976).
115. Hegel, PR, para 195. Hannah Arendt's attempt to pose a clear distinction between labour (*Arbeit*) and work (*Werk*) cannot therefore apply to Hegel's argument here. She argues that labour (*Arbeit*) is distinguished by the fact that it has an 'unequivocal connotation of pain and trouble' whereas work (*Werk*) need not. Hegel's point, however, is that labour as 'toil' contains a higher form of labour existing within itself. H. Arendt, *The Human Condition* (University of Chicago Press, Chicago and London, 1958), p. 80, n. 3.
116. Hegel, PR, para 195.
117. Hegel, PR, para 195.

118. Hegel, PR, para 196A.
119. Hegel, PR, para 196.
120. Hegel, PR, para 197 and 197A.
121. Hegel, PR, para 198.
122. Hegel, PR, para 198.
123. Hegel, PR, para 199.
124. Hegel, PR, para 200.
125. Hegel, PR, para 201; *Werke*, Vol. VII, p. 354.
126. Hegel, PR, para 201A.
127. Hegel, PR, para 202.
128. Hegel, PR, para 203.
129. Hegel, PR, para 203 and 203R.
130. Hegel, PR, para 203A.
131. Hegel, PR, para 203A.
132. Hegel, PR, para 204.
133. Hegel, PR, para 204.
134. Hegel, PR, para 204; *Werke*, Vol. VII, p. 357.
135. Hegel, PR, para 204.
136. Hegel, PR, para 204.
137. Hegel, PR, para 204A.
138. Hegel, PR, para 204A.
139. Hegel, PR, para 205.
140. Hegel, PR, para 205.
141. Hegel, PR, para 206.
142. Hegel, PR, para 206R.
143. Hegel, PR, para 207.
144. See S. B. Smith, 'What is "Right" in Hegel's *Philosophy of Right?*', *American Political Science Review*, 83, 2, 1989; S. B. Smith, *Hegel's Critique of Liberalism*, (University of Chicago Press, Chicago and London, 1991).
145. Hegel, PR, para 208.
146. Hegel, PR, para 208.
147. Hegel, PR, para 209A.
148. Hegel, PR, para 209A.
149. Hegel, PR, para 230.
150. Hegel, PR, para 230A.
151. Hegel, PR, para 235.
152. Hegel, PR, para 235.
153. Hegel, PR, para 236R.
154. Hegel, PR, para 236.
155. Hegel, PR, para 236.
156. Hegel, PR, para 236R.
157. Hegel, PR, para 236A.
158. Hegel, PR, para 238 and 238A.
159. Hegel, PR, para 241.
160. Hegel, PR, para 241.
161. Hegel, PR, para 242.
162. Hegel, PR, para 243.
163. Hegel, PR, para 243; *Werke*, Vol. VII, p. 389. Translation modified. I follow Knox here in translating '*Not*' as 'distress' rather than 'want' as Nisbet does.

164. Hegel, PR, para 243.
165. Hegel, PR, para 204.
166. Hegel, PR, para 244.
167. Hegel, PR, para 244.
168. Hegel, PR, para 244.
169. Hegel, PR, para 244A.
170. Hegel, PR, para 244A.
171. Hegel, PR, para 244A.
172. Hegel, PR, para 244A; *Werke*, Vol. VII, p. 390.
173. Hegel, PR, para 244.
174. Hegel, PR, para 245.
175. Hegel, PR, para 245.
176. Hegel, PR, para 245.
177. Hegel, PR, para 246.
178. Hegel, PR, paras 247 and 248.
179. Hegel, PR, para 248A.
180. Hegel, PR, para 249.
181. Hegel, PR, para 250.
182. Hegel, PR, para 251.
183. Hegel, PR, para 252 and 253.
184. Hegel, PR, para 254A.
185. Hegel, PR, para 255.
186. Hegel, PR, para 255.
187. Hegel, PR, para 256.
188. Hegel, PR, para 256R.
189. Hegel, PR, para 256R.
190. Hegel, PR, para 183; *Werke*, Vol. VII, p. 340.
191. J. Schmidt, 'A Paideia for the "Burger als Bourgeois": The Concept of "Civil Society" in Hegel's Political Thought', *History of Political Thought*, II, 3, Winter, 1981, p. 471.
192. S. Avineri, 'The Paradox of Civil Society in the Structure of Hegel's Views of Sittlichkeit', *Philosophy and Theology*, 3, Winter, 1988, p. 171.
193. Avineri, 'The Paradox of Civil Society', p. 171.
194. Hegel, PR, para 260.
195. Hegel, PR, para 260.
196. Hegel, PR, para 257.
197. Hegel, PR, para 33A
198. Hegel, PR, para 198.
199. G. W. F. Hegel, *Hegel and the Human Spirit*, trans. L. Rauch (Wayne State University Press, Detroit, 1983), p. 121; G. W. F. Hegel, *Gesammelte Werke 8: Jenaer Systementwürfe III*, (eds) R.-P. Horstman with J. Henrich Trede (Felix Meiner Verlag, Hamburg, 1976), pp. 224–5. Translation modified. Cf. G. Lukács, *The Young Hegel. Studies in the Relation Between Dialectics and Economics* (Merlin, London, 1975), pp. 328–9.
200. G. W. F. Hegel, *System of Ethical Life and First Philosophy of Spirit*, trans. H. S. Harris and T. M. Knox (State University of New York Press, Albany N Y, 1979), p. 247; G. W. F. Hegel, *Gesammelte Werke 6: Jenaer Systementwürfe I*, (eds.) K. Düsing and H. Kimmerle (Felix Meiner Verlag, Hamburg, 1975), p. 321. Translation modified. Cf. Lukács, *The Young Hegel*, p. 330.

201. Hegel, *Hegel and the Human Spirit*, p. 139; *Gesammelte Werke 8*, p. 243. Translation modified. Cf. Lukács, *The Young Hegel*, p. 331.

202. Adam Smith himself noted various negative aspects of the division of labour. For a discussion see S. Hollander, *The Economics of Adam Smith* (Heinemann, London, 1973), p. 215.

203. Cf. Springborg, *Problem of Human Needs*, p. 88, who fails to see automation as a crucial foundation for the proper satisfaction of 'spiritual needs'.

5

HEGEL'S AESTHETIC NEED

The previous two chapters displayed how Hegel understands 'natural needs' and their satisfaction taking particular forms in society. Analysing forms captures, therefore, the dialectical movement of universal and particular conceptions of need. From a basic level of need-satisfaction, humans progress through the mediations of labour, machinery and money to satisfy a number of different needs in many diverse ways. So great is this diversity that Hegel suggests needs can take the form of 'opinions' – mere whims and fancies. Hegel also recognises that the contradictions of civil society reduce many people to satisfying their basic or 'natural needs' at a very simple level. Within this very process, however, 'spiritual needs' emerge, but their full satisfaction is only possible beyond the realm of natural necessity.

Such a conflict between nature and spirit, and the importance Hegel attaches to the notion of form, are a recurring theme in his *Aesthetics*. Previous writers have examined this text first as aesthetic theory, and second to determine its place in Hegel's system.[1] My main concern is how the *Aesthetics* can illuminate the way Hegel understands the concept of need.[2] Such an understanding, for Hegel, centres on three main questions. First, why is there a need for a philosophy of art? Second, why do humans need to produce art? Third, why do humans need to contemplate art?

Hegel also discusses the concept of need when examining the particular forms of art in certain historical periods. He comprehends these forms through the satisfaction of humans' 'natural needs', or humans' relation to nature, and their more spiritual concerns. As we shall see, for Hegel, the 'higher' or 'spiritual needs' of humans actually emanate from their 'natural needs'. The modes of existence of certain 'natural needs' are 'spiritual needs'. So an aesthetic need is a form 'natural needs' can take. Hegel's emphasis on understanding needs as forms, therefore, gains further support from an examination of needs in his *Aesthetics*.

THE NEED FOR A PHILOSOPHY OF ART

Hegel first mentions the concept of need in his *Aesthetics* from a comparison between art in his own time and art in ancient societies. He bluntly states that 'art no longer affords that satisfaction of spiritual needs (*geistigen Bedürfnisse*) which earlier ages and nations sought in it'.[3] The ancient Greeks may have venerated and worshipped works of art, but society in Hegel's time has gone beyond this. 'Art, considered in its highest vocation, is simply and remains for us a thing of the past.'[4] The emphasis is now on reflection and judgement, and not simply the immediate enjoyment of art.[5] For Hegel, the content of art, its means of presentation, and the suitability of the one to the other are now the main concerns of aesthetics.[6] Moreover, the fact that art no longer satisfies a 'spiritual' or 'highest need' (*höchstes Bedürfnisse*)[7] leads itself to a further need. As Hegel states:

> The *philosophy* of art is . . . a greater need in our day than it was in the days when art by itself as art yielded full satisfaction. Art invites us to intellectual considera- tion, and that not for the purpose of creating art again, but for knowing philosophically what art is.[8]

Philosophical reflection was not really necessary for the ancient Greeks because they recognised the spiritual significance of art and held it in deep esteem. With the veneration of art no longer present, a philosophy of art now becomes an urgent need. We require a 'higher touchstone and a different test' for works of art than the immediate spiritual satisfaction that sufficed for the ancient Greeks.[9] This subjection of art to philoso- phical analysis is itself 'satisfying the need of the spirit's inmost nature'.[10] This is because thought expresses itself through art and thereby aligns art with the realm of conceptual thinking. Spirit, which is 'the ego, the permanent universal centre of all our experience',[11] only satisfies itself when 'it has permeated all products of its activity with thought . . . and . . . made . . . them genuinely its own'.[12] Works of art are thus evidence of thought manifesting itself in the world as an embodiment of spirit's essential nature. Only through philosophical reflection, however, can art acquire its 'real ratification'.[13]

Hegel's prescription of the content for a philosophy of art is a clear example of his emphasis on uniting the abstract with the concrete, theory with practice, which we highlighted in the discussion of his method in Chapter 2. He stresses how the scientific treatment of art has, on the one hand, been content to take works of art as they are and arrange them into a 'history of art'.[14] On the other hand, it has also contented itself with general abstractions of what constitutes beauty with little or no reference to particular works of art.[15] For Hegel, Plato's treatment of artistic forms is a prime example of the latter approach.[16] Consequently, Hegel argues for the dialectical unity of these two opposing views, which can then conceive Plato's idea of the beautiful – his abstract universalisations of artistic forms – 'more concretely, more profoundly'; that is, in their particularity.[17] Universal and particular must come into a contradictory unity because Platonic ideas of abstract beauty can no longer satisfy 'the richer philosophical needs of our spirit today'.[18] Satisfying these needs requires the universal ideas of art to become particular, and the particular itself to embody aspects of the universal. The concept of art is then both a universal abstraction *and* a concrete, particular entity.[19] A philosophy of art begins with this concept of art but cannot just assume it; instead it must show the concept to be necessary.[20] This is a 'higher scientific need' (*höhere wissenschaftlichen Bedürfnis*), which involves proving that art is the consequence of some 'antecedent' universal concept of art.[21]

However, as Hegel notes, the starting point is concrete not abstract. There has to be an examination of 'the different ideas of the beautiful and art held by ordinary people, or [that] have formerly been accepted by them'.[22] Ordinary ideas of art must be subject to analysis and critique, whereas the system of philosophy itself simply presupposes a universal concept of art.[23] So Hegel is analysing the form art takes, from which he can then draw out the universal concept. Analysis or method of inquiry begins, therefore, with the concrete and not an abstract universal. So, as we elucidated in Chapter 2 when discussing Hegel's method, analysing forms is his starting point. We analyse forms, need-forms, art-forms, from which we can then draw out a universal concept. For Hegel, the universal concept of 'natural need' exists in many different forms. Similarly, the universal concept of art also exists in many different forms. By analysing the forms art takes in particular periods, Hegel will deduce why art itself no longer satisfies our 'highest need'. Before that, however, Hegel discusses the human need to produce and contemplate art.

THE NEED TO PRODUCE AND CONTEMPLATE ART

In his discussion of the human need to produce works of art, Hegel notes how some interpret artistic production simply as a product of human fancy.[24] He also recognises that humans may have even higher interests which art cannot satisfy. Despite such views, however, Hegel does think that art emanates from a 'higher impulse' (*höheren Triebe*) and satisfies 'higher needs' (*höheren Bedürfnissen*).[25] Indeed, at particular times, art satisfies 'the highest and absolute needs' (*absoluten Bedürfnis*) because 'it is bound up with the most universal views of life and the religious interests of whole epochs and peoples'.[26] Hegel indicates that the 'universal and absolute need' for producing art originates in the fact that the individual is a '*thinking* consciousness'.[27] Humans become conscious of themselves both theoretically and in practice. The theoretical aspect refers to humans being conscious of their emotions and feelings – 'whatever moves, stirs and presses in the human breast'.[28] 'Man' needs to be cognisant of his inner self so he can 'represent himself to himself' and thereby become an 'explicit self'.[29] The practical side of 'man' as a 'thinking consciousness' involves giving this 'explicit self' an 'outward reality'.[30] He achieves this through '*practical* activity', which involves 'altering external things' to allow 'the external realization of himself'.[31] Such a need is present, according to Hegel, in the 'most diversiform phenomena'; from a child's 'impulse' (*Trieb*) to throw a stone in a river and watch the resultant circles as an effect of her or his own actions, to the production of works of art themselves.[32]

Hegel concludes, then, that 'the universal need for art . . . is man's rational need to lift the inner and outer world into his spiritual consciousness as an object in which he recognises again his own self'.[33] Not just art but 'all acting and knowing' have their origin in this 'free rationality of man'.[34] So art is one particular form that the need for external self-realisation can take. This is important, because the implication of Hegel's comments is that many different ways of objectifying our inner self are examples of satisfying our 'spiritual needs'. The seemingly commonplace activity of a child throwing a stone into a river is one mode of existence of the natural need for self-realisation. This changing of the external environment is a moment of a 'spiritual need'. The production of a work of art is a further manifestation of the human need for self-realisation; as such it is an even greater moment of a 'spiritual need'. Even major works of art, therefore, are a form of humans' 'natural need' for self-realisation – a mode of existence of the need to objectify themselves and shape their external environment. In tracing the inner connection between phenomena, Hegel is indicating how the production of art relates to the very basic needs of humans.

In terms of humans' need to contemplate art, Hegel examines the common argument that art's purpose is to arouse feelings of pleasure.[35] He reports how this led many thinkers to investigate the type of feelings that art should arouse. Hegel quickly dismisses such a task. He argues that feeling is simply an 'emotional state of mind' and as such is 'an entirely empty form of subjective affection'.[36] Feelings are vague and differ from subject to subject. Consequently, any investigation of such feelings is itself vague because it is examining only the particular manifestation of a subject's emotions to a work of art. Instead, it is the work of art that demands examination to escape the 'indefiniteness and emptiness' of subjective feeling.[37] Hegel observes how certain thinkers attempted to escape this vagueness by specifying only one type of feeling for examination – the '*feeling* of the beautiful'.[38] The emphasis now centred on the discovery of taste. The aim was to educate people to see which works of art were tasteful and which not. Yet this was still one-sided and superficial because it related only to the external appearance of an object. Even worse, it was so vague in its operation that almost anything could qualify as being beautiful.[39] Such a failure led to the development of the connoisseur, whose concern was not simply to study works of art for the education of taste but also to exhibit taste himself.[40] One advantage of the advent of the connoisseur is that it did involve knowledge of the whole character of a work of art. The disadvantage was that it only analysed the 'external aspects' of artistic products, such as the technical or historical elements. It did not penetrate to the 'true nature of the work of art'.[41]

In contrast to the one-sided emphasis on the sensuous apprehension of art, Hegel stresses the importance of uniting such sensuousness with '*spiritual* apprehension'.[42] Works of art should affect humans' spirit as well as their senses. For Hegel, the sensuous aspect of a work of art should only be present in terms of its relation to humans' spirit. Sensuous apprehension is the 'least adequate to spirit' because it is in an 'appetitive relation' to the external world.[43] In this 'mode of apprehension', humans relate to any object rudimentarily as they are driven by particular 'impulses and interests' in the form of desire.[44] Objects are simply 'destroyed and consumed' as humans become determined by their desires, which themselves become determined by these external objects.[45] Hegel argues for the elimination of this form of desire when considering works of art. The work of art must be free to exist in its own form and not simply be consumed or destroyed. Consequently, humans must relate themselves to an object of art without desire. They must refer to 'the contemplative side of spirit alone'.[46] If humans are to satisfy their 'purely spiritual interests' then they have to supersede the sensuousness that works of art present.[47] So art can, and does, appear to humans sensuously, but they have to rise above that level of presentation and fulfil their spiritual concerns through contemplation.

A second way in which sensuousness relates to spirit is through '*intelligence*'.[48] In contrast to sense-perception and practical desire, intelligence is a 'theoretical study of things' which does not consume objects. Instead, intelligence comes to know objects in their 'universality', discovering their 'inner essence and law, and conceiving them in accordance with their Concept'.[49] Interestingly, however, Hegel suggests that art cannot follow this 'work of science' in transforming the object into a universal concept distinct from its appearance as a sensuous object.[50] Art has an interest in an object in its 'individual existence' and not in terms of its universal aspect.[51]

There is a very close link between humans' need to produce art and contemplate it, because the sensuous nature of art is the form in which spirit itself appears. Humans make objects of art to try to satisfy 'higher spiritual interests'.[52] So art itself only exists because it has arisen from 'spiritual productive activity'. Yet this spiritual aspect must unite with the sensuous aspect of art. Hegel indicates, for instance, how only bad poetry can result where a poet begins with a thought and then adds poetical images and rhyme to it. These cannot be separate but must be in an 'undivided unity'.[53] The poet needs to unite the spiritual and sensuous aspects of his or her artistic production together. It is 'activity of artistic imagination' that exists as the 'rational element' – as spirit – when it propels itself into consciousness through the mediation of sensuousness. So humans' need to produce art arises from the general need to objectify themselves in the world in some way and make manifest their spirit. Humans' very contemplation of art is a form in which they satisfy their 'spiritual needs'. Spirit appears in a sensuous form through artistic production. Humans contemplate this sensuous form through their own senses, but these senses need dissipating so humans can apprehend art spiritually. On one side, the human spirit exists in its sensuous form in an art object. On the other, the human spirit contemplates the work of art in its sensuous form. There is a reciprocation, therefore, between the need to produce art and the need to contemplate art.

For Hegel, then, humans have a need to produce and contemplate art to satisfy their 'spiritual' or 'higher needs'. Concerning the need to produce art, Hegel points out that almost anyone can reach a particular level.[54] 'Art proper', however, only begins beyond this level and rests on an 'inborn, higher talent' that can only be present in a minority of people.[55] This implies that although everyone has a need to produce art, real or 'proper art' is the preserve of the few. Not everyone can be a Mozart or a Matisse, but everyone has the need to make her or his inner self externally explicit in some way. Externalisation can take the mundane form of throwing stones in a river or that of creative work. Art is one particular and important form in which humans satisfy this need for externalisation.

Concerning the need to contemplate art, Hegel clearly thinks that a real 'spiritual need' is being satisfied. Yet what of those who have no interest in contemplating works of art? Hegel would have to say that they are not satisfying their 'spiritual needs'. This is why he thinks that art should be open to everyone.[56] Not only can anyone produce art in some form, anyone can also contemplate art. 'We must make clear', he states:

> that works of art are not to be composed for study or for the learned . . . For art does not exist for a small enclosed circle of a few eminent *savants* but for the nation at large and as a whole.[57]

Art should not be elitist; it should allow all people to appreciate works of art and thereby satisfy their 'spiritual needs'. However, Hegel does add a caveat in that the appreciation of art from different historical periods and cultures requires some knowledge of the concerns and interests of these civilisations.[58] So if people lack this knowledge there could be limitations on their capacity to contemplate artistic works properly.

THE AIM OF ART

Having established the human need both to produce and to contemplate art, need next arises in Hegel's consideration of the aim of art. He rejects the commonplace thought that the aim is to imitate nature. He thinks this is a forlorn task because works of art cannot compare with nature. Moreover, it is a superfluous activity because we can simply go and look at the real thing. Imitative art can only produce 'one-sided deceptions' which depict a 'pretence of life'.[59] Consequently, art imitating nature is 'like a worm trying to crawl after an elephant'.[60] Imitative skill is restrictive in its delight. In contrast, the 'free productive power of man' requires that he takes delight in what 'he produces out of himself'.[61] Imitative art is simply on a par with 'the trick of the man who had learnt to throw lentils through a small opening without missing'.[62]

Another common opinion on the aim of art suggests that it brings to our senses and feeling 'everything which has a place in the human spirit'.[63] On this view, art awakens our passions and draws out all our varied emotions so that we become moved by the experiences of life. Yet the problem with seeing art's aim in this way, according to Hegel, is that the experience felt is not real but an appearance of reality; it is deception. Moreover, the idea of arousing myriad feelings within us gives art no explicitly fixed task. Any type of emotion or feeling that a work of art arouses would therefore be art's aim. For Hegel, this is so wide as to be meaningless, because it would include 'every possible kind of content and worth'.[64] This 'jumbled diversity' is not the end or aim of art but must

itself be penetrated to uncover a 'higher' and 'more universal end'.[65]
Hegel attempts to understand what this 'end' of art is through the concept
of need.

Hegel notes how some writers have interpreted the aim of art as being a
form of moral instruction and guidance.[66] He totally rejects this as a
possible end of art because it actually makes art a means – a means to the
end of moral instruction.[67] Moreover, such a 'modern moralistic view'
holds the spiritual, universal will in a 'fixed opposition' to the particular,
sensuous will.[68] Instead of attempting a reconciliation of these opposites,
the 'moralistic view' sees only a 'reciprocal battle' between them, with the
spiritual being preferred over the sensuous.[69] Hegel's concern is to
reconcile these opposites. He observes how such an opposition between
the sensuous and the spiritual emerges for consciousness, not simply in
moral action, but in every aspect of human existence. In its abstract form,
it is the opposition of universal and particular. In its concrete form, it is in
nature as the opposition of 'abstract law' to the 'abundance of individual
phenomena'.[70] In spirit, it takes the form of the opposition between the
sensuous and the spiritual in humans. These oppositions have become
increasingly heightened in modern culture, and have resulted in an
opposition that makes the human an 'amphibious animal' living in
'two worlds which contradict one another'.[71] One of these worlds sees
'man imprisoned' in 'reality and earthly temporality, borne down by need
and poverty, hard pressed by nature, enmeshed in matter, sensuous ends
and their enjoyment, mastered and carried away by natural impulses and
passions'.[72] In the other world, 'man':

> lifts himself to eternal ideas, to a realm of thought and freedom, gives to
> himself, as *will*, universal laws and prescriptions, strips the world of its
> enlivened and flowering reality and dissolves it into abstractions, since the
> spirit now upholds its right and dignity only by mishandling nature and denying
> its right, and so retaliates on nature the distress and violence which it has
> suffered from itself.[73]

A problem with 'modern culture' is that it wants to resolve these two
contradictory worlds by arguing that one is preferable to the other. In
contrast, Hegel argues that the task of philosophy is to supersede these
oppositions to show that neither one nor the other possesses truth.
Finding this truth depends on the 'reconciliation and mediation' of
both of these worlds.[74] For Hegel, philosophy 'shows how truth is just
the dissolving of opposition', not so that these opposites do not exist at all,
but so that they 'exist reconciled'.[75] For Hegel, then, art's vocation is to
'unveil the *truth* in the form of sensuous artistic configuration, to set forth
the reconciled opposition just mentioned, and so have its end and aim in

itself, in this very setting forth and unveiling'.[76] Art must 'reduce to unity' the 'opposition and contradiction between the abstractly self-concentrated spirit and nature'.[77] This opposition between nature and spirit now takes centre stage in Hegel's philosophy of art.

ART, NATURE AND SPIRIT

To explain how art fits into the 'entire sphere of natural and spiritual life', Hegel examines the 'whole field of our existence', which he understands in terms of needs.[78] He notes how we have a system of physical needs that we satisfy through 'trade, shipping and technologies', the state, the 'need of religion', and the 'activity of science', which 'comprehends everything'.[79] The need for 'artistic activity' and a 'spiritual satisfaction in artistic creations' arises amongst these spheres.[80] How, though, does the need for art relate to these realms? Hegel offers an answer through the importance of recognising an 'inner connection' between these spheres of need. He suggests that they appear to be 'simply present as such', and their relation to each other is seemingly in terms of utility. However, they do 'complement one another', as one sphere contains 'higher modes of activity' than the other. In discovering the 'necessity of an inner connection', the lower sphere 'presses on above itself', searching for the 'deeper satisfaction of wider-ranging interests' and securing these satisfactions by thus entering a higher sphere.[81]

Expanding on this point, Hegel reiterates that the concept of art has a content or a meaning and a realisation or appearance of this content.[82] The meaning or content is 'abstract in form' and has to become concrete to realise itself in appearance.[83] For the 'conscious subject', this realisation is initially an 'unsatisfied need', as it remains in the abstract.[84] The content is simply subjective and inside the 'conscious subject'. The need is to make this abstract content concrete – to objectify it. For Hegel, this opposition between subject and object is a 'universal characteristic running through everything'.[85] Humans are initially in the 'one-sided form of subjectivity', which, as a restriction, becomes manifest in 'unrest' and 'grief' as a negative. Overcoming or negating this contradiction can allow life to become 'affirmative'.[86]

Hegel points out that within the subject the highest content is freedom, but it exists there only in the abstract. In reality, humans as subjects are 'confronted by the unfree' object of the 'necessity of nature'.[87] Obviously, then, they have to reconcile this opposition. The subject must overcome the object as nature. Yet such a conflict also exists within the subject himself. Humans' concern is for the '*immediate* satisfaction' of their 'sensuous needs' (*sinnlichen Bedürfnisse*), such as hunger and thirst.[88]

Eating and drinking overcome this opposition, but as this is the 'natural sphere of human existence' satisfaction is not absolute. Consequently, a 'new neediness (*Bedürftigkeit*) arises continually and restlessly' because 'hunger and weariness begin again on the morrow'.[89] Humans engage in a 'struggle to cancel this situation of unfreedom', driven by the 'impulse of curiosity' and the 'pressure for knowledge'. The aim is 'to make the world one's own in one's ideas and thought'.[90]

Tied to finitude and necessity, humans seek 'a higher, more substantial, truth in which all oppositions and contradictions in the finite can find their final resolution, and freedom its full satisfaction'.[91] Oppositions, such as those between freedom and necessity, disappear at this level of absolute truth. Instead, three realms of absolute spirit are present: art, religion and philosophy.[92] They each bring the absolute to consciousness, but do so in different forms. Art, as the first form, does so through '*sensuous* knowing'.[93] Religion, the second form, brings knowledge of the absolute through '*pictorial* thinking'.[94] Finally philosophy, the third form, is the '*free* thinking of absolute spirit'.[95]

Examining these in turn, Hegel asserts that art 'sets truth before our minds in the mode of sensuous configuration'.[96] Art appears in this sensuous form and has a 'loftier, deeper sense and meaning'.[97] It is the 'first and immediate satisfaction of absolute spirit' and can offer people an awareness of truth.[98] For Hegel, Greek art is one example of this because it represented the gods to the people and so gave them a concrete idea of the 'behaviour, life and effectiveness of the Divine'.[99] Hence, religion itself used art to bring an awareness of religious truth to people. So art does bring some manifestation of the absolute and truth to people, but its limitations require its transcendence. Art no longer stands as the highest mediation of truth. Only very early in history did it fulfil this function, but as civilisation develops 'art points beyond itself.'[100] Christianity used art for the depiction of Christ's life and death, but the 'urge for knowledge and research, and the need for inner spirituality' dissipated its use in this form. The Reformation meant that the presentation of religious ideas no longer assumed a sensuous form, but instead reverted to an 'inner self'.[101] Spirit's 'need' now satisfies itself inwardly and not outwardly. Hegel argues, therefore, that in his time 'the form of art has ceased to be the supreme need of spirit'.[102] Objects of art, even if they portray divine images of God and Christ, have lost their influence over us: 'we bow the knee no longer [before these artistic portrayals]'.[103]

It is the sphere of religion that transcends the sphere of art. The absolute is now manifest in 'pictorial thinking' within the subject, and not outside in objects of art.[104] Whereas art presents truth or spirit in a sensuous form as an object, religion instead internalises the content of this object. The absolute now exists as an '*inner* presence in ideas and depth of feeling', which manifests itself in worship.[105]

Philosophy is the final form of absolute spirit.[106] The 'untrammelled *thinking*' of philosophy is the 'purest form of knowledge', which surpasses the 'inwardness' present in religion's pictorial thinking and the 'heart's worship'.[107] Philosophy unites the objectivity of art with the subjectivity of religion. The objectivity of art exchanges its 'external sensuousness' for the 'form of thought'. Religion now purifies into the 'subjectivity of thinking'. On the one side, we have thinking, which is the 'most inward, closest, subjectivity'. On the other is 'true thought', which is the most 'objective universality'.[108] Philosophy, as the 'purest form of knowledge', reconciles them both.[109]

On the basis of this overview of aesthetics, Hegel postulates a universal, particular and individual understanding of art. The universal aspect refers to the beauty or ideal of art. The particular relates to the forms art can take: symbolic, classical and romantic. The individual refers to the five main types of art, which, for Hegel, are architecture, sculpture, painting, music and poetry. We can now examine how the concept of need appears within these universal, particular and individual moments, beginning with the universal ideal of art.

BEAUTY OR IDEAL OF ART

It is in Hegel's discussion of the relation of art to the external world that needs again come to the fore. Hegel argues that humans' 'relation of *dependence*' to nature ties them to the activity of satisfying their needs.[110] Humans can only become an object for art by ending this dependence. On the one side, nature supplies humans with what they need, but on the other side, 'man has needs and wishes which nature is in no position to satisfy directly'.[111] Humans in this case have to satisfy their needs by taking possession of the objects nature offers, and changing these objects through their 'self-won skillfulness'.[112] Uniting this 'spiritual skillfulness' with 'the friendliness of nature', however, is one way to overcome the 'harshness and dependence of struggle' that besets humans.[113] Such a reconciliation between humans and nature allows the 'purest relationship' to exist.

Even so, the distress caused by having to satisfy our basic needs leads Hegel to conclude that such an activity should be 'banished' from the 'ideal ground of art'.[114] He maintains that a 'situation in which poverty and labour vanish, not merely momentarily but entirely', coincides with the 'Ideal'. However, he realises that art cannot totally dispense with the 'sphere of needs' tied to finitude.[115] The capacity to pursue art is dependent on the 'externals of life', such as the basic needs for food and drink. These needs are also present in the 'inner life', where they become 'manifold' in their form and satisfaction. Hegel concludes, however, that for art:

> the genuine ideal consists not only in man's being in general lifted above the grim seriousness of dependence on these external circumstances, but in his standing in the midst of a superfluity which permits him to play freely and cheerfully with the means put at his disposal by nature.[116]

To partake in this artistic creativity, humans must abolish the realm of natural necessity. For example, Hegel reports how the ancient Greeks poured an immense amount of wealth into artistic production, instead of using such wealth to feed poor Athenians or to ransom slaves. He therefore stresses how art should demand that 'distress and poverty' be 'set aside'. Art can then rise above the 'distress of reality' and use natural things for '*contemplative* satisfaction'.[117]

In contrast to this form of artistic pursuit is humans' use of external things to satisfy their 'practical needs'.[118] Humans have to work to satisfy their 'physical needs', which themselves 'stir up a broad and variegated range of activities' that gives humans an 'inner power'.[119] It is out of this 'feeling' that humans develop even more 'deeper interests and powers'.[120] This idyllic or golden age of art, as Hegel terms it, now finds itself opposed by what he refers to as 'universal culture'.[121] The tremendous productive developments in society lead to a situation where all individuals lose their independence and become 'tied down in an endless series of dependence on others'.[122] Humans no longer engage themselves actively with nature to satisfy their own 'physical needs'. Instead, their activity becomes 'purely mechanical'. 'Industrial civilization', with its 'mutual exploitation' and with 'people elbowing other people aside', results in the 'harshest cruelty of poverty'. A positive effect of this development, however, is that 'individuals who are freed from working to satisfy their needs . . . can now devote themselves to higher interests' – humans are no longer 'stuck in the sordiness of gain'.[123] Ironically, though, Hegel recognises how even this causes problems because individuals are not at home in a world they have not created. 'Man' takes his goods from what other people have produced 'through a long chain of efforts and needs foreign to himself'.[124] Consequently, an alternative exists which stands between the idyllic and golden ages and modern industrialised civil society, namely, the 'Heroic' or 'ideal age'.

In this 'Heroic age' people still satisfy their 'immediate needs' (*unmittelbaren Bedürfnisse*) themselves. So they do not encounter 'alienated objects' that they have not worked on.[125] Hegel stresses how the individual's labour in satisfying these needs should avoid 'painful drudgery' and instead be 'easy, satisfying work that puts no hindrance and no failure in his way'.[126] Works of art by Homer depict such a way of life, where 'man has present before his eyes the power of his arm, the skill of his hand, the cleverness of his own spirit, or a result of his courage and bravery'.[127] The 'Heroic age' sees humans satisfying their 'natural needs' themselves in a spiritual manner through work. The 'spiritual relation-ships' of ethical life appear here as 'custom, usage and habit', not as the distinct moments of 'religion, law, morality, . . . political organisation, the constitution, law courts, family, public and private life, sociability, etc.'.[128] Nature and spirit become entwined. We must now consider, however, the tensions between these two elements that give rise to Hegel's classification of the main forms of art.

SYMBOLIC, CLASSICAL AND ROMANTIC FORMS OF ART

Hegel specifies the differences between the symbolic, classical and romantic forms of art through meaning and form, and humans' relation to nature. These art-forms arise in particular historical and social periods, and are a reflection of the concerns of that particular society.[129] The symbolic art-form, and the symbol in particular, 'constitute the beginning of art' and relate to eastern nations such as Egypt and India.[130] The symbolic art-form is the first manifestation of the universal concept as a stage in the progression to 'genuine art'.[131] The main deficiency of the symbolic form of art is that meaning and its appearance either separate from each other, or unite together only symbolically.[132] Symbolism in Egyptian art, for instance, 'confusedly intertwines meaning and shape' and makes one symbol into an 'ensemble of symbols'.[133] Meaning can therefore only appear imperfectly, as is the case in the symbol of the sphinx. The latter takes so many forms in Egyptian society that it ends up a riddle in Greek mythology. Hegel argues that the symbol cannot properly articulate the meaning of spirit. Even the famous pyramids are a poor symbol for the 'realm of death and the invisible', which, Hegel purports, is their inner meaning.[134]

The symbolic art-form arises in a period that sees humans under the power of nature while at the same time trying to change nature to satisfy their needs.[135] Humans' relation to nature exacerbates this separation between the meaning of spirit and its form. Humans relate to nature in this historical period reverentially, interpreting nature's objects, such as seas, rivers, mountains, etc., as divine.[136] Humans, in objectifying themselves by shaping the objects of nature, see in these objects a form of spirit. Yet it is only an 'inkling' of this universal aspect.[137] Thus a

contradiction emerges between spirit and nature, reflecting the contradiction between meaning and shape. It is the classical form of art that
resolves this contradiction.

Hegel contends that the 'cleavage' between 'meaning and shape'
actually produces the 'proper need for art', which is the attempt to
unite these disparate aspects.[138] The classical art-form in ancient Greece
is where such a unity takes place.[139] With Greek mythology, for instance,
the 'inmost and deepest convictions' of the Greeks became manifest 'not
in the form of thought but in shapes devised by imagination without
separating the universal abstract ideas from the concrete pictures'.[140] The
universal meaning exists in the shape of the pictures. Understanding
meaning and shape separately, and not as a contradictory unity, creates a
division that only art can heal.[141] The attempt to reconcile meaning and
the shape of that meaning or content and the form of that content is the
'proper need for art'. Yet such a reconciliation must also take place
between spirit and nature.

Hegel makes the distinction between the 'immediate aims of life',
related to the satisfaction of 'primary needs' (nächsten Bedürfnisse), and
the realm of political organisation concerned with 'ethics, law, property
rights, freedom and community'.[142] In the 'Heroic age', as we have just
seen, these are both entwined. Hegel observes how Greek mythology
plays out this opposition using the Titans and the Olympians. Prometheus was a Titan because he provided people with the 'cunning to
master things in nature and use them as a means to human satisfaction'.[143]
Prometheus gave humans 'fire and skills' but nothing spiritually or
ethically. Only Zeus offered humans a more ethical basis to life, providing
'respect for others and a sense of justice'.[144] On the one side, humans satisfy
their 'lower needs' (menschlichen Bedürfnisse)[145] or 'primary needs'. On the
other side, humans have 'spiritual needs' that they can only satisfy through
the system of ethical life. This conflict between nature and spirit is
sublated. The realm of merely satisfying 'natural needs' (Naturbedürfnis) is 'put into the background',[146] but this realm is also preserved because
the 'satisfaction of needs' (Befriedigung der Bedürfnisse) – which Prometheus's fire has contributed to – is 'an essential feature in human
existence'.[147] Consequently, we have to understand the realm
of natural necessity and the realm of spirit as a contradictory unity.[148]
In artistic representation, Greek society dialectically overcomes this
opposition.

Under the symbolic form of art, humans immersed themselves in, and
worshipped, the objects of nature. Although this did allow humans some
grasp of their own spirituality, they still remained tied to nature.
Overcoming the split between nature and spirit, and meaning and

form, requires a society where the classical form of art is prevalent. The period of the classical art-form was one in which 'the perfection of art reached its peak' precisely because 'it idealised the natural and made it into an adequate embodiment of spirit's own substantial individuality'.[149] For Hegel, 'nothing can be or become more beautiful'.[150] Yet a third form of art, the romantic, arises because spirit no longer finds satisfaction in the external form of its existence.[151] Instead, it finds reconciliation within itself. The development of Christianity, and in particular the Reformation, emphasised an inward satisfaction of the human spirit compared to an outer satisfaction in objects of art. The 'true content of romantic art is absolute inwardness', and its form is 'spiritual subjectivity with its grasp of its independence and freedom'.[152] Romantic art has, therefore, a spiritual realm within and an external realm, which is simply 'empirical reality'.[153] In the classical form of art 'empirical reality' was the form in which the content of spirit appeared. Romantic art rejects 'external appearance' in favour of inner 'mind and feeling'.[154] This turning of spirit into itself means that it can no longer find its true existence in the 'mere contingency' of nature.[155] Consequently, inner and outer become separate and art can no longer offer us the 'apprehension of truth'.[156] We must seek truth in 'higher forms', which, as we have seen, are religion and, ultimately, philosophy itself. Hegel's next concern, however, is the manifestation of these art-forms into the individual arts of architecture, sculpture, painting, music and poetry.

THE INDIVIDUAL ARTS

Art-forms 'acquire their determinate existence' through the individual arts.[157] Architecture is the first manifestation of art and actually arises from the material necessity of building a hut or a house.[158] Such a construction is based on 'a need lying indeed outside art, and its appropriate satisfaction has nothing to do with fine art and does not evoke any works of art'.[159] Humans in their practical activity build houses to satisfy their 'specific needs' (*bestimmter Bedürfnisse*) for shelter.[160] For Hegel, such constructions are indicative of an 'external aim and need' – the aim of building a house to satisfy the need for shelter.[161] The making of such edifices is not to affirm the human spirit, but simply a means to satisfy human needs. Architecture, however, must 'fashion external nature . . . into beauty by art out of the resources of the spirit'.[162] The 'meaning' of the building, therefore, is in the building or object itself, and not in the human need for shelter or a place of worship. As Hegel explains:

> When architecture serves a purpose, the real purpose is there independently as a statue or, more particularly, as human individuals assembled as a community or

nation for ends which are universal, i.e. religious or political, and which do not now
issue from the satisfaction of physical needs (*physischer Bedürfnisse*).[163]

Hegel's hostility to the tyranny of having constantly to satisfy our
'natural needs' is again present here. In relation to art, natural necessity is
an impediment to true aesthetic production and appreciation. The
satisfaction of humans' higher, 'spiritual needs' depends on eschewing
ends which relate to 'physical needs'. However, the very 'starting point'
for architecture is precisely the 'real needs' (*eigentlichen Bedürfnisse*) of
people in their practical activity.[164] So the spiritual arises initially from
the material needs of humans. This theme is a guiding thread through the
other individual arts that express the greater development of humans'
'spiritual needs' within the aesthetic realm.

Sculpture, the next type of art Hegel considers, gives an independence
to spirit that is not fully present in architecture.[165] The tendency of the
latter to be enmeshed in external purposes, such as satisfying 'natural
needs', means that it is a lesser type of art than sculpture. Sculpture gives
spirit a 'corporeal shape' that is 'purposive' and 'independent in itself'.[166]
For Hegel, the 'sculptural form' of the human figure is a perfect example
of this.[167] He argues that the 'human attitude and face . . . is expressive of
the spirit'.[168] This is in contrast to 'the animal which does not go beyond
the expression of animated natural life in its firm connection with natural
needs (*Naturbedürfnissen*) and with the animal organism's structure that is
designed for their satisfaction'.[169] Again, Hegel emphasises the spiritual
aspect assigned to humans in distinction from nonhuman animals, which,
as ever, remain tied to the realm of natural necessity.

Hegel thinks this is particularly evident in the sculptural impressions of
the head in Classical Greece. He suggests that in the formation of the
animal head the mouth is 'predominant' because it is the 'tool for
chewing'.[170] All the other animal's organs are simply 'servants and
helpers' to the mouth – the nose sniffs out food whilst the eye simply
spies it.[171] Consequently, the prominence of these organs which are
'exclusively devoted to natural needs (*Naturbedürfnis*) and their satisfaction gives the animal head the appearance of being merely adapted to
natural functions and without any spiritual ideal significance'.[172] Tied to
the realm of natural necessity, and dependent on the 'merely material
aspect of nourishment', the animal has a complete 'spiritual absence'.[173]
These characteristics that are so prominent in the animal 'must be in the
background in man' if he is to emphasise his spiritual aspect.[174]
Accordingly, Hegel suggests it is the 'intellectual brow' and the 'eye,
expressive of the soul' through which humans' 'spiritual relation to things
is manifested'.[175] This 'theoretical and spiritual brow' is in contrast to the

'practical organ of nourishment', the mouth.[176] The connection between these two is the nose, which in its 'natural function as the organ of smell stands in between our theoretical and practical relation to the external world'.[177] Hegel recognises that in this activity of smelling the nose still belongs to an 'animal need' (tierischen Bedürfnis).[178] Yet it can acquire a more 'spiritual expression and character' the more the nose is 'drawn up' towards the forehead.[179] Hegel thinks this is evident even in everyday activities, such as screwing up one's nose quickly to express a 'spiritual judgement'.[180] Similarly, the 'natural purpose' of the mouth is to serve as a 'tool for eating and drinking'.[181] Sculptural representations of the human mouth should, therefore, 'remove . . . what is purely sensuous and indicative of natural needs (Naturbedürfnisse)' to give the mouth a more 'spiritual bearing'.[182]

What Hegel's comments display here is the recurring theme of emphasising 'spiritual' over 'natural needs'. However, he also recognises the dialectical relationship between these two moments. The mouth is an organ of natural necessity but also an organ of spirituality, as it is the 'seat of speech'.[183] 'Spiritual needs', therefore, emanate out of 'natural needs', but to be truly spiritual, to be expressive of the human essence, the aspect of natural necessity must be eliminated or at least drastically reduced. Through the further developments of the individual arts, spirituality eschews its initial immersion in nature and properly manifests the human spirit. The romantic arts of painting, music and poetry are these very developments.

Hegel believes painting imparts a greater expression of human 'inner life' than does sculpture.[184] He is critical of classical sculpture in particular for depicting humans in their 'natural aspect . . . only in figures that are half man and half animal'.[185] Instead, the nonhuman animal aspect of humans should be 'recalled into subjective consciousness and negatived there'.[186] Painting does this through a greater emphasis on subjectivity – 'the essential nature of spirit' which 'withdraws out of the external world into an existence within'.[187] Consequently, the task of painting is to portray this inner existence of humans.[188] Hegel suggests that this manifestation of an inner life allows a greater insight into 'men and human nature'.[189] In particular, he praises the Dutch painters for displaying the 'essential ingredient' of all art, namely, 'the vision of what man is as man, what the human spirit and character is'.[190] Such an expression of the human spirit becomes even greater with the individual art of music.

Music offers a more extensive withdrawal into subjectivity, and also overcomes the spatial limits of painting.[191] Music, unlike painting, 'relinquishes the element of an external form and a perceptible visibility'.[192] The task of music is, therefore, to make humans' inner life, their feelings, 'echo . . . in notes'.[193] For Hegel, Rossini is particularly adept at this task because he composes music which is 'full of feeling and genius, piercing the mind and heart'.[194] However, it is this very emphasis on feeling that indicates the limited nature of music as an individual art.[195] Spirit cannot be 'completely characterized qualitatively by a note'.[196] Music requires a 'more exact meaning of words' to express humans' inner life, and poetry – 'the art of speech' – is the medium that can achieve this.[197]

Hegel suggests that the origins of poetry are present in humans' attempt to satisfy their 'natural needs'. He states:

> Poetry began when man undertook to express *himself*; for poetry, what is spoken is there only to be an expression. When once, in the midst of his practical activity and necessity (*Not*), man proceeds to collect his thoughts and communicate himself to others, then he immediately produces a coined expression, a touch of poetry.[198]

Within the realm of natural necessity a moment of human 'spiritual need' is present. To become a 'sphere of its own' poetry does have to 'separate itself from ordinary speech'.[199] It then becomes a spiritual need, but initially, it exists as a moment – a 'touch' in humans' natural necessity.[200] In its proper existence, beyond natural necessity, poetry has to communicate its 'inner conceptions' through language but also transform language itself through the 'choice, placing and sounds of words'.[201] The highest art of poetry exists within the realm of natural necessity, and indeed develops dialectically from this realm. Through this development, art itself becomes a 'liberation of the spirit', and an objectification of human 'inner life'.[202]

CONCLUSION

The *Aesthetics* therefore offers a valuable insight into Hegel's understanding of needs, and affirms the importance of analysing forms for the investigation of such phenomena. Humans' need to produce art is an aspect of the basic need to objectify themselves in the external world. Art is one form in which they accomplish this; it is one mode of existence of this basic need for self-realisation. 'Spiritual needs', therefore, are characterised by this objectification of human essence or 'inner life', as Hegel refers to it. Even when this realisation takes a very mundane form – such as throwing stones in a river – a moment of 'spiritual need' is still present, according to Hegel. Understood dialectically, Hegel seems to suggest that we should analyse everyday human activities to discover the positive moments within the negative – the spiritual within the non-spiritual. This is particularly prevalent in his understanding of the forms of art in certain historical periods through the opposition between nature and spirit. Such an opposition is a reflection of the constant battle between the realm of necessity and the realm of freedom, which Hegel highlights through his discussion of needs. As we argued in the previous chapter, Hegel sees this dichotomy between spirit and nature being overcome through technological developments that limit the realm of natural necessity. Humans still have to satisfy their 'natural needs' while also satisfying their more spiritual concerns, but increased automation will attend to the former whilst humans can pursue the latter. Through the dialectical movement of needs and their satisfaction emerges a real moment which can allow humans to develop to a proper realm of freedom.

The examination of the concept of need in Hegel's writings here, and in the previous two chapters, clearly establishes the importance he attaches to understanding needs as forms. The dialectical movement between the universal and particular moments of need through the manifestation of the Will – the self-activity of human beings – is readily evident. Attention to form allows Hegel to grasp needs not statically, but in their movement and transition from 'natural need' to 'opinion' and to 'spiritual need'. Against modern need theory, which has a tendency to hold universal and particular need in static opposition to one another, Hegel attempts to comprehend needs in their mediation – universal to particular, particular to universal. A similar understanding of need will now become evident in the next two chapters as attention turns to Marx's discussion of this concept.

NOTES

1. See for example, C. Karelis, 'Hegel's Concept of Art: An Interpretative Essay', in *Hegel's Introduction to Aesthetics*, trans. T. M. Knox (Clarendon Press, Oxford, 1979); S. Bungay, *Beauty and Truth* (Oxford University Press, Oxford), 1984; S. Houlgate, *Freedom, Truth and History: An Introduction to Hegel's Philosophy* (Routledge, London, 1991), Ch. 4; R. Wicks, 'Hegel's Aesthetics: An Overview', in F. C. Beiser (ed.) *The Cambridge Companion to Hegel* (Cambridge University Press, Cambridge, 1993).

2. G. Rose, *Hegel Contra Sociology* (Athlone, London, 1981), Ch. 4, offers some discussion of needs but more in terms of the *Aesthetics* than of the needs themselves.

3. G. W. F. Hegel, *Aesthetics Lectures on Fine Art*, trans. T. M. Knox, (Clarendon Press, Oxford, 1974–5), Volumes I and II (hereafter denoted as A, I or A, II), A, I, p. 10. G. W. F. Hegel, *Werke*, Volumes XIII, XIV and XV (Suhrkamp Verlag, Frankfurt, 1970), Vol. XIII, p. 24.

4. A, I, p. 11.

5. A, I, p. 11.

6. A, I, p. 11.
7. A, I, p. 11; *Werke*, Vol. XIII, p. 24.
8. A, I, p. 11.
9. A, I, p. 10.
10. A, I, p. 13.
11. P. T. Murray, *Hegel's Philosophy of Mind and Will* (Edwin Mellen Press, Lewiston, Queenston and Lampeter, 1991), p. x.
12. A, I, p. 13.
13. A, I, p. 13.
14. A, I, p. 14.
15. A, I, p. 14.
16. A, I, pp. 21–2.
17. A, I, p. 22.
18. A, I, p. 22.
19. A, I, p. 22.
20. A, I, p. 23.
21. A, I, p. 24; *Werke*, Vol. XIII, p. 42.
22. A, I, p. 25.
23. A, I, p. 25.
24. A, I, p. 30.
25. A, I, p. 30; *Werke*, Vol. XIII, p. 50.
26. A, I, p. 30; *Werke*, Vol. XIII, p. 50.
27. A, I, p. 31.
28. A, I, p. 31.
29. A, I, pp. 31–2.
30. A, I, p. 32.
31. A, I, p. 31.
32. A, I, p. 31; *Werke*, Vol. XIII, p. 51.
33. A, I, p. 31.
34. A, I, p. 32.
35. A, I, p. 32.
36. A, I, p. 33.
37. A, I, p. 33.
38. A, I, p. 33.
39. A, I, p. 34.
40. A, I, p. 34.
41. A, I, p. 35.
42. A, I, p. 35.
43. A, I, p. 36.
44. A, I, p. 36.
45. A, I, p. 36.
46. A, I, p. 37.
47. A, I, p. 37.
48. A, I, p. 37.
49. A, I, p. 37.
50. A, I, p. 37.
51. A, I, p. 38.
52. A, I, p. 39.
53. A, I, p. 40.

54. A, I, p. 41.
55. A, I, p. 41.
56. A, I, p. 273.
57. A, I, p. 273.
58. A, I, p. 273; cf. Houlgate, *Freedom, Truth and History*, pp. 155–6.
59. A, I, p. 42.
60. A, I, p. 43.
61. A, I, p. 43.
62. A, I, p. 44.
63. A, I, p. 46.
64. A, I, p. 47.
65. A, I, p. 48.
66. A, I, pp. 50–3.
67. A, I, p. 55.
68. A, I, p. 53.
69. A, I, p. 53.
70. A, I, p. 53.
71. A, I, p. 54.
72. A, I, p. 54.
73. A, I, p. 54.
74. A, I, p. 55.
75. A, I, p. 55.
76. A, I, p. 55.
77. A, I, p. 56.
78. A, I, p. 94–5.
79. A, I, p. 95.
80. A, I, p. 95.
81. A, I, p. 95.
82. A, I, p. 95.
83. A, I, p. 96.
84. A, I, p. 96.
85. A, I, p. 96.
86. A, I, p. 97.
87. A, I, p. 97.
88. A, I, p. 98. Hegel uses the term 'physical needs' (*physischen Bedürfnisse*) interchangeably with 'sensuous needs' (*sinnlichen Bedürfnisse*). *Werke*, Vol. XIII, pp. 135–6.
89. A, I, p. 98; *Werke*, Vol. XIII, p. 135. Translation modified. Knox oddly translates '*Bedürftigkeit*' as 'want', but 'neediness' captures more precisely Hegel's emphasis here in terms of the constant burden of having to satisfy 'physical needs'.
90. A, I, p. 98.
91. A, I, p. 99.
92. A, I, p. 100–1.
93. A, I, p. 101.
94. A, I, p. 101.
95. A, I, p. 101.
96. A, I, p. 101.
97. A, I, p. 101.
98. A, I, p. 102.
99. A, I, p. 102.

100. A, I, p. 103.
101. A, I, p. 103.
102. A, I, p. 103.
103. A, I, p. 103. Terms in square brackets in the original translation.
104. A, I, p. 103.
105. A, I, p. 104.
106. A, I, p. 104.
107. A, I, p. 104.
108. A, I, p. 104.
109. A, I, p. 104.
110. A, I, p. 256.
111. A, I, p. 256.
112. A, I, p. 257.
113. A, I, p. 257.
114. A, I, p. 257.
115. A, I, p. 257.
116. A, I, p. 257.
117. A, I, pp. 258–9.
118. A, I, p. 259.
119. A, I, p. 259.
120. A, I, p. 259.
121. A, I, p. 260.
122. A, I, p. 260.
123. A, I, p. 260.
124. A, I, p. 260.
125. A, I, p. 261; *Werke*, Vol. XIII, p. 337.
126. A, I, p. 261.
127. A, I, p. 261.
128. A, I, p. 263; cf. Rose, *Hegel Contra Sociology*, pp. 129–30.
129. See Rose, *Hegel Contra Sociology*, p. 122.
130. A, I, p. 303.
131. A, I, p. 311.
132. A, I, p. 426.
133. A, I, p. 360.
134. A, I, p. 356.
135. A, I, p. 315.
136. A, I, pp. 315–16.
137. A, I, p. 315.
138. A, I, p. 333.
139. A, I, p. 427.
140. A, I, p. 311.
141. A, I, p. 333.
142. A, I, p. 461; *Werke*, Vol. XIV, p. 56.
143. A, I, p. 462.
144. A, I, p. 461.
145. A, I, p. 462; *Werke*, Vol. XIV, p. 57.
146. A, I, p. 467; *Werke*, Vol. XIV, p. 64.
147. A, I, p. 470; *Werke*, Vol. XIV, p. 67. Translation modified. Knox has 'human needs'.
148. A, I, p. 471.

149. A, I, p. 517.
150. A, I, p. 517.
151. A, I, p. 518.
152. A, I, p. 519.
153. A, I, p. 527.
154. A, I, p. 527.
155. A, I, p. 524.
156. A, I, p. 529.
157. A, II, p. 614.
158. A, II, p. 631.
159. A, II, p. 632.
160. A, II, p. 632; *Werke*, Vol. XIV, p. 268.
161. A, II, p. 632.
162. A, II, p. 633.
163. A, II, p. 655; *Werke*, Vol. XIV, p. 296.
164. A, II, p. 659; *Werke*, Vol. XIV, p. 302.
165. A, II, p. 702.
166. A, II, p. 702. However, Hegel recognises that a sculpture has to be placed in specific surroundings. Consequently, sculpture 'retains a permanent relation with spaces formed architecturally' and its independence is not total.
167. A, II, p. 723.
168. A, II, p. 723.
169. A, II, p. 723; *Werke*, Vol. XIV, p. 377.
170. A, II, p. 728.
171. A, II, p. 728.
172. A, II, p. 728; *Werke*, Vol. XIV, p. 384.
173. A, II, p. 728.
174. A, II, p. 729.
175. A, II, p. 729.
176. A, II, p. 729.
177. A, II, p. 729.
178. A, II, p. 729; *Werke*, Vol. XIV, p. 385.
179. A, II, p. 730.
180. A, II, p. 730.
181. A, II, p. 736.
182. A, II, p. 736; *Werke*, Vol. XIV, p. 394.
183. A, II, p. 736.
184. A, II, p. 795.
185. A, II, p. 791.
186. A, II, p. 791.
187. A, II, p. 792.
188. Wicks, 'Hegel's Aesthetics: An Overview', p. 357.
189. A, II, p. 887.
190. A, II, p. 887.
191. A, II, p. 889.
192. A, II, p. 890.
193. A, II, p. 902.
194. A, II, p. 949.
195. A, II, p. 960.

196. A, II, p. 960.
197. A, II, p. 960.
198. A, II, p. 974; *Werke*, Vol. XV, p. 241. Translation modified.
199. A, II, p. 974.
200. A, II, p. 974.
201. A, II, p. 969.
202. A, II, p. 1236.

6

MARX AND THE NEED-FORM

In Chapter 2, we illustrated the importance Marx attaches to the analysis of forms. The contention of this chapter is that we can only properly elucidate Marx's understanding of needs by grasping the importance of form. I will show that Marx operates with an understanding of basic or 'natural needs' that take particular forms in society. These need-forms exist within a circuit of needs that express the contradictory presence of a working individual within capitalism.

To develop a coherent need theory from Marx's writings, I draw from both his early and later texts. An initial problem, however, is that Marx only fully worked out the importance of analysing forms in 1857, so how can it illuminate the concept of need in his works prior to this date? As Cowling observes, in Marx's early writings 'the development of one abstraction from another, as found in Hegel or as discussed subsequently by Marx in the Introduction to the *Grundrisse*, is absent'.[1] This may indeed be the case, but an emphasis on the importance of form is clearly evident in Marx's early works despite there being no specific use of the terms 'general' and 'determinate' abstractions. Indeed, Marx himself points out how his early writings on Hegel in 1843 allowed him to conclude that 'political *forms* . . . originate in the material conditions of life'.[2] It is the analysis of these 'material conditions' and 'forms' that Marx undertakes even in his earliest works, especially the 'Economic and Philosophical Manuscripts'.[3] Attention to form, then, is crucial for developing a coherent need theory from Marx's writings both early and late. This will become readily evident once we establish the inner connections between the various need-forms in this and the following chapter.

Agnes Heller is one of the main theorists to have embarked on a rigorous study of needs in Marx's writings. Much of my discussion will therefore be a response to Heller's analysis. In particular, I will show that problems arise with Heller's interpretation because of a lack of attention to form. This is evident in her overall interpretation of needs in Marx's writings. She contends, for instance, that capitalism alienates the needs of the working class by constantly reducing their needs to the needs of capital.[4] She argues that a non-alienated form of needs can occur only in a society of 'associated producers' where the structure of need changes through the creation of abundance and labour becomes a vital need. The distribution of goods is on the basis of need, and people pursue 'higher activities', treating each other not as a means to some other end but as ends in themselves. Heller concludes, therefore, that for Marx, needs are not economic categories but historical-philosophical or anthropological ones, which are impossible to define within the capitalist economic system. Consequently, Heller asserts that an analysis of the economic categories of capitalism as a system of alienated needs is only possible through a contrast with a more positive system of non-alienated needs – the society of 'associated producers'.[5]

Heller certainly makes a valid point in seeing a problem with the economistic interpretation of needs – an interpretation which is particularly prevalent amongst bourgeois economists. However, her assertion that we can only understand the category of need through a contrast with the society of 'associated producers' is less convincing. By focusing on the form needs take in capital, indications of the possibility of alternatives within existing society, and not some future one, are discernible.[6] Communism, or the society of 'associated producers', is not, then, some far-off future order but is present within the movement of the contradictions of capitalism.[7] Analysing the form of these contradictions can reveal the possibility of transcendence within existing society. This now becomes clear as we elucidate the core need concepts in Marx's writings, beginning with the fundamental concept of 'natural need'.

NATURAL NEEDS

In the 'Economic and Philosophical Manuscripts' of 1844, Marx declares that:

> Hunger is a natural need (*natürliches Bedürfniß*); it therefore requires a nature and an object outside itself in order to satisfy and still itself. Hunger is the acknowledged need of my body for an *object* which exists outside itself and which is indispensable to its integration and to the expression of its essential nature.[8]

Hunger is an expression of one of the most basic needs that a person has to satisfy to live. Marx argues that on the one side 'man' has '*vital powers*' that exist within him as '*drives*'.[9] On the other side, outside him exist the object of these drives. These are 'objects of his *need*, essential objects, indispensable to the exercise and confirmation of his essential powers'.[10]

Without the objects to satisfy their basic needs humans are obviously going to die. In this way 'natural needs' are clearly those that are essential to continue human existence.

Within the 'Manuscripts' Marx uses the concept of 'natural need' only once, but its meaning recurs in other terms such as 'bodily needs' (*Leibesbedürfnisse* or *körperlichen Bedürfnisse*)[11] or 'physical needs' (*physischen Bedürfnisses*).[12] Marx's concern is to analyse and elucidate the forms 'natural needs' take in capitalist society through a critique of classical political economy. From the analysis of Marx's method in Chapter 2, 'natural needs' are a general abstraction. Such needs are universally present in all societies and must be satisfied for people to continue living. Consequently, Marx concludes that 'the first historical act' is the 'production of the means to satisfy [the] needs . . . of eating and drinking, housing, clothing and various other things'.[13] The satisfactions of such needs are a 'fundamental condition of all history' and are essential in order to 'sustain human life'.[14] 'Natural needs' exist universally in all societies but in divergent forms of satisfaction. Different societies are going to satisfy these 'natural needs' in diverse ways. As Marx notes: 'what could be more varied than the objects that form the staple food of different peoples?'[15] So the movement from the general to the determinate abstraction is required to focus on the forms these needs take in a society in a particular historical period.

Marx's understanding of the general abstraction of 'natural needs' relates to the position of humans in capital. For Marx, human existence in capitalist society is one of incessant dehumanisation. He argues that the process of capital accumulation reduces humans to 'the level of a machine' due to the repetitive nature of their labour.[16] An individual transmogrifies 'from being a man . . . [to] become an abstract activity and a stomach'.[17] 'Man' as 'man' ceases to exist in capitalism and instead becomes an abstraction. Political economy itself reflects this in seeing a human being '*not as a man* but *as a worker*'.[18] Consequently, those who are outside this working relationship are simply 'nebulous figures' who are the problem of 'doctors, judges, grave-diggers, beadles, etc.', and are not the concern of political economy.[19] This allows the latter to reduce the requirements of the worker 'down to one', which is 'the *need to support him while he is working* and prevent the *race of workers* from dying out'.[20] For capitalists and political economists, humans are workers, no more and no less. As workers they have to reproduce themselves in order to be able continually to sell their labour-power to the capitalist. So the very satisfaction of the workers' 'natural needs' is an imposition on capital as well as on the workers themselves.

Such an understanding of 'natural needs' re-emerges in Marx's later writings. In Volume 1 of *Capital* he notes how 'man's' 'natural needs, such as food, clothing, fuel and housing . . . must . . . be sufficient to maintain him in his normal state as a working individual'.[21] Again, 'natural needs' are those needs which humans must satisfy to exist. Marx discusses these 'natural needs' within the context of the sale and purchase of labour-power.[22] He explains that it is through the expenditure of labour-power that individual workers use up 'a definite quantity of human muscle, nerve, brain, etc.', which they have to replace for the valorisation process to begin anew.[23] Marx argues, as he had in his early writings, that the subsistence needed is for a 'working individual' and not simply an individual as a human being.[24] The problem for the individual as a human being in capitalism is that he or she cannot directly satisfy these needs because the means of production are under private ownership. This implies that capital has to satisfy the 'natural needs' of the worker. Capital has to ensure that there is a supply of labour-power which will create surplus-value on the market. If capital did not allow the satisfaction of the 'natural needs' of the workers, then this supply would dissipate, threatening the production and extraction of surplus-value.[25] So 'natural needs' in capitalism are not simply the needs of individuals, but the needs of 'working individuals' to reproduce themselves and their family as labour-power for capital.

This explication of 'natural needs' means we are now in a position to examine Heller's interpretation. She also construes Marx's concept of 'natural needs' as those needs which humans must satisfy for their self-preservation.[26] However, she also argues that such needs are 'not identical' with the needs of nonhuman animals even though both have to preserve themselves.[27] For Heller, humans have certain needs, such as 'warmth, clothing', for which the '[nonhuman] animal has no "need"'.[28] 'Natural needs', then, are an 'existential limit', beyond which survival is 'passed', that is 'different for different societies' and different for nonhuman animals compared to humans.[29] Heller contends that these needs are almost irrelevant for Marxist theory today. However, she concludes that the occurrence of mass deaths from famine in particular countries means that we cannot ignore 'natural needs' as a 'limit concept'.[30]

There are clear problems with Heller's understanding of 'natural needs', which mainly arise from her failure to comprehend them as a general abstraction taking particular forms in society. First, Heller mistakenly suggests that the 'natural needs' of humans are not identical with the 'natural needs' of nonhuman animals. However, as a general abstraction, human and nonhuman animals do share 'natural needs' because both have needs that they must satisfy in order to exist. The determinate abstraction or form these 'natural needs' take is where a difference could arise. Heller's example of the need for clothing is certainly peculiar to humans, but she fails to realise that such a need is simply a form of the 'natural need' for warmth – a 'natural need' which humans share with nonhuman animals despite Heller's strange attempt to suggest otherwise.

Second, she suggests that 'natural needs' can differ *between* societies but ignores the fact that they can also differ *within* societies. Marx himself grasps this in a comparison between the requirements of a prisoner and those of the average family *within* Belgium – a country considered by 'English capitalists' to be a 'workers' paradise' during Marx's time.[31] Drawing on the work of the Belgian inspector-general of prisons and charitable institutions, Marx notes how a prisoner has a higher level of need-satisfaction than the average family within that society. The prisoner satisfies his 'natural needs' in a form which is at a greater level than the 'natural needs' of the family. Marx argues that such an outcome is due to the pressure on workers to economise consistently in order to survive in the harsh environment of capital. Only when the family are at a stage where they can no longer economise do they reach a level of severe deprivation. For Marx, such a level, in this case at least, is not death but pauperism.[32] Consequently, 'natural needs' are not just a 'limit concept' differing between countries, as Heller suggests; they also differ *within* countries and have various levels of satisfaction.

Attention to form clearly highlights the problems of Heller's understanding of 'natural needs'. 'Natural needs' are the fundamental general abstraction that Marx examines the form of in capitalist society. This will become even more evident as we now consider the concept of 'necessary needs'.

NECESSARY NEEDS

To understand properly the concept of 'natural need' and how it differs from 'necessary need' requires a critical examination of Heller's interpretation. This is because Heller suggests that Marx equated 'necessary' and 'natural needs' in the *Grundrisse* but differentiated between them in *Capital*.[33] For Heller, Marx posits this disparity in terms of 'necessary needs' not being dictated by mere survival and including a historical and moral element.[34] She suggests that 'necessary needs' contain not only material needs, but also needs of a non-material kind such as education. However, the satisfaction of these needs is through the form of money, which suggests they are 'necessary needs' and therefore require inclusion in the value that accrues to labour-power to satisfy such needs.[35] So necessary needs for Marx, at least on Heller's interpretation, have to be 'averaged' and 'purchasable'.[36]

For Heller, 'necessary needs' are constantly growing out of material production which itself remains, even in a communist society of 'associated producers', a realm of necessity. The opposite to such needs, then, is what Heller calls 'spiritual and moral needs', which are needs that are not purchasable and exist properly in the realm of freedom as 'free needs'.[37] Heller is quite correct to link 'necessary needs' with the mediations of labour-power and money; however, her suggestion that 'necessary' and 'natural needs' are different in *Capital* but the same in the *Grundrisse* does raise a number of problems. This will become apparent as we examine Marx's comments on these concepts in these works.

NATURAL AND NECESSARY NEEDS IN THE *GRUNDRISSE*

An examination of the *Grundrisse* reveals that Marx first briefly mentions 'natural needs' to draw a distinction not from 'necessary needs' but from what he calls 'socially created needs' (*Societät geschaffnen Bedürfnissen*).[38] Elucidating this contrast later in the work, Marx indicates how capital's thirst for surplus-value drives labour beyond the level of necessity. Production reaches such a level that goods become produced in greater abundance. The end result is that 'natural necessity in its immediate (*unmittelbaren*) *form* has disappeared; because a historically created need has taken the place of a natural one'.[39]

Workers start off with the intention of producing their necessary labour, but have to produce a surplus which capitalists appropriate. 'Capital's ceaseless striving towards the general form of wealth drives labour beyond the limits of its natural paltriness.'[40] This means that 'natural needs' no longer appear in their 'immediate form' as the need for food or housing, etc. They begin to take the form of, or are mediated through, what Marx calls 'historic' or 'social' needs.[41] These needs are the 'offspring of social production and intercourse' and they become 'posited as *necessary*, the higher the level to which real wealth has become developed'.[42] Marx states that these 'social needs' are 'created by production itself', which suggests that as society develops new products emerge that people see they need.[43] Yet these 'social needs' also affect the 'specific manner' in which people satisfy their needs.[44] As Marx notes, 'hunger is hunger, but the hunger gratified by cooked meat eaten with a knife and fork is a different hunger from that which bolts down raw meat with the aid of hand, tooth and nail'.[45]

So developments in production create new needs and new ways of satisfying those needs. Marx's meaning of 'social needs' in this instance is fairly evident, but it raises the question of the distinction between 'luxury' and 'social needs'. Returning to Marx's own example can elucidate this distinction. Before the creation of knives and forks from production, people simply ate with their fingers. Once invented, knives and forks become a 'social need', which is historically created at a particular stage of development. That is, then, the example of a 'social need'. When knives and forks first appear on the market however, they *appear* as a 'luxury need'. The mass of people will not be able to afford them, or they may not even see the need for them, as their fingers do the job pretty well anyway. However, as wealth increases, and more of these knives and forks are produced and used, 'the manner of consumption' changes.[46] What was formerly a luxury good now becomes 'posited as necessary'.[47] The availability of knives and forks increases and they become more easily attainable due to increased wealth. Coupled with this is a cultural development which makes people want to eat with knives and forks rather than with their hands. This is the effect of capitalist development that emanates from the search for ever greater quantities of surplus-value.

So Marx has intimated, but not clearly stated, the concept of 'necessary need' through his understanding of particular goods being 'posited as necessary'. His actual definition of 'necessary needs' (*Nothwendige Bedürfnisse*) is 'those of the individual himself reduced to a natural subject'.[48] Heller takes this to mean that Marx is equating 'natural needs' with 'necessary needs'.[49] On the previous page, however, Marx talks of 'necessary needs' as developmental. He states that 'necessity is itself subject to changes, because needs are produced just as are products and the different kinds of work skills. Increases and decreases do take place within the limits set by these needs'.[50] 'Necessary needs' do not correspond to the fixed nature that Heller supposes 'natural needs' to have. In contrast, both 'natural' and 'necessary needs' have gradations within them, and both contain a cultural or moral element. What constitutes them differs not only *between* particular countries, as Heller recognises, but also *within* countries, which she does not.

It should also be noted that Marx is saying 'natural subject' and not 'natural need'. What can he mean by 'natural subject'? If we refer back to the earlier example, we saw that a 'luxury need' – knife and fork – came to take the form of a 'necessary need'. On Heller's interpretation, this would mean that the 'necessary need' for a knife and fork is that of an individual reduced to the level of a 'natural subject'. This in turn would imply that the acquisition of knives and forks is something basic or tied to survival. Yet this makes no sense, because humans have moved beyond the level of satisfying their hunger with their hands. Heller's attempt to equate 'natural' and 'necessary needs' must fail. The only way Marx's comments can make proper sense here is to understand the 'necessary need' as the form of the 'natural need'. The 'natural need' for food takes the form of a 'necessary need'. What figures as a 'necessary need' depends on 'the higher . . . level to which real wealth has become developed'.[51] Yet real wealth for workers is in the form of their wage, which allows them to satisfy their 'natural need' for food. This takes different forms depending on the development or lack of development of society. A knife and fork become a 'necessary need', but this is the form in which people satisfy the 'natural need' for food. The lack of an understanding of the need-form, therefore, leads Heller's interpretation into contradiction. With these points clear we can now see how Marx uses these distinctions in *Capital* itself.

NATURAL AND NECESSARY NEEDS IN *CAPITAL*

Marx does not actually use the term 'necessary needs' (*Nothwendige Bedürfnisse*) anywhere in *Capital*. Heller translates '*nothwendiger Lebens- mittel*'[52] as 'necessary needs', but '*Lebensmittel*' generally translates as 'means of subsistence'.[53] There is, however, a clear reference to 'natural needs' (*natürlichen Bedürfnisse*).[54] The crucial passage is as follows:

> His [the worker's] natural needs, such as food, clothing, fuel and housing, vary according to the climatic and other physical peculiarities of his country. On the other hand, the number and extent of his so-called necessary means of subsistence (*nothwendiger Lebensmittel*), as also the manner in which they are satisfied, are themselves products of history, and depend therefore to a great extent on the level of civilisation attained by a country; in particular they depend on the conditions in which, and consequently on the habits and expectations with which, the class of free workers has been formed. In contrast, therefore, with the case of other commodities, the determination of the value of labour-power contains a historical and moral element. Nevertheless, in a given country at a given period, the average amount of the necessary means of subsistence (*nothwendigen Lebensmittel*) for the worker is a known *datum*.[55]

Marx is using 'necessary means of subsistence' in the same way as he used 'necessary needs' in the *Grundrisse*. So Heller correctly interprets the meaning of 'necessary means of subsistence' without being precise in using the term. Marx states that both their 'number and extent', along with the way they are satisfied, are products of history and the level of development in a particular society. This has an exact parallel with the *Grundrisse* in terms of 'social' or 'historic needs' that arise out of production and then take the form of 'necessary needs'. A new need is created and so is a new 'manner in which [such needs] are satisfied'.[56] The question then turns on why Marx puts the adjective 'necessary' before the 'means of subsistence'. In other words, what is the difference between the 'means of subsistence' and the 'necessary means of subsistence'?

Marx links 'means of subsistence' with 'natural needs'. For instance, on the following page he refers to 'some of the means of subsistence, such as food and fuel'.[57] As we have seen, for Marx, food and fuel are objects of 'natural needs'. Moreover, in the appendix to *Capital* he defines 'means of subsistence' as 'a particular *form* of material existence in which capital confronts the worker before he acquires them through the sale of his labour-power'.[58] The only way people can satisfy their 'means of subsistence' in capital is through the sale of labour-power. This is because the capitalist owns the means of production and thereby the 'means of subsistence'.[59] The wage payment itself is nothing but the 'money *form* of the means of subsistence'.[60] So it is only through the selling of labour-power that people can satisfy their 'means of subsistence' and so posit such needs as necessary – as 'necessary means of subsistence'. What differentiates 'natural needs' ('means of subsistence') and 'necessary needs' ('necessary means of subsistence'), therefore, is that the satisfaction of the former in capital is through the sale of labour-power, the wage, and hence in the form of 'necessary needs'. As Marx states, the wage 'belongs to the *worker* as soon as it has assumed its true shape of the means of subsistence destined to be consumed by him'.[61] The wage is the mediated form of the 'means of subsistence'. Only when the wage is spent on goods does the 'true shape' of the 'means of subsistence' emerge. However, this is still in the form of the 'necessary means of subsistence', which itself is the value of labour-power.[62]

Marx encapsulates the important aspect of labour-power that demarcates 'necessary' from simple 'means of subsistence' as follows:

> When we speak of capacity for labour, we do not abstract from the necessary means of subsistence. On the contrary, their value is expressed in its value. If his capacity for labour remains unsold, this is of no advantage to the worker. He will rather feel it to be a cruel nature-imposed necessity that his capacity for labour has required for its production a definite quantity of the means of subsistence, and will continue to require this for its reproduction.[63]

Marx directly links labour-power – the 'capacity for labour' – with the 'necessary means of subsistence' in terms of its value. If individuals cannot sell their labour-power then they have to find a different form of satisfaction of their 'means of subsistence' ('natural needs'). Without the means of production to satisfy her or his 'means of subsistence', the worker now 'vegetates on public alms' and enters the world of official pauperism.[64] 'Outside the workshop', outside the sale of labour-power, the individual worker depends on the mercies of charity and begging.[65] However, this does not simply mean survival, as Heller asserts, because gradations exist within the band of 'means of subsistence' ('natural needs'), as I illustrated in the previous section.

Heller errs, therefore, in suggesting that the difference between 'necessary' and 'natural needs' in *Capital* centres on the former developing historically and the latter being dictated by mere survival. As I have illustrated, workers satisfy 'natural needs' ('means of subsistence') in capitalism through the sale of labour-power and the receipt of a wage. When this wage is spent on commodities they become posited as 'necessary' if the mass of workers can afford them. These goods satisfy 'necessary needs' and are the 'necessary means of subsistence'. The only difference between 'necessary' and 'natural needs' is not that one is about survival and the other not, as Heller suggests; it is obvious that they both are when reduced to their lower limits. The difference is rather that 'necessary needs' involve the mediation of labour-power. The worker uses the value of this labour-power to satisfy 'natural' and 'necessary needs' – needs that a bearer of labour-power must satisfy to exist and allow the valorisation process to continue. As we have seen, Heller herself realises how 'necessary needs' are satisfied through the mediation of labour-power and money. However, she fails to recognise these needs as the mode of existence of 'natural needs' and thereby misses their inner connection.

So people are born with 'natural needs' that they have to satisfy in order to live. To satisfy these needs individuals have to become workers and sell themselves as labour-power. The value of this labour-power will determine the workers' 'necessary needs'. These 'necessary needs' will be the greater the higher the value of labour-power, prices remaining constant. The 'natural needs' are therefore being satisfied, but this will be in a qualitatively, and quantitatively, different way. A high value of labour-power could offer the possibility of accruing meat instead of gruel, for instance, or a rented house instead of a hut. 'Necessary needs' are the form that the satisfaction of 'natural needs' take in capital. 'Natural needs' are satisfied through the sale of labour-power and in the form of 'necessary needs'. When workers cannot sell their labour-power, they have to satisfy the 'natural need' in a form that is not mediated through the wage. They have now entered 'official pauperism, or the part of the working class which has forfeited its condition of existence (the sale of labour-power)'.[66] They have become part of the '*faux frais*'[67] of capitalist production, as Marx calls it, and are thereby reduced to the satisfaction of their 'natural needs' in their 'immediate form'. No positing of 'necessary needs' is therefore possible at this level of need-satisfaction.

This examination of the contrast between 'natural' and 'necessary needs' has been crucial for understanding the general abstraction of 'natural needs' in the determinate form of 'necessary needs'. We have also shown that Heller mistakenly interprets 'natural needs' only as a 'limit concept' and wrongly equates 'natural' and 'necessary' needs in the

Grundrisse. Attention to form highlights the inner connection between 'natural need' and 'necessary need'. For Marx, therefore, 'natural needs' exist in the form of 'necessary needs'. The task now is to examine the previously mentioned concepts of 'luxury' and 'social needs'. This will further emphasise the importance of the need-form and complete the circuit of needs as experienced by the worker in capital.

LUXURY NEEDS

Marx first talks of a 'luxury need' (*Luxusbedürfnis*) in his critique of Proudhon in the *Poverty of Philosophy*.[68] In this work, he contrasts 'luxury needs' with 'necessary needs'. The latter are the need for 'indispensable objects' of 'prime necessity . . . like corn, meat, etc', while the former are the need for 'luxury articles, like artichokes, asparagus, etc.'[69] Interestingly, Marx argues that the difference between a 'luxury' and a 'necessary need' is not one of price. He notes how luxury articles such as artichokes can actually be cheaper than necessary articles.[70] So a 'luxury need' on this interpretation is one that the working class does not posit as necessary through the selling of labour-power and the wage.

In Volume 2 of *Capital*, however, Marx contradicts this understanding of 'luxury needs' by arguing that '*luxury* means of consumption . . . enter the consumption only of the capitalist class, i.e. can be exchanged only for the expenditure of surplus-value, which does not accrue to the workers'.[71] There seems to be a shift in Marx's understanding of what constitutes a 'luxury need'. In the *Poverty of Philosophy* he suggested that luxury consumption was possible for the working class because certain luxury items were even cheaper than necessary items. Now, in *Capital*, Marx is saying that luxury consumption is the preserve 'only of the capitalist class'. However, Marx then reverts to his original formulation when he argues that in situations of 'prosperity' the 'working class . . . takes a temporary share in the consumption of luxury articles that are otherwise for the most part "necessary" only for the capitalists'.[72] How can we make sense of these comments?

Heller opts for the interpretation which suggests that what constitutes a 'luxury need' is whether an article is used or possessed by the majority of the population or not.[73] In this way 'no specific product or need *possesses* the quality of being a luxury product or luxury need'.[74] On Heller's view, then, 'luxury need' is a transient concept, which, as Marx himself suggests, allows the working class to posit 'luxury needs' as necessary in situations of prosperity. Such a tendency for luxury goods to be posited as necessary was evident in our earlier discussion of 'natural' and 'necessary needs' in the *Grundrisse*.[75] How, though, can this be equated with Marx's comment that luxury goods 'do not accrue to the workers'?

What Marx means here, I suggest, is that at a certain time luxury goods are those which are out of reach of the working class. However, with increases in productivity and spending power these luxuries can, in time, be made 'necessary'. So when Heller suggests that 'luxury needs' posited as necessary 'cease to be luxury needs', some care is required.[76] Reference to form means that 'luxury needs' posited as necessary have not 'ceased to be' luxury needs but exist in the mode or take the form of 'necessary needs'. This is important because it allows us to understand the 'inner connection' of all need concepts and trace this connection back to class conflict in the production process. As Marx points out, such 'production is founded on the antagonism of orders, estates, classes and finally on the antagonism of accumulated labour and immediate labour'.[77] Such an antagonism is mediated through the various forms needs take in capital. 'Luxury needs', as the preserve of the capitalist class at a point in time, are posited as 'necessary' by the working class. Initially, these needs seem diametrically opposed. However, attention to form indicates how they can mediate into different modes of existence of each other. Recognition of such forms is therefore crucial for a proper understanding of needs in Marx's writings.

The final need-forms that will be now be considered in this chapter are 'social' and 'true social need'. This will then allow us to illustrate the circuit of needs that exist for the worker in capitalism.

SOCIAL NEED AND TRUE SOCIAL NEED

In the discussion of 'natural' and 'necessary needs' in the *Grundrisse*, it was noted how Marx referred to a 'social need' which was 'socially created' through developments in the process of production.[78] In this section we want to consider two contrasting 'social need' concepts, namely, 'social' and 'true social need'. In Volume 3 of *Capital*, Marx defines 'social need' (*gesellschaftliche Bedürfnis*) as 'the quantity [of commodities] for which the society is able to pay the market value'.[79] 'Social need', in this sense, is effective demand–demand backed up by the ability to pay. In contrast, a 'true social need' (*wirklichen gesellschaftlichen Bedürfnis*) is 'the quantity that would be demanded at other money prices, or with the buyers being in different financial and living conditions'.[80] So the market recognises 'social need' in the form of effective demand but does not recognise 'true social need'.

Heller also recognises the distinction Marx is attempting to make here, but she actually reduces 'true social need' to the concept of 'necessary need'.[81] She argues that the former is simply an average of individual needs which are historically developed and handed down through custom and habit.[82] Yet this is problematic, because when Marx talks of 'necessary needs' he refers to them as 'the average amount of the means of subsistence necessary for the worker . . . in a given country at a given period'.[83] 'Necessary needs' are those needs which keep workers in a fit state to offer their labour-power to capital and are a definite quantity, a 'known *datum*', as Marx expresses it.[84] Historical and moral factors suggest that what constitutes a 'necessary need' will change, but it will be an accepted standard of living at a particular point in time that the working class has posited as necessary. The point about 'true social needs' is that they are not a 'known *datum*' because they are not expressed on the market. So it is difficult to see how Heller can equate them with 'necessary needs'.

If Heller has a problem in conflating these two needs then Lebowitz has difficulty in trying to keep them apart. In contrast to Heller, Lebowitz, who also talks of the 'true social need' in the sense of it being 'hidden', thinks that there is a clear distinction between the historically determined 'necessary needs' and 'true social needs'.[85] For Lebowitz 'true social needs' exceed the level of 'necessary needs' and are therefore 'not customary'.[86] He sees this distinction as highlighting a major failure of capitalism, namely, the limitations it puts on the satisfaction of people's needs. However, what Lebowitz does not realise is that 'true social needs' do not necessarily have to 'exceed' the limitations of 'necessary needs'. The 'true social need' that is not expressed could include those people who cannot even sell their labour-power and so cannot posit needs as 'necessary'. Indeed, Marx himself makes this very point using the example of paupers, 'whose "demand" is . . . below the narrowest limits of their physical need'.[87] Hence, the 'hidden' or 'true social need' could consist of those who want to reach the level of 'necessary needs' as well as those who want to go beyond it. Lebowitz's attempt to distinguish between the two leads him to ignore those members of society who cannot even sell their labour-power.

The concept of 'true social need' causes further problems for Lebowitz. Although he recognises Marx's distinction between 'true social need' and 'social need',[88] he uses the latter at times to refer to both types of social need.[89] To make proper sense of his discussion, therefore, I will impose the distinction of these needs into his comments.

Lebowitz links 'social needs' into the idea of immiseration by suggesting that the gap between 'necessary needs' and 'true social needs' is indicative of the level of immiseration of the worker.[90] The more wages workers get the less their immiseration, because the gap between workers' 'necessary need' and 'true social need' diminishes. However, Lebowitz then argues that '[true] social needs . . . are not mere wishes in the heads of workers [but] are a real moment of economic life', as they force workers to 'posit those [true] social needs as necessary'.[91] 'Unsatisfied [i.e. true] social needs' are at the bottom of workers' struggle for a higher wage, according to Lebowitz, which is a struggle in opposition to the interests of capitalists.[92] So more money 'permits the production of the worker as an altered human being, one richer in quality, one for whom more historic and social needs are "posited as necessary"'.[93] What can Lebowitz mean when he says that 'true social needs' exist as 'real' and not just as a 'wish' in the heads of workers? He suggests that these needs are 'part of the very nature' of workers and are 'finite' at any given point in time.[94] So a 'definite quantity of commodities' exist which would be demanded if prices, income levels, and the way workers rank their needs were all different.[95] There are, however, some severe weaknesses in Lebowitz's analysis here.

First, Lebowitz's emphasis on the importance of struggling for higher wages, which he sees as allowing a greater development of the individual, seems very debatable. Why should receiving more money alter the individual in a good way? Is it not imaginable that more money can corrupt certain individuals? What if the extra money earned led to heroin addiction? Would Lebowitz say that this made the worker 'richer in quality'?[96] The mere existence of wage struggles suggests to Lebowitz that by having more money a need is satisfied and the individual becomes qualitatively richer in the process. Yet to decide whether this is so we have to understand just what the need is and how it is being satisfied. Drawing such contradictory conclusions from Lebowitz's argument is possible because he does not concentrate on the form a particular need takes or analyse its positive and negative moments.

Second, although Lebowitz is attempting to reassert working-class spontaneity and struggle against objective interpretations of Marxism, his own account of 'social needs' also contains a determinist aspect. As we have seen, he suggests that 'true social needs' are a part of the nature of the worker, and to this end he quotes Marx: 'If I am determined, forced, by my needs, it is only my own nature, this totality of needs and drives, which exert a force upon me.'[97] It seems, then, that 'true social needs' determine the actions of the worker. However, Lebowitz seems unaware that this comment from Marx takes place in a discussion not of 'social needs' but of 'natural needs'.[98] Marx is looking at the simple relation between two individuals who meet for exchange to satisfy the other's 'natural need' and not a 'true social need'.[99] In Marx's discussion at this point there are no unsold goods on the market, because he is positing direct, one-for-one exchange. Evidently, then, the 'true social need' does not exist, as no quantity of articles corresponds to such a need. Lebowitz has not only misinterpreted Marx here, but he is also mistaken in seeing 'true social needs' as a determining part of human nature. There is a determinate aspect to 'natural needs' in that the human organism has to receive sufficient quantities of food or water to go on living. Yet this does not alter the fact that such needs can be overridden, which Marx himself suggests with his use of the word 'if' in the quotation cited.

Obviously, then, there are some real problems in the way certain Marxists, such as Lebowitz, use Marx's understanding of 'true social need'. However, the important insight that Marx offers is the counter to bourgeois political economy's understanding of 'social need' only as effective demand. With this final need-form elucidated it is now possible to illustrate the circuit of need that emerges from the presence of an individual within capitalism.

THE NEED-FORM AND THE CIRCUIT OF NEEDS

An emphasis on the need-form in Marx's writings reveals a circuit of needs as illustrated in Figure 6.1. Marx presents 'natural needs' as the general abstraction, that is, needs in general. What form do these needs take in capital? As capitalism is a system of private property, workers cannot immediately satisfy their needs, so workers have to sell their labour-power first. The process of determinate abstraction has begun. We move from the general to the concrete, from the simple to the complex. The concrete forms that 'natural needs' begin to take are mediated through the sale of labour-power. The 'cruel nature-imposed necessity' is that workers have to sell their labour-power to satisfy their 'natural needs'.[100] Once the 'natural needs' take on this form a further mediation arises – the value of labour-power. The latter is determined by the socially necessary labour time required for workers to reproduce themselves. However, the wage workers receive can be above or below this level depending on class struggle. It is here that 'natural needs' take on the more concrete form of 'necessary needs'. So if the wage or money received is greater than the value of labour-power the workers' 'necessary needs' increase. This may allow the new form of 'luxury needs' to come into existence and be satisfied. If the converse happens then workers could be forced back onto the lower limit of 'necessary needs'. If workers cannot sell their labour-power, they could fall even further to the level of 'natural needs' proper. 'Natural needs' take the form of 'necessary needs', which in turn take the form of 'luxury needs'. Those needs considered as luxury at one time can, with social development and increased wages, become necessary, and, due to changing circumstances, necessary goods may even become luxury goods. Similarly, depending on societal development, 'necessary needs' could become 'natural needs'. New needs are 'socially created' through developments in the production process, and these appear on the market in the form of 'luxury needs'. The total or collective expression of need takes two forms: 'social' and 'true social need'. The former appears on the market in the form of effective demand, whilst the latter remains hidden as a potential level of need that people could satisfy if prices and their own incomes and living conditions were different. In this sense, the market and bourgeois political economy do not recognise 'true social needs'.

Figure 6.1   The need-form and the circuit of needs.

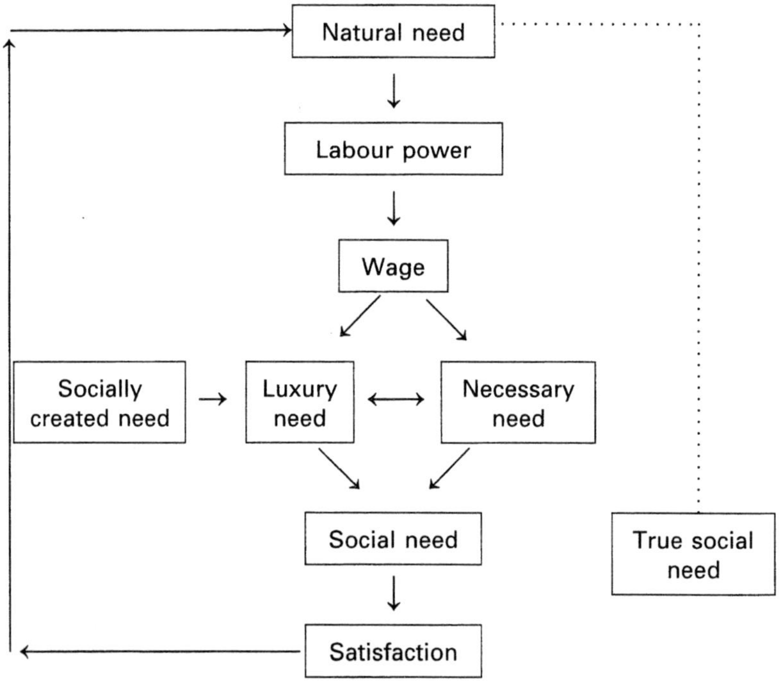

The need-form in Marx's schema is, therefore, a 'concentration of many determinations'.[101] They are contradictions within a unity. 'Luxury need' appears as the opposite to 'necessary' and 'natural', but can also take the form of 'natural' and 'necessary'. Hard and fast distinctions do not apply because the forms are in motion, 'natural' to 'necessary', 'necessary' to 'natural', 'luxury' to 'necessary' – contradictions within a unity. Analysing forms allows us to see the 'inner connection' between these concepts of need and relate them to the struggle of the worker's existence within capital.

NOTES

1. M. Cowling, 'Marx's Conceptual Framework from 1843–5: Hegelian Dialectic and Historical Necessity versus Feuerbachian Humanistic Materialism?', *Studies in Marxism*, 2, 1995, p. 45.

2. K. Marx, *A Contribution to the Critique of Political Economy*, (trans.) S. W. Ryazanskaya (Progress Publishers, Moscow, 1977), p. 20. Emphasis added. Cf. L. Wilde, *Marx and Contradiction* (Avebury, Aldershot, 1989), pp. 28–9.

3. See L. Wilde, 'Logic: Dialectic and Contradiction', in T. Carver (ed.) *The Cambridge Companion to Marx* (Cambridge University Press, Cambridge, 1991), pp. 279–80.

4. A. Heller, *The Theory of Need in Marx* (Allison and Busby, London, 1976), p. 23.

5. Heller, *Theory of Need in Marx*, pp. 26–7.

6. H. Cleaver, 'The Inversion of Class Perspective in Marxian Theory: From Valorisation to Self-Valorisation', in W. Bonefeld, R. Gunn and K. Psychopedis (eds) *Open Marxism. Volume II: Theory and Practice* (Pluto, London, 1992), pp. 125–8; K. Soper, 'The Needs of Marxism', *Radical Philosophy*, 15, 1977, p. 41.

7. K. Marx and F. Engels, *Collected Works*, Volume 5 (Lawrence and Wishart, London, 1976), p. 49.

8. K. Marx, 'Economic and Philosophical Manuscripts', in K. Marx, *Early Writings*, (trans.) R. Livingstone and G. Benton (Penguin, Harmondsworth, 1992), p. 390; K. Marx and F. Engels, *Gesamtausgabe (MEGA)*, I.2 (Dietz Verlag, Berlin, 1982), p. 408.

9. Marx, 'Economic and Philosophical Manuscripts', p. 389.

10. Marx, 'Economic and Philosophical Manuscripts', pp. 389–90.

11. Marx, 'Economic and Philosophical Manuscripts', p. 290; *MEGA*, I.2, p. 334.

12. Marx, 'Economic and Philosophical Manuscripts', p. 329; *MEGA*, I.2, p. 369.

13. Marx and Engels, *Collected Works*, Vol. 5, pp. 41–2.

14. Marx and Engels, *Collected Works*, Vol. 5, p. 42. Soper suggests that Marx contradicts himself here, because he also argues that the 'creation of new needs' is the 'first historical act'. K. Soper, *On Human Needs: Open and Closed Theories in a Marxist Perspective* (Harvester Press, Brighton, 1981), p. 46; Marx and Engels, *Collected Works*, Vol. 5, p. 42. However, as Marx himself points out only a few pages later, which Soper does not refer to, these 'aspects' of 'social activity' he has identified 'are not to be taken as . . . different stages'. Instead, Marx suggests, in an Hegelian refrain, that they should be understood as 'moments', which have existed simultaneously since the dawn of history'. Marx and Engels, *Collected Works*, Vol. 5, p. 43. The production of means to satisfy needs and the creation of new needs exist simultaneously and both, therefore, are 'first historical acts'. For example, the project of sharpening a stone in order to cut meat better is both the production of the means to satisfy a need (for food or meat) and also the creation of a new need (for a sharp stone). Marx is therefore dialectically tracing the inner connections between the moments of need and their satisfaction. He is trying to avoid a static approach which demarcates needs into particular 'stages'. Instead, Marx is emphasising the importance of understanding needs in their movement and transition within and between each other. Consequently, the production of means to satisfy needs and the creation of new needs coexist. This is why he can refer to them both as 'first historical acts'.

15. K. Marx and F. Engels, *Collected Works*, Volume 6 (Lawrence and Wishart, London, 1976), p. 117.

16. Marx, 'Economic and Philosophical Manuscripts', p. 285.

17. Marx, 'Economic and Philosophical Manuscripts', p. 285.

18. Marx, 'Economic and Philosophical Manuscripts', p. 355.

19. Marx, 'Economic and Philosophical Manuscripts', p. 355.

20. Marx, 'Economic and Philosophical Manuscripts', p. 355.

21. K. Marx, *Capital*, Volume 1, (trans.) B. Fowkes (Penguin, Harmondsworth, 1988), p. 275. The German word '*Bedürfnis*' can be translated as either 'need' or 'want'. Hence, the Moscow translation of *Capital* has 'wants' (*Capital*, Volume 1, (trans.) S. Moore, and E. Aveling (Lawrence and Wishart, London, 1961), p. 171) but the more recent Penguin translation has 'needs'. Heller, *Theory of Need in Marx*, p. 30, modifies the translation of the Moscow edition by replacing 'wants' with 'needs'.

22. Marx, *Capital*, Vol. 1, Ch. 2.

23. Marx, *Capital*, Vol. 1, p. 274.

24. Marx, *Capital*, Vol. 1, p. 275.

25. This is indeed the reason Marx gives for the introduction of the ten-hour working day in the nineteenth century. See Marx, *Capital*, Vol. 1, Ch. 10.

26. Heller, *Theory of Need in Marx*, p. 31.

27. Heller, *Theory of Need in Marx*, p. 31.

28. Heller, *Theory of Need in Marx*, p. 31.

29. Heller, *Theory of Need in Marx*, pp. 32–3.

30. Heller, *Theory of Need in Marx*, pp. 32–3.

31. Marx, *Capital*, Vol. 1, p. 825.

32. Marx, *Capital*, Vol. 1, p. 827.

33. Heller, *Theory of Need in Marx*, p. 33.

34. Heller, *Theory of Need in Marx*, p. 33; Marx, *Capital*, Vol. 1, p. 275.

35. Heller, *Theory of Need in Marx*, pp. 33–4.

36. Heller, *Theory of Need in Marx*, pp. 33–4.

37. Heller, *Theory of Need in Marx*, p. 34.

38. K. Marx, *Grundrisse*, (trans.) M. Nicolaus (Pelican, Harmondsworth, 1973), p. 93; K. Marx and F. Engels, *Gesamtausgabe (MEGA)*, II.1.1 (Dietz Verlag, Berlin, 1976), p. 30.

39. Marx, *Grundrisse*, p. 325; *MEGA*, II.1.1, p. 241. Emphasis added. Translation modified.

40. Marx, *Grundrisse*, p. 325.

41. Marx, *Grundrisse*, p. 527.

42. Marx, *Grundrisse*, p. 527.

43. Marx, *Grundrisse*, p. 527.

44. Marx, *Grundrisse*, p. 93.

45. Marx, *Grundrisse*, p. 92.

46. Marx, *Grundrisse*, p. 92.

47. Marx, *Grundrisse*, p. 527.

48. Marx, *Grundrisse*, p. 528; K. Marx and F. Engels, *Gesamtausgabe (MEGA)*, II.1.2 (Dietz Verlag, Berlin, 1981), p. 427.

49. Heller, *Theory of Need in Marx*, p. 30.

50. Marx, *Grundrisse*, p. 527.

51. Marx, *Grundrisse*, p. 527.

52. K. Marx, and F. Engels, *Gesamtausgabe (MEGA)*, II.5 (Dietz Verlag, Berlin, 1983), p. 124.

53. Fowkes translates it as 'requirements' while even more misleadingly Moore and Aveling use 'wants'. Elsewhere throughout *Capital*, however, both Fowkes and Moore and Aveling translate '*Lebensmittel*' as 'means of subsistence'. When the whole phrase '*nothwendigen Lebensmittel*' appears again later in *Capital*, Fowkes simply misses the 'necessary' out altogether whereas Moore and Aveling translate it as 'necessaries of life'.

See Marx, *Capital*, Vol. 1, Penguin edition, p. 655, and Lawrence and Wishart edition, p. 519; Marx and Engels, *MEGA*, II.5, p. 420.

54. *MEGA*, II.5, p. 123; Marx, *Capital*, Vol. 1, p. 275.
55. Marx, *Capital*, Vol. 1, p. 275; *MEGA*, II.5, pp. 123–4. Translation modified.
56. Marx, *Capital*, Vol. 1, p. 275.
57. Marx, *Capital*, Vol. 1, p. 276.
58. Marx, *Capital*, Vol. 1, p. 1004. Emphasis added.
59. Marx, *Capital*, Vol. 1, p. 1003.
60. Marx, *Capital*, Vol. 1, p. 1005. Emphasis added.
61. Marx, *Capital*, Vol. 1, p. 984.
62. Marx, *Capital*, Vol. 1, p. 274.
63. Marx, *Capital*, Vol. 1, p. 277.
64. Marx, *Capital*, Vol. 1, p. 807.
65. Marx, *Capital*, Vol. 1, p. 807.
66. Marx, *Capital*, Vol. 1, p. 807.
67. Marx, *Capital*, Vol. 1, p. 797.
68. Marx and Engels, *Collected Works*, Vol. 6, p. 132; K. Marx and F. Engels, *Werke*, Volume 4 (Dietz Verlag, Berlin, 1969), p. 91. Translation modified. The original translation actually has 'need for luxury'.
69. Marx and Engels, *Collected Works*, Vol. 6, p. 133.
70. Marx and Engels, *Collected Works*, Vol. 6, p. 133.
71. K. Marx, *Capital*, Volume 2, (trans.) D. Fernbach (Penguin, Harmondsworth, 1992), p. 479.
72. Marx, *Capital*, Vol. 2, p. 488.
73. Heller, *Theory of Need in Marx*, p. 37.
74. Heller, *Theory of Need in Marx*, p. 37.
75. Marx, *Grundrisse*, pp. 527–8.
76. Heller, *Theory of Need in Marx*, p. 37.
77. Marx and Engels, *Collected Works*, Vol. 6, p. 132.
78. Marx, *Grundrisse*, pp. 92–3, 527.
79. K. Marx, *Capital*, Volume 3, (trans.) D. Fernbach (Penguin, Harmondsworth, 1991), p. 281; K. Marx and F. Engels, *Werke*, Volume 25 (Dietz Verlag, Berlin, 1964), p. 190; see also, K. Marx, *Theories of Surplus Value*, Part II (trans.) R. Simpson (Lawrence and Wishart, London, 1968), pp. 527–35.
80. Marx, *Capital*, Vol. 3, p. 290; Marx and Engels, *Werke*, Vol. 25, p. 198. Translation modified. The original translation has 'genuine social need'.
81. Heller, *Theory of Need in Marx*, p. 71.
82. Heller, *Theory of Need in Marx*, p. 71.
83. Marx, *Capital*, Vol. 1, p. 275.
84. Marx, *Capital*, Vol. 1, p. 275.
85. M. Lebowitz, *Beyond Capital: Marx's Political Economy of the Working Class* (Macmillan, London, 1992), p. 27.
86. Lebowitz, *Beyond Capital*, p. 27.
87. Marx, *Capital*, Vol. 3, p. 290.
88. Lebowitz, *Beyond Capital*, p. 27.
89. Lebowitz, *Beyond Capital*, p. 28.
90. Lebowitz, *Beyond Capital*, pp. 28–30.
91. Lebowitz, *Beyond Capital*, p. 30.
92. Lebowitz, *Beyond Capital*, p. 30.

93. Lebowitz, *Beyond Capital*, pp. 97, 98.
94. Lebowitz, *Beyond Capital*, p. 28.
95. Lebowitz, *Beyond Capital*, p. 28.
96. Lebowitz, *Beyond Capital*, p. 97.
97. Marx, *Grundrisse*, p. 245; Lebowitz, *Beyond Capital*, p. 28.
98. Marx, *Grundrisse*, p. 242.
99. Marx, *Grundrisse*, pp. 242–5.
100. Marx, *Capital*, Vol. 1, p. 277.
101. Marx, *Grundrisse*, p. 101.

7

MARX AND HIGHER NEEDS

With the circuit of needs clearly elucidated, and the importance of the need-form readily evident, this chapter considers Marx's use of need concepts that relate to what I define as human 'higher needs'. Marx sees these higher needs existing in some form within the contradictions of the circuit of needs in capitalist society, and not just in a future society of the associated producers, as Heller suggests. Against the arguments of many commentators, therefore, I show how analysing forms allows Marx to understand these needs in the dialectical mediation between their universal and particular moments. I illustrate the mistaken basis of those arguments which suggest that Marx privileges a universal conception of need over a particular, or that he is in some way confused between the two. Marx's attention to the need-form rules out such a one-sided or muddled understanding of needs and their satisfaction. I also demonstrate Marx's emphasis on the human need to overcome the realm of natural necessity and reach the true realm of freedom, and the role technology plays in allowing this to happen. For Marx, the defeat of natural necessity and the creation of a realm where humans can fully develop and satisfy their higher needs are imperative if people are to be truly free. It is attention to form that highlights how moments of this realm exist contradictorily within capitalism, and points to the possibility of their full realisation beyond such a system. This will now become clear through the analysis of Marx's crucial concept of 'human need'.

HUMAN AND NONHUMAN ANIMAL NEED

For Marx, 'human needs' have two general characteristics. First, they are distinct from the needs of nonhuman animals; second, they constitute the self-realisation of the human essence. To distinguish 'human need' from 'nonhuman animal need' Marx uses the concept of 'species-being'. He argues that whereas animals cannot choose their own 'life activity' – for instance, a rabbit has to dig its burrow – humans, through their own 'will and consciousness', can do so. Through 'conscious life activity' humans can choose what they want to do or be.[1] As a 'conscious being', 'man' 'reproduces himself . . . actively and actually . . . in a world he himself has created'.[2] By working on the material world humans give evidence of their 'conscious species-being'. Animals also produce things themselves, but what Marx wants to emphasise is that they do so 'only when physical need compels them', whereas 'man produces even when he is free from physical need and truly produces only in freedom from such need'.[3] Accordingly, Marx argues that whereas animals produce 'one-sidedly' humans produce 'universally'; to produce 'universally' is, therefore, to produce free from the constraint of one's 'immediate physical need'.[4] For Marx, therefore, humans, unlike nonhuman animals, are thinking beings that can go beyond the satisfaction of their 'immediate physical needs' to satisfy higher needs. Through creative labour, humans can truly produce and concretely assert their own essence. So Marx's specification of 'human needs' is very much dependent on this human/nonhuman animal distinction. However, he also develops the concept of 'human need' through another need that he calls 'egoistic'.

EGOISTIC NEED

Marx refers to 'egoistic need' as being in conflict with 'social need', which, as we saw in the previous chapter, is the need of society as a whole expressed in the form of effective demand. So a 'cobbler, for instance, satisfies a social need' (*sociales Bedürfniß*) through making shoes for others.[5] Marx contends that such 'social needs' can have a very negative effect on the worker who becomes determined by these 'social needs' (*gesellschaftlichen Bedürfnisse*), which are 'alien to him and which act upon him with compulsive force'.[6] The worker submits to this force of 'social need . . . from egoistic need (*egoistischem Bedürfniß*), from necessity'.[7] This leads Marx to contrast the 'social need' of society with the 'egoistic need' of the individual.[8]

Marx argues that society sees the worker as 'only the slave that satisfies its needs'.[9] Similarly, workers themselves look to society only for the satisfaction of their own 'egoistic needs'. Individuals are recognised not as human beings – as ends in themselves – but simply as a means to fulfil the ends of others. Even the labouring activity of 'man' is not an end in itself, because it is reduced to nothing more than the 'maintenance of his individual existence'.[10] Humans' labours are simply a means to the end of ensuring their own physical survival.

For Marx the realm of private property inevitably reduces an individual to an 'egoistic man' of civil society, who has 'private desires and interests that are separated from the community'.[11] The only bonds that hold individuals together are 'natural necessity, need and private interest, the conservation of their property and their egoistic persons'.[12] Individuals relate to each other not as human to human, but merely as means to the end of satisfying their 'egoistic needs'. They 'subordinate' themselves to the 'alien substance' of money, which is the very 'estranged essence of man's work and existence'.[13] Money acts as a '*pimp* between need and object, between life and man's means of life'.[14] The object needed becomes secondary to the prior need for money. Consequently, money, and not the object, becomes the 'real need' of all individuals in the perverted realm of private property.[15]

Only in communist society can 'human needs' be properly satisfied. However, communism or the 'true community', which is the 'essence of man', actually 'arises out of the *need* and the *egoism* of individuals'.[16] The 'true community of man' contains the 'real, conscious and authentic existence' of man's 'species-activity' and 'species spirit' through '*social* activity and *social* enjoyment'.[17] As the realm of private property does not allow humans to recognise themselves as humans or 'give the world a human organization, this *community* appears in the form of estrangement (*Form der Entfremdung*)'.[18] So even in the alienated form of a system of private property, elements of the 'true community' are present. In the very satisfaction of 'egoistic needs' moments of 'human need' are also being satisfied, but in an estranged form. To overcome this estrangement properly and establish a 'true community' fully, 'human need' has to replace 'egoistic need' totally. In terms of analysing forms, therefore, 'human need' in capitalism takes the form of 'egoistic need'. Consequently, moments of 'human need' exist within the alienated form of 'egoistic need', and analysing forms is the way to uncover such moments. The mode of existence or determinate abstraction of 'human need' in capitalism is 'egoistic need'.[19]

The preceding discussion has given a general indication of what Marx conceives 'human needs' to be. The most salient are self-realisation, creative labour and freedom from necessity. The task now is specifically to elucidate these very important needs.

SELF-REALISATION

For Marx, the need for the self-realisation of the essence of 'man' is a crucial 'human need'. In capitalism, of course, such a realisation 'appears as the de-realization of his life'.[20] The 'fulfilment of his personality' or the 'realization of his natural talents and spiritual goals' becomes 'wholly *accidental* and *unimportant*'.[21] Humans in capitalism are workers, sellers of labour-power, a mere commodity. Overcoming such 'de-realization' is imperative for Marx because 'man' is '*in need* of a totality of vital human expression; he is the man in whom his own realization exists as inner necessity, as *need*'.[22] Humans have a need to realise their self, the very essence that makes them truly human. In doing so 'man' becomes aware that he is:

> a *total* being and as a *total* being his needs stand in an *inner* relation to the products of others – for the need for a thing is the most obvious, irrefutable proof that the thing is part of *my* essence, that its being is for me and that its *property* is the property, the particular quality peculiar to my essence.[23]

Self-realisation leads to a situation where 'man' experiences 'his greatest wealth – the *other* man – as need'.[24] In socialism, humans' inner need is to realise themselves and recognise other humans as the '*source*' of their own life.[25] We look to others not as means to an end, not as an external imposition on the satisfaction of our own needs, but as fellow human beings. To highlight such a fact, Marx argues that 'the relation of man to woman' is the 'most *natural* relation of human being to human being'.[26] He asserts that such a relation 'demonstrates the extent to which man's *needs* have become *human* needs' because the '*other*, as a human being, has become a need for him'.[27] Consequently, Marx indicates that even when 'man' is 'in his most individual existence he is at the same time a communal being'.[28] There is a recognition of the 'other' as human, rather than just as an object, once estrangement in the realm of private property ends.

For Marx, then, people have a 'human need' for self-realisation that becomes manifest in their 'personality', 'natural talents' and 'spiritual goals'. Moreover, the need for an object is an 'inner relation' not an external imposition. Self-realisation itself leads to a recognition of others as human beings rather than things or objects to use for pursuing particular ends. One way humans mediate such self-realisation is through their shaping of the world with fulfilling, creative labour.

LABOUR

The need for fulfilling, creative labour is also the mediation of the need for self-realisation. Marx argues that in the 'true community of man', where people could produce as human beings, labouring activity would be a form of self-affirmation through objectifying individuality.[29] 'Human need' would replace 'egoistic need', with the production of an object now 'corresponding to the needs of another *human being*'.[30] In capitalism, however, labouring activity, instead of being the '*free expression*' and '*enjoyment of life*', simply becomes a 'torture', nothing more than '*forced* labour imposed . . . *not* through an *inner necessity* (*innere nothwendige Noth*) but through an *external* arbitrary need (*äusserliche Zuffällige Noth*)'.[31] Only in a fully communist society will 'need or enjoyment' lose their '*egoistic* nature' and nature lose its 'mere *utility* in the sense that its use has become *human* use'.[32] 'Man' creates, and is at home in, the world which represents the '*objectification of himself*' as a realisation of his 'essential powers'.[33] This is because the whole of world history is 'nothing more than the creation of man through human labour, and the development of nature for man'.[34] Humans mediate their 'human need' for self-realisation through creative and fulfilling labour that is itself a vital 'human need'. Truly fulfilling labour is dependent, however, on the human capacity to overcome external necessity. Labour may be the 'living, form-giving fire'[35] through which humans realise themselves, but it quickly becomes a deathly activity under the tyranny of natural necessity. Marx makes this quite clear when he contrasts natural necessity with the true realm of freedom.

NECESSITY AND FREEDOM

As the discussion of 'species-being' indicated, Marx thinks that the individual 'truly produces only in freedom from . . . physical need'.[36] Marx's later writings replicate such a contention with even greater emphasis. In Volume 3 of *Capital*, for example, he states:

> The realm of freedom really begins only where labour determined by necessity and external expediency ends; it lies by its very nature beyond the sphere of material production proper. Just as the savage must wrestle with nature to satisfy his needs, to maintain and reproduce his life, so must civilised man, and he must do so in all forms of society and under all possible modes of production. This realm of natural necessity expands with his development, because his needs do too; but the productive forces to satisfy these expand at the same time. Freedom in this sphere, can consist only in this, that socialised man, the associated producers, govern the human metabolism with nature in a rational way, bringing it under their collective control instead of being dominated by it as a blind power; accomplishing it with the least expenditure of energy and in conditions most worthy and appropriate for their human nature. But this always remains a realm of necessity. The true realm of freedom, the development of human powers as an end in itself, begins beyond it, though it can only flourish with this realm of necessity as its basis. The reduction of the working day is the basic prerequisite.[37]

For Marx, it is self-evident that all societies have to reproduce themselves to survive; they have to satisfy their 'natural needs'. The labour performed in doing this is not totally 'free' labour because it does not involve the development of human powers as an end in themselves.

Rather, such labour is a means to an end – the end of satisfying the essential, 'natural needs' of all of society. The only way an element of freedom can exist in this sphere of necessity is to accomplish these necessary tasks with the minimum of effort and in pleasurable surroundings.[38] Even if they meet these conditions, however, humans are still in the realm of necessity and not 'true' freedom. Only in the latter realm can human powers develop as ends in themselves and not just as a means to satisfy 'natural needs'. The path to the true realm of freedom begins, therefore, with a reduction in the working day – a reduction in necessary labour. This allows us to pursue activities that we want to pursue as human beings, and not as mere cogs in a production process. The satisfaction of our 'natural needs' is a constant burden, but its diminution is possible with the development of the productive forces. As Marx argues in the *Grundrisse*, such a reduction of necessary labour time 'corresponds to the artistic, scientific etc. development of the individuals in the time set free'.[39] Such 'free time – which is both idle time and time for higher activity – has naturally transformed its possessor into a different subject, and he then enters into the direct production process as this different subject'.[40]

Even with the development of the productive forces to high levels of automation, humans will still have to enter the realm of natural necessity to satisfy the 'social needs' of society. This is still the realm of unfreedom, but we perform labour there as a 'different subject'. We realise we are satisfying the needs of others, who in turn are satisfying our needs as fellow human beings. Marx, though, perceptively points out that the capacity for technological developments means that even this minimal '*direct labour* . . . cease[s] to be the basis of production [because] it is transformed more into a supervisory and regulatory activity'.[41] The onset of automatic work processes means that human involvement in the realm of necessity and unfreedom will be very minimal indeed.[42]

Necessary labour is not free labour and must therefore be decreased. 'True' labour, labour that involves the development of human powers as ends in themselves, stands above and beyond such necessary labour. There is a big difference, therefore, in mass-producing tables by standing at a machine all day and working on a piece of wood to develop the article itself. The latter is far more an expression of the human essence or species-being than the former, because it is an activity separate from producing under the burden of natural necessity.[43] Any suggestion, therefore, that 'the satisfaction of aesthetic and cognitive needs does not require the performance of further practice, over and above the practices through which physical needs are met'[44] is obviously mistaken. The person making the table with her or his own skill and attention is outside the pressure to produce to satisfy a 'natural need' – the need to have a table from which to eat. Rather she or he is expressing her or his own essence in the creative act of making the table. The satisfactions of such higher needs are qualitatively different from the satisfactions of 'natural needs'. This is because when people are producing 'truly', they are doing what they want to do; whereas in the satisfaction of 'natural needs', it is what people have to do that is the issue. Yet it is in doing what you want to do, in expressing your own identity in whatever form you wish, that you can satisfy your higher needs. So the 'human need' for free time in which we can be 'idle' and 'creative' is dependent on the reduction and eventual abolition of the working day.[45]

HIGHER NEED-FORMS

With the importance of the need for self-realisation established, we now have to consider the status of 'human needs' through the notion of general and determinate abstractions. This raises the issue of how analysing forms can illuminate the 'inner connections' between 'natural', 'human' and 'egoistic' needs. As I have already argued in the previous chapter, for Marx, 'natural needs' are a general abstraction. They are needs that have to be satisfied in all societies, and in all different historical periods, for the human race to continue in existence. In capital, people accomplish this through the selling of labour and the receipt of a wage or, alternatively, some form of welfare. Within capitalism the 'natural needs' of individuals take an 'egoistic' form in society. Individuals look to other people simply as a means to their own end and not as an end in themselves. The 'other' is simply a means to satisfy their own needs. One mode of existence of 'natural needs' therefore is 'egoistic'. The determinate abstraction of 'natural needs' – the needs specific to a particular society and historical period – are 'egoistic needs' in capital. Yet, as Marx points out, within this estranged form the very possibility of transcendence to the satisfaction of 'human needs' is possible. In fact, 'human needs' exist contradictorily within the capitalist system. They appear in the mode of existence of 'egoistic needs'. The question is, however, whether these 'human needs' are 'natural needs'. Are such 'human needs' essential requirements for the continued existence of human beings? To resolve this matter we have to examine some comments made by Marx on the status of 'human needs'.

In his early writings he offers a long list of examples of what he considers are 'human needs'. These are the 'human need' to 'eat, drink, buy books, go to the theatre, go dancing, go drinking, think, love, theorize, sing, paint, fence, etc.'.[46] Nonhuman animals also share some of these needs, not least the need to eat and drink. However, Marx is not

equating human and nonhuman animal needs. What makes the needs to
eat and drink distinctly 'human', for Marx, is the form in which these
needs are satisfied.[47] As Marx asserts, when man is a 'prisoner of crude
practical need (*rohen praktischen Bedürfniß*)' then he is satisfying his
'natural needs' in their 'crudest form'.[48] It follows, therefore, that eating
or drinking in such an immediate form is a 'crude need' on a par with the
eating and drinking activity of nonhuman animals. Instead, humans have
to 'transform crude need into *human* need'.[49] Such a need is made human
by its satisfaction taking a more refined form.[50] Eating and drinking can
then be designated as 'human needs'.[51] Marx's discussion of labour in
Volume 1 of *Capital* is particularly enlightening in this respect. He notes
how labour is a 'process, by which man, through his own actions,
mediates, regulates and controls the metabolism between himself and
nature'.[52] In this very process of changing 'external nature' and subjecting it to his 'own sovereign power', 'man' 'simultaneously changes his
own nature' and 'realizes his own purpose' in such activity.[53]

Marx then makes a crucial comment to distinguish such labouring
activity:

> We are not dealing here with those first instinctive forms of labour which remain on
> the animal level. An immense interval of time separates the state of things in which
> a man brings his labour-power to market for sale as a commodity from the situation
> when human labour had not yet cast off its first instinctive form. We suppose
> labour in a form in which it is an exclusively human characteristic.[54]

Marx is arguing that when human labour was simply a matter of instinct
this was congruent with the labour of nonhuman animals. The nonhuman
animal is trapped by the instinct to satisfy its 'physical needs' immediately
and must hunt to do so. Humans as savages, are no different in that they
hunt to live and live to hunt, making mere instinct and the drive of
necessity the basis of their labour. Yet within this process 'human labour'
exists, as a moment, in its 'instinctive form'. For Marx, what makes such
labour human is that 'at the end of every labour process, a result emerges
which had already been conceived by the worker at the beginning, hence
already existed ideally'.[55] The human aspect is the individual being
conscious of a purpose to his or her labouring activity. Hence, 'what
distinguishes the worst architect from the best of bees is that the architect
builds the cell in his mind before he constructs it in wax'.[56] Humans at the
level of the savage are like the bee, simply driven by instinct to construct
what they need to satisfy their 'natural needs'. At this level, human labour
– the labour of human beings – is in its 'instinctive form'. Eventually,
however, as humans develop their relation with nature, the 'instinctive
form' of human labour is 'cast off'; labour now becomes more human.

Ironically, however, even in more advanced societies human labour, the self-realisation of human creativity, still exists contradictorily. Capitalism actually reduces such labour to the valorisation process, thereby making it take an estranged form.

Marx's argument implies that 'human needs' emanate from human interaction with nature and other human beings. The determinate existence or form 'human needs' take in a primitive society is limited due to the rudimentary stage of such development. Human need is still present but only in an 'instinctive form'. As society progresses, labour takes on a more human characteristic. Humans are not necessarily prisoners of their 'crude' and 'immediate physical needs'. They are conscious of their labouring activity as they use and shape the objects of their environment for a specific purpose.

How, though, do these 'human needs' relate to 'natural needs'? To consider this we can examine Marx's discussion in the *Grundrisse* of two individuals engaging in the simple exchange of commodities. In an analysis of why these individuals exchange particular goods Marx observes:

> Both have the need to breathe; for both the air exists as atmosphere; this brings them into no social contact; as breathing individuals they relate to one another only as natural bodies, not as persons. Only the differences between their needs and between their production gives rise to exchange.[57]

Humans have the 'natural need' to breathe, and despite sharing the atmosphere this is no reason for them to come into a social relation with each other. Although they share the 'natural need' to breathe, they relate to each other not as 'persons', not as human beings, but simply as 'natural bodies'. For Marx what unites the two of them together in a social relation is that 'each of them reaches beyond his own particular need etc., as a *human being*, and that they relate to one another as human beings; that their common species-being is acknowledged by all'.[58] The italicised and singular 'human being' is simply a 'natural body' that satisfies its 'natural needs'. It develops and 'goes beyond' this simple level of satisfaction by producing for another human being, who in turn also produces for it. When these two individuals stand in a relation to each other, each needing the other's product, they become 'human beings'. They are no longer simply 'natural bodies' labouring in isolation to satisfy only their own needs, but have become 'persons', real people, real human beings.

Marx's argument implies that the satisfaction of 'natural needs' with production aimed solely at one's self is not properly human. It becomes more human with exchange, when people produce not just for themselves but for others.[59] Consequently, the 'human need' for fulfilling labour is an incipient tendency in the self-production of individuals. At a low level of development this takes a merely 'instinctual form'. As society develops and individuals produce for others this labour takes on a more human form. The particular needs of the individual assume a more universal aspect for the species of humans as a whole. 'Human needs', therefore, are a developmental tendency within humans. These needs arise out of the satisfaction of 'natural needs'. The 'natural need' to eat takes the form of the human need to dine at a restaurant. The need to labour to satisfy hunger takes the form of a 'human need' to direct labouring activity consciously towards the satisfaction of the needs of others. The need for self-realisation arises out of the very need to satisfy 'natural needs'. So 'human needs' are a form, or mode of existence, of 'natural needs'. The former emerge out of humans' interaction with nature and other human beings. The need for self-realisation develops and manifests itself in different forms through humans' activity and their relation to nature. In the form of estrangement it is 'egoistic need', whilst its non-alienated form is expressive of human creativity and talents.

Marx's emphasis on analysing the forms needs take in society means that he is not presupposing a conception of universal need. Instead, he is examining the form 'natural needs' assume and deducing 'inner connections' between these need-forms. A failure to recognise this emphasis on form can lead to misinterpretations of Marx's theory of need. Kate Soper, for instance, accuses Marx of having 'internal inconsistencies' in his statements on needs.[60] She argues that on the one hand, he suggests that 'our needs are always historic and relative'; whilst on the other, he proceeds to 'specify our absolute need for labour, for all round development, for rich individuality'.[61] Yet as we have seen from the preceding analysis, Marx does not posit these needs as universal or absolute. He deduces them from human practical activity that has posited them as absolute and universal. The needs for fulfilling labour, for self-realisation, etc., emanate from the interaction of humans with nature and their fellow human beings. Analysing the forms needs take in society exposes the existence of 'human needs'. Such needs are 'historically created' from particular needs – the universal arises out of the particular. Labour as fulfilling activity arises out of its lesser 'instinctive form', just as the need for free time is present and arises within non-free time.

Ironically, Soper thinks that Marx's 'inconsistencies' are valuable, because even if they offer no solutions to problems of human needs, they at least pose questions that demand an answer.[62] As examples she offers the 'tensions between relativism and essentialism, between 'forms' common to our needs and their irreducible 'contents'.[63] As we have seen, however, it is these very tensions that Marx himself is exploring. Any

'solutions' arise from human beings themselves in their natural development. Marx is not positing universal or essentialist notions of need over
particular or relative notions. Instead, he is seeing how the universal or
essential need emerges out of the particular or relative. He understands
universal and particular not as polar opposites, but as existing in a
dialectical unity. We, human beings, make particular needs universal
in many diverse and relative forms. For Marx self-realisation is an
essential and universal 'human need'. He has not started his analysis
by assuming such a need but has deduced it from human activity. Of
course, even a universal need such as self-realisation is going to take many
different forms itself, and in this way a universal will have a mode of
existence as a particular. This, however, is exactly Marx's point. Universal and particular must relate to each other dialectically, as a contradictory unity. The mode of existence of a universal need can be very
particular indeed. Hence, Marx is not in any way inconsistent because he
understands universal and particular as a totality, not one-sidedly, and
deduces this from human self-activity.

The attempt to impose a needs/wants distinction on Marx also misses
the importance of how attention to form illuminates Marx's understanding of needs. Archibald, for instance, attempts to interpret Marx
as distinguishing between needs and wants, although he also admits that
at times Marx elided the two.[64] For Archibald, 'needs' are linked to
biological factors, food, drink, etc., whereas 'wants' are the 'myriad of
things individuals through the ages have desired – but not necessarily
needed'.[65] The distinction Archibald is attempting to impose mirrors
the approach of certain modern need theorists that we discussed in
Chapter 1.[66] Needs are being seen as essential and wants as superficial. Marx, however, clearly rejects such a rigid, undialectical understanding of needs. Dichotomising 'needs' and 'wants', as Archibald does,
ignores the possibility of such 'wants' existing as 'needs' and *vice versa*.
For instance, luxuries, which Archibald would see as wants, Marx refers
to as needs because the working class can eventually posit such luxuries as
'necessary needs'. By understanding needs as forms, Marx grasps how
'natural needs' become posited as 'necessary needs' and as 'luxury needs'.
Moreover, he is able to highlight the inner connection between these
forms of need, which a static understanding of needs, such as Archibald's,
cannot comprehend.[67]

Analysing forms, therefore, holds the key to a proper understanding of
needs in Marx's writings. Attention to form also highlights the mistaken
basis of many criticisms of Marx's need theory. Marx is not privileging
universal over particular needs or particular over universal. Instead, he is
capturing the dialectical movement between these moments of need

through human self-activity in the world. This becomes even more evident when Marx indicates how 'human needs' develop into another need-form, namely, 'radical needs'. Agnes Heller has rightly attached great importance to this type of need; it is through a critique of her own interpretation that we will now elucidate and analyse this need-form.

RADICAL NEEDS

For Heller, 'radical needs' emanate out of the contradictions of capitalism as individuals become conscious of their alienation. She argues, therefore, that 'radical needs' are already in existence in capitalism but people cannot satisfy them.[68] Instead, these needs offer the potential for the creation of a 'collective Ought' which allows consciousness to 'exceed its bounds'.[69] People can then transcend capitalism and create an alternative system, thus overcoming the 'simple consciousness of alienation'.[70] Heller stresses that the consciousness exceeding its bounds is not the same as the consciousness of being in poverty or misery. The latter is only an 'empirical consciousness', whereas the former achieves the highest level of consciousness by recognising the social relations of production as alienated.[71]

There are a number of problems with Heller's account of 'radical needs', not least in her assertion that their satisfaction is only possible in the society of 'associated producers' and not in capitalism. On this view, Heller would have to declare that workers' struggles for higher wages are of little importance because they do not transcend the capital/wage relation. Yet, as Lebowitz rightly points out, even though Marx recognised the limitations of wage struggles, he also saw them as important in allowing the working class to develop some notion of class consciousness.[72] Locating 'radical needs' only in a society of the future means that Heller ignores important moments of transcendence within capitalism.[73]

Heller's position becomes even more curious with her assertion that even if workers overturned a social order they would still not be bearers of 'radical needs'. This is because they have merely taken over the current system of needs and not gone beyond it.[74] She wants to suggest that a 'radical need' can only be radical if it is not satisfied in any way within any given society.[75] By definition, this implies that a 'radical need' can only have existed in a given society in the heads of people or workers. How, then, does such a 'mental' need arise? Heller suggests that the development of the productive forces creates needs which belong to capitalism's 'Being' but not to its system of needs.[76] She contends that this is also the case for Marx, giving his example of free time which allows people to transform themselves as human beings.[77] Yet what Heller ignores is that free time as a 'real' need, and not a 'mental' need, also exists in capitalism. People do experience free time in capitalism as a reality. Obviously, the quality of this free time is dependent on its duration and the economic resources available; but it is still a need that people can satisfy within the existing system – even if in an imperfect way. Heller, therefore, fails to see the contradictory nature of need-satisfaction within capitalism. Instead, she posits a false division between this world and the future world of the 'associated producers'. Yet as Marx himself said:

> communism is . . . not a *state of affairs* which is to be established, an *ideal* to which reality [will] have to adjust itself. We call communism the *real* movement which abolishes the present state of things. The conditions of this movement result from the now existing premise.[78]

So transcendence of capitalism is present not simply in the heads of workers, but in their everyday actions in capitalism through resisting the imposition of work and constituting their own autonomy. The idea of self-valorising activity by workers, that is, the positive 'power to constitute new practices' within capital, has no place in Heller's analysis.[79] She thus actually misses forms of transcendence within existing capitalism.[80]

The actual bearers of 'radical needs' cause further problems for Heller's analysis. As Lebowitz recognises, Heller's constant emphasis on needs as consumptive activity leads her to see students and young people as such bearers because they reject the materialism of capitalist society.[81] Not surprisingly, then, the working class as an agent grasping for the 'new' society drops out of Heller's analysis. In contrast, Lebowitz argues that the needs of workers to control the use and production of their labour clearly makes the working class a bearer of 'radical needs' and human liberation. Heller's preoccupation with consumption rather than production makes her overlook this. Lebowitz suggests, therefore, that formulating needs in his way overcomes the uncertain relationship between Heller's 'radical needs' and the real process of transcending capitalism.[82]

The validity of Lebowitz's criticisms of Heller cannot conceal the fact that both are one-sided in their analysis. Marx is not emphasising production over consumption or *vice versa*, but wants to understand them as contradictions within a unity.[83] Again, it is through an emphasis on the need-form that a fuller understanding is available. The movement from production to consumption is the movement of the need-form through 'natural', 'necessary' and 'luxury' to satisfaction. Disconnecting these moments into production and consumption, and not grasping them as a totality, separates the form a need takes in exchange from the social relations of production. Understanding needs in capital as forms re-emphasises this social basis and reveals its antagonistic nature. Such an emphasis will now become clear in the examination of the origins of 'radical needs' in Marx's writings.

As Heller herself notes, it is in the 'Contribution to the Critique of Hegel's Philosophy of Right. Introduction' that Marx first develops the concept of 'radical needs'. Her main contention is that 'radical needs' are qualitative needs which go beyond capitalism. She offers the abolition of the wage system as an example of such a need.[84] As we shall now see, however, an analysis of Marx's text cannot support Heller's understanding of 'radical needs'. Marx's concern in the whole piece is the relationship between theory and practice. He argues that radical theory – philosophy – becomes actualised in people through practice. As he states: 'just as philosophy finds its material weapons in the proletariat so the proletariat finds its intellectual weapons in philosophy'.[85] He asserts that Germany is like a theory that is separate from practice, and so political emancipation is at a lower level than in other nations.[86] He argues that a revolution can only occur if a '*passive* element' or '*material* basis' is present, namely, the 'people's needs'.[87] Consequently, Marx then makes a distinction, not mentioned by Heller, between 'theoretical' and 'practical' needs. Marx asks:

> Will the enormous gap that exists between the demands of German thought and the responses of German reality now correspond to the same gap both between civil society and the state and civil society and itself? Will the theoretical needs be directly practical needs? It is not enough that thought should strive to realise itself; reality must itself strive towards thought.[88]

So Marx is positing a 'gap' between theory and practice that exists in Germany at his time of writing, namely, 1843–4. This 'gap' resembles the separation between civil society and the state, which arises because Germany is behind other modern nations in terms of political emancipation and industrialisation.[89] No bourgeois class has come forward in civil society in Germany to enact a political revolution.[90] What we have instead is opposing classes causing civil society to be in conflict within itself.[91] Such is the backward nature of German society that partial emancipation of a bourgeois form is no longer possible except with a class that is 'under the compulsion of its *immediate* situation, of *material* necessity and of its *chains themselves*'.[92] That class is the proletariat: 'a class of civil society which is not a class of civil society'.[93] For Marx, this is the only type of liberation that is practically possible for Germany if it is to cast off its feudal ties completely.[94] The discord within civil society, along with its separation from the state, will then disappear.[95]

The emphasis on material necessity links back to Marx's comment on the 'material basis' needed for a revolution. However, the problem then centres on his use of the terms 'theoretical' and 'practical' needs. According to Chris Arthur, Marx has not yet fully worked out his relationship between theory and practice.[96] Arthur interprets Marx as keeping theory and practice separate and not showing their 'interdependence . . . in a dialectically conceived totality'.[97] What Arthur means here is that Marx posits theory as separate from practice. Instead, we should understand theory and practice as being in a unity with each other. What is important for our purposes is that Arthur is interpreting Marx as understanding theory as philosophy, and practice as the proletariat, which he interprets as the 'material basis'.[98] However, as I have already indicated, it is not the proletariat that is this material basis but the people's needs. If philosophy is theory, then a theoretical need is a philosophical need. The philosophical or theoretical need that Marx seems to put forward in this context is the need for human emancipation and economic development. To realise itself, this theoretical need has to take the form of a practical need. The proletariat is the agent that Marx thinks can accomplish this task. It cannot just think about realising these needs but actually has to satisfy them practically. The proletariat has to stand in an 'all-sided opposition to the premises of the German political system' and declare 'man to be the supreme being for man'.[99] Yet there is another important need which is a spur to satisfying the need for human emancipation, and that is the very 'material necessity', the 'chains', which compel a class to satisfy such a need. According to Marx, the chains of necessity in the German case are attached to the proletariat and as such become 'radical chains'.[100] Material needs are therefore at the root of revolutionary action.

So we finally come to Marx's first mention of the concept of radical needs. 'A radical revolution', he states, 'can only be the revolution of radical needs, but the preconditions and seedbeds for such needs appear to be lacking.'[101] Marx argues that 'to be radical is to grasp things by the root. But for man the root is man himself.'[102] German theory was radical, for instance, in that it transcended religion to arrive at the position of the individual. It also had a 'practical energy' with the Reformation. So a theory that starts in the head of, in this case, Luther can have radical consequences in actuality as well as in the realm of thought. The main point to note is that *both* theory *and* practice can be radical, but it is the actualisation of theory that makes changes in the world. That said, how can this help us to understand Marx's comment on 'radical needs'? If 'radical' means going to the root of things then 'radical needs' can only mean going to the root of needs – the needs of humans. These needs in theory are the need for human emancipation and a change in the 'material basis' – the means by which needs are satisfied. The material basis for the satisfaction of human needs is minimal because Germany itself is not as economically advanced as countries such as France and England.[103] Similarly, the low level of industrial development in Germany means that the 'proletariat is only beginning to appear', but it is only this class that can achieve the emancipation of Germany itself.[104] However, the factors just mentioned suggest that there is little prospect of such needs appearing.

It is fairly obvious, therefore, that Heller errs in positing 'radical needs' as only qualitative and distinct from material considerations. They also contain quantitative aspects in terms of the 'material basis' upon which needs are built. Such a basis is the development of the productive forces in society at any particular time. Without a sufficient level of development of production, human emancipation is simply theoretical. Humans are still tied to necessity. They can only make their freedom practical as increases in productivity reduce the necessary labour time for society.

It is interesting that Heller attempts to make such a demarcation between qualitative and quantitative needs within the concept of 'radical needs'. She repeats the split between production and consumption made earlier. Understanding needs as forms, however, disallows any demarcation between consumption and production. 'Radical needs' are needs that attempt to go beyond capital, but their roots are firmly in its practical existence. A society that drastically minimises necessary labour is a society with a high degree of development in its productive forces. Hence, qualitative and quantitative inform one another – distinctions in a unity. Moreover, 'radical needs' themselves do take practical effect in capital through self-valorising activity by workers. Only through struggling within and against capital is it possible to get beyond it. Heller's exclusive focus on the 'beyond' and her neglect of the 'material basis' of 'radical needs' reveals the weakness of her interpretation of such needs from Marx's writings.

This leaves the question of how 'radical needs' relate to 'human needs'. The inference from Marx's comments is that 'radical needs' are a form of 'human needs'. This is particularly evident in Marx's emphasis on the need for emancipation by the proletariat, which he expresses in terms of the distinctly human. For instance, he declares the proletariat to be a 'sphere of society that can no longer lay claim to a *historical* title, but merely to a *human* one'.[105] Similarly, Marx also argues that the proletariat 'cannot emancipate itself without emancipating itself from – and thereby emancipating – all the other spheres of society, which is, in a word, the *total loss* of humanity and which can therefore redeem itself only through the *total redemption of humanity*'.[106] The proletariat is the agent of the truly human, whose mission is the 'total redemption of humanity'. So the satisfaction of 'human needs' within the contradictory relations of capitalism manifests itself as 'radical needs'. Consequently, 'radical needs' are the mode of existence of 'human needs' that are indicative of heightened class consciousness. For instance, the 'human need' for self-realisation takes the form of a 'radical need' when the satisfaction of such a need poses a threat to capital; that is, when a worker is engaging in self-valorising activity and not the valorising of the capitalist system. The 'human need' for free time, for instance, becomes 'radical' through absenteeism, strikes, go-slows, and sabotage of machinery – all of which can inflict severe damage on the capitalist production process. 'Human need' thus becomes 'radical' through its rupturing potential in, against and potentially beyond capital.

CONCLUSION

This discussion of higher needs reaffirms Marx's understanding of needs as forms within capitalism that we developed in the previous chapter. As humans offer themselves on the market as a commodity in order to satisfy their 'natural needs', moments of 'human needs' emerge. These can become manifest in an estranged form as 'egoistic needs' or in their own right as moments of self-valorisation. When such activity poses a threat to the capitalist system then 'human need' takes the form of 'radical need'. Analysing forms, therefore, reveals the 'inner connection' between these phenomena. The implications of Marx's argument for any theory of needs are therefore quite substantial. He would reject any privileging of either universal or particular conceptions of needs. Instead, it is the dialectical interaction between the two that has to be the focus. For Marx, needs can be posited as universal, but this is by the subjects themselves in their interaction with other human beings and the natural world. In the very positing of a universal need, the particular mode of existence of its satisfaction can take many different forms. So the constant interaction of universal and particular, both alienated and human, reverberates in and against the capitalist system.

For humans, the potential for subordination to a very miserable level of need-satisfaction exists alongside the potential for a much greater level of enjoyment. Technological developments offer increased free time from necessary labour, and the opportunity for humans to become rich in needs and their satisfaction, just as these developments also offer the opportunity for degrading labour and unemployment. Hence, Marx's theory of needs can highlight the positive moments within the negative manifestations of humans' contradictory development in their interaction with each other and the natural world. In this way a movement beyond capital, into a realm where human needs are properly satisfied, can become a real possibility.

NOTES

1. K. Marx, 'Economic and Philosophical Manuscripts', in K. Marx, *Early Writings*, (trans.) R. Livingstone and G. Benton (Penguin, Harmondsworth, 1992), pp. 328–9.
2. Marx, 'Economic and Philosophical Manuscripts', p. 329.
3. Marx, 'Economic and Philosophical Manuscripts', pp. 328–9
4. Marx, 'Economic and Philosophical Manuscripts', p. 329. Sensitive to the case for animal rights, Ted Benton argues for a more naturalistic interpretation of Marx's comments in an attempt to overcome any negative implications of designating nonhuman animals a lesser species than humans. See his 'Humanism = Speciesism: Marx on Humans and Animals', *Radical Philosophy*, 50, 1988, and *Natural Relations: Animal Rights and Social Justice* (Verso, London, 1993), Ch. 2. In any case, as Lawrence Wilde points out, keeping Marx's distinction does not inevitably result in the insensitive treatment of nonhuman animals, as many of Marx's positive comments concerning nonhuman animals and nature indicate. See L. Wilde, 'Marx's Concept of Human Essence and its Radical Critics', *Studies in Marxism*, 1, 1994, pp. 36–8.
5. K. Marx, 'Critique of Hegel's Doctrine of the State', in Marx, *Early Writings*, p. 189; K. Marx and F. Engels, *Gesamtausgabe (MEGA)*, 1.2 (Dietz Verlag, Berlin, 1982), p. 129.
6. K. Marx, 'Excerpts from James Mill's *Elements of Political Economy*' in Marx, *Early Writings*, p. 269; K. Marx and F. Engels, *Gesamtausgabe (MEGA)*, IV.2 (Dietz Verlag, Berlin, 1981), p. 455.
7. Marx, 'James Mill', p. 269; *MEGA*, IV.2, p. 455.
8. Marx, 'James Mill', p. 269.
9. Marx, 'James Mill', p. 269.
10. Marx, 'James Mill', p. 269.
11. K. Marx, 'On the Jewish Question', in Marx, *Early Writings*, p. 230.
12. Marx, 'Jewish Question', p. 230. See also K. Marx and F. Engels, *Collected Works*, Volume 4 (Lawrence and Wishart, London, 1975), p. 113.
13. Marx, 'Jewish Question', pp. 241, 249.
14. Marx, 'Economic and Philosophical Manuscripts', p. 375.
15. Marx, 'Economic and Philosophical Manuscripts', p. 358.
16. Marx, 'James Mill', p. 265.
17. Marx, 'James Mill', p. 265.
18. Marx, 'James Mill', p. 265; *MEGA*, IV.2, p. 452. Translation modified.
19. W. Leiss, 'Marx and Macpherson: Needs, Utilities, and Self-Development', in A. Kantos (ed.) *Powers, Possessions and Freedom* (University of Toronto Press, Toronto, Buffalo and London, 1979), pp. 121–2, is wrong to suggest, therefore, that Marx's early writings are 'a one-sided attack on capitalist society, asserting that it denies all "human needs"'. For a more accurate account of how 'human need' is present within 'egoistic need', see A. Chitty, 'The Early Marx on Needs', *Radical Philosophy*, 64, 1993, p. 29. However, Chitty does not account for Marx's notion of 'natural needs', which, as we saw in the previous chapter, appear mostly in the early writings as 'physical' or 'bodily' needs. Consequently, the inner connection between 'egoistic', 'human' *and* 'natural' need remains unexplored.
20. Marx, 'James Mill', p. 266.

21. Marx, 'James Mill', p. 269.
22. Marx, 'Economic and Philosophical Manuscripts', p. 356.
23. Marx, 'James Mill', p. 267; *MEGA*, IV.2. p. 454. Translation modified. The Penguin translation has 'felt need for a thing' but the word 'felt' does not appear in the original German. For a more correct translation, see D. McLellan (ed.) *Karl Marx: Selected Writings* (Oxford University Press, Oxford, 1977), p. 116.
24. Marx, 'James Mill', p. 267.
25. Marx, 'James Mill', p. 267.
26. Marx, 'Economic and Philosophical Manuscripts', p. 347.
27. Marx, 'Economic and Philosophical Manuscripts', p. 347.
28. Marx, 'Economic and Philosophical Manuscripts', p. 347.
29. Marx, 'James Mill', p. 277.
30. Marx, 'James Mill', p. 277.
31. Marx, 'James Mill', p. 278; *MEGA*, IV.2, p. 466.
32. Marx, 'Economic and Philosophical Manuscripts', p. 352.
33. Marx, 'Economic and Philosophical Manuscripts', pp. 352–3.
34. Marx, 'Economic and Philosophical Manuscripts', p. 357.
35. K. Marx, *Grundrisse*, (trans.) M. Nicolaus (Pelican, Harmondsworth, 1973), p. 361.
36. Marx, 'Economic and Philosophical Manuscripts', p. 329.
37. K. Marx, *Capital*, Volume 3, (trans.) D. Fernbach (Penguin, Harmondsworth, 1991), pp. 958–9.
38. For a more positive view of labour in the realm of necessity, see S. Sayers, 'The Need to Work', *Radical Philosophy*, 46, 1987, and 'Work, Leisure and Human Needs', in T. Winnifrith and C. Barrett (eds) *The Philosophy of Leisure* (Macmillan, London, 1989).
39. Marx, *Grundrisse*, p. 706.
40. Marx, *Grundrisse*, p. 712.
41. Marx, *Grundrisse*, p. 709.
42. N. Mobasser, 'Marx and Self-Realization', *New Left Review*, 161, January/February, 1987, pp. 122–3, also recognises the qualitative difference in performing necessary labour, but ignores the role of automation as a possible basis for eventually making work in this realm superfluous.
43. Cf. H. Lefebvre, *Critique of Everyday Life*, Volume 1 (Verso, London, 1991), pp. 173–5.
44. Benton, 'Humanism = Speciesism', p. 14.
45. A. Cohen, 'Marx – From the Abolition of Labour to the Abolition of the Abolition of Labour', *History of European Ideas*, 17, 4, 1993, suggests that the political reality of the failed revolutions of 1848 reconciled Marx to arguing only for the minimisation of necessary labour rather than its complete abolition. However, Cohen ignores the fact that the eventual abolition of labour is dialectically present in the minimisation of labour itself through increased automation. Marx's support for the minimisation of necessary labour is therefore not antithetical to the abolition of such labour. On the contrary, minimisation is a necessary stepping stone to the true realm of freedom.
46. Marx, 'Economic and Philosophical Manuscripts', p. 361.
47. Cf. N. Geras, *Marx and Human Nature: Refutation of a Legend* (Verso, London, 1983), p. 114, who suggests that the 'common need for food' is indicative of a 'common *human* nature' without realising that such a need is 'common' to nonhuman animals also. Emphasis added.
48. Marx, 'Economic and Philosophical Manuscripts', p. 353; *MEGA*, I.2, p. 394.
49. Marx, 'Economic and Philosophical Manuscripts', p. 359.

50. Marx actually refers to a 'refined need', which he links to the consumptive activities of the rich, and therefore offers a possible connection with a 'luxury need'. Marx, 'Economic and Philosophical Manuscripts', p. 363.

51. With some justification, Benton criticises Marx on this matter for 'exaggerat[ing] both the fixity and limitedness of scope in the activity of other [nonhuman] animals'. Benton, 'Humanism = Speciesism', p. 9.

52. K. Marx, *Capital*, Volume 1, (trans.) B. Fowkes (Penguin, Harmondsworth, 1988), p. 283.

53. Marx, *Capital*, Vol. 1, pp. 283–4.

54. Marx, *Capital*, Vol. 1, pp. 283–4.

55. Marx, *Capital*, Vol. 1, p. 284.

56. Marx, *Capital*, Vol. 1, p. 284. Cf. above, p. 64, n. 43.

57. Marx, *Grundrisse*, p. 242.

58. Marx, *Grundrisse*, p. 243.

59. Of course, these human moments exist in an alienated form within exchange, especially when they are subject to the imposition of 'social needs'.

60. K. Soper, *On Human Needs: Open and Closed Theories in a Marxist Perspective* (Harvester Press, Brighton, 1981), p. 213.

61. Soper, *On Human Needs*, p. 213; cf. P. Springborg, *The Problem of Human Needs and the Critique of Civilisation* (Allen and Unwin, London, 1981), p. 109.

62. Soper, *On Human Needs*, p. 214.

63. Soper, *On Human Needs*, p. 214.

64. W. P. Archibald, *Marx and the Missing Link: Human Nature* (Humanities Press, Atlantic Highlands NJ, 1989), p. 93.

65. Archibald, *Marx and the Missing Link*, p. 90.

66. See above, pp. 13–14.

67. Cf. C. Bay, 'Human Needs, Wants and Politics: Abraham Maslow, Meet Karl Marx', *Social Praxis*, 7, 1980, p. 239, who suggests that Marx's need theory requires 'a second concept "want" so it can offer a truly dialectical analysis . . . between manifest wants and evolving human needs'. That Marx is actually carrying out this task by analysing forms, but beyond the restrictions of needs/wants distinctions, is in no way recognised.

68. A. Heller, *The Theory of Need in Marx* (Allison and Busby, London, 1976), pp. 94–5.

69. Heller, *Theory of Need in Marx*, p. 95.

70. Heller, *Theory of Need in Marx*, p. 95.

71. Heller, *Theory of Need in Marx*, p. 95.

72. M. A. Lebowitz, 'Heller on Marx's Concept of Needs', *Science and Society*, 3, Fall, 1979, p. 351.

73. L. Boella, 'Radicalism and Needs in Heller', *Telos*, Fall, 1978, p. 114, argues that as Heller's work was linked with the democratic reforms in Hungary and Czechoslovakia in the 1960s this criticism is unfounded. However, if this is indeed the case it is even more odd that such important moments of transcendence are not included in the *Theory of Need in Marx*.

74. Heller, *Theory of Need in Marx*, p. 97.

75. Heller, *Theory of Need in Marx*, p. 97.

76. Heller, *Theory of Need in Marx*, p. 98; cf. J. Cohen, 'Review of Agnes Heller, *The Theory of Need in Marx*', *Telos*, 33, Fall, 1977.

77. Heller, *Theory of Need in Marx*, p. 98.

78. K. Marx and F. Engels, *Collected Works*, Volume 5 (Lawrence and Wishart, London, 1976), p. 49. Term in square bracket in the original translation.

79. H. Cleaver, 'The Inversion of Class Perspective in Marxian Theory: From Valorisation to Self-Valorisation', in W. Bonefeld, R. Gunn and K. Psychopedis (eds) *Open Marxism. Volume II: Theory and Practice* (Pluto, London, 1992), p. 129. The autonomist Marxist tradition is most notable for emphasising the importance of self-valorisation for Marxist discourse. For background, see H. Cleaver, *Reading Capital Politically* (Harvester, Brighton, 1979), particularly, pp. 43–66. For a more recent overview, see N. Witheford, 'Autonomist Marxism and the Information Society', *Capital and Class*, 52, Spring, 1994.

80. Heller is to some extent replicating the 'one-sided' analysis of Marcuse which is particularly encapsulated in his own notion of 'false needs'. For Marcuse, such needs are those which are 'superimposed upon the individual by particular social interests in his repression: the needs which perpetuate toil, aggressiveness, misery, and injustice'. H. Marcuse, *One-Dimensional Man* (Beacon Press, Boston, 1964), pp. 10–11. The tendency to overemphasise capital's domination of labour through the creation and imposition of so-called 'false needs' neglects the positive moments of transcendence by workers through their needs in and against capital. As O'Connor notes, consumption is not only 'another capitalist weapon in the class war', it is also 'another Achilles' heel of the capitalist system'. J. O'Connor, *Accumulation Crisis* (Blackwell, Oxford, 1986), p. 151. Moreover, the designation of certain needs as 'false' can also lead to the imposition of objective or universal needs against the particular needs of individuals. The dialectical mediation between the universal and particular is thereby lost. For a useful, and relatively sympathetic, discussion of Marcuse's argument, see B. Agger, 'Marcuse's "One-Dimensionality": Socio-Historical and Ideological Context', *Dialectical Anthropology*, 13, 4, 1988.

81. Lebowitz, 'Heller on Marx's Concept of Needs', pp. 351–2.

82. Lebowitz, 'Heller on Marx's Concept of Needs', p. 352. However, it should be noted that Lebowitz's exclusion of students and young people from the 'working class' could also be criticised. For a response to changes in working-class formation and a wider understanding of the notion of the 'working class' see M. Hardt and A. Negri, *Labour of Dionysus: A Critique of the State-Form* (University of Minnesota Press, Minneapolis, 1994).

83. Marx, *Grundrisse*, p. 99. Heller, *Theory of Need in Marx*, p. 76, does mention this important fact but then fails to accommodate it.

84. Heller, *Theory of Need in Marx*, p. 89.

85. K. Marx, 'A Contribution to the Critique of Hegel's Philosophy of Right. Introduction', in Marx, *Early Writings*, p. 257.

86. Marx, 'Contribution to the Critique', p. 251.

87. Marx, 'Contribution to the Critique', p. 252.

88. Marx, 'Contribution to the Critique', p. 252.

89. On the low level of German industrialisation at this time, see J. H. Clapham, *The Economic Development of France and Germany, 1815–1914* (Cambridge University Press, Cambridge, 1955), p. 82. On both economic and political backwardness see E. M. Wood, *The Pristine Culture of Capitalism* (Verso, London, 1991), pp. 26, and 105.

90. Marx, 'Contribution to the Critique', pp. 253–4.

91. Marx, 'Contribution to the Critique', p. 255.

92. Marx, 'Contribution to the Critique', p. 256.

93. Marx, 'Contribution to the Critique', p. 256.

94. As Marx notes in a colourful phrase: 'If I negate powdered wigs I am still left with unpowdered wigs. If I negate the situation in Germany in 1843, then according to the

French calendar I have barely reached 1789, much less the vital centre of our present age.'
Marx, 'Contribution to the Critique', p. 245.

95. Marx, 'Contribution to the Critique', p. 245.

96. This is to be accomplished in the 'Theses on Feuerbach' a year later. See C. Arthur, 'Introduction', in K. Marx and F. Engels, *The German Ideology* (Lawrence and Wishart, London, 1991), p. 14.

97. Arthur, 'Introduction', p. 14.

98. Arthur, 'Introduction', p. 14.

99. Marx, 'Contribution to the Critique', pp. 256–7.

100. Marx, 'Contribution to the Critique', p. 256.

101. Marx, 'Contribution to the Critique', p. 252.

102. Marx, 'Contribution to the Critique', p. 251.

103. Marx, 'Contribution to the Critique', p. 248.

104. Marx, 'Contribution to the Critique', p. 256.

105. Marx, 'Contribution to the Critique', p. 256.

106. Marx, 'Contribution to the Critique', p. 256.

8

HEGEL, MARX AND THE
NEED-FORM

At the outset, I argued that this study would depict a Hegel and Marx in agreement rather than opposition in their understanding of needs. This chapter makes this agreement explicit by drawing the main points of the book together in comparing their understanding of the concept. The three main areas of comparison correspond to the major themes that I outlined in the introduction: their respective methods; their concern about the human need to be free from necessity; and how their own understanding of needs makes a cogent contribution to debates in modern need theory. All three themes will illustrate the similarities rather than the differences between these two great thinkers.

DIALECTIC AND FORM

Hegel and Marx share the same dialectical method. Marx operates with general and determinate abstractions which find direct correspondence in Hegel's universal and particular concept. Both thinkers understand the determinate abstraction and the particularisation to be forms; that is, the mode of existence of the general abstraction or universal concept in society. Both begin by analysing these forms to discover their inner connection. The detailed examination of needs in the preceding chapters has indicated the power of understanding the concept of need on the basis of this method. 'Natural needs' – needs that are universally present in all societies and which humans must satisfy to subsist – are the universal concept and general abstraction for Hegel and Marx respectively. They both analyse the forms this universal notion of need takes in society. For Hegel, the focus is on the Will, human beings, who have to satisfy their 'natural needs' in order to exist. The satisfaction of these 'natural needs' passes through various mediations: immediate satisfaction, labour, tools and machinery, surplus, and money. The Will's movement through these mediations can take the form of a universal which can then take the form of a particular and so on.

165

Similarly, Marx follows the form 'natural needs' take through the antagonistic presence of labour in capital. He too emphasises the mediation of need through the moments of labour, machinery, surplus and money.[1] For both thinkers there is an initial mention of 'drives'. Beginning with the subjective satisfaction of individual needs, Hegel emphasises the importance of the human 'drive' towards ethical life.[2] Such a drive manifests itself in the form of need, which is itself a 'feeling of separation'.[3] Humans have to overcome this 'feeling of separation' to satisfy their 'natural needs' in order to exist. For Hegel, therefore, the 'drive' towards ethical life takes the form of a need. However, the individual is also a *'dialectic* of drives' that she or he is constantly trying to satisfy.[4] For Hegel, the individual must try and master these drives if she or he is to be free. For Marx, 'drives' exist within humans as 'vital powers'. The objects of these drives are external. Such 'drives' quickly take the form of 'natural needs', for Marx, as humans have to satisfy such needs in order to exist.[5]

Hegel and Marx both frown upon the immediate satisfaction of such needs because it suggests that humans are on a par with nonhuman animals. They therefore emphasise the important mediation of labour to satisfy 'natural needs'. Both grasp how labour leads to productive developments that can result in the creation of a surplus. Both also realise that control over the surplus produced leads to exchange and forms of domination which are rooted in human needs. The direct correspondence between an individual's need and an object becomes broken through exchange. For Hegel, the creation of a surplus leads to a form of domination which he captures through the master/servant relation. Control over the surplus leads to certain people dominating others. Needs are the persistent, reverberating presence in this process, culminating in the form of money as an 'abstract sign' of need.[6] The tensions present in Hegel's system of needs give rise to forms of mediation that attempt to unite particular with universal. Humans begin by satisfying their 'contingent' or 'subjective' needs alone, but eventually come into contact with others through exchange. In this way humans unite their particular needs with the universal needs of other people.

Hegel's introduction of the concept of 'opinion' – mere whim and fancy – indicates the level to which need-satisfaction can develop. At the same time, however, Hegel also notes how a mass of people have to satisfy their 'natural needs' in a very rudimentary form. The poor remain outside any mediating institutions. Even worse, a section of the poor become a 'rabble'. Their state is a result of the contradictions inherent in a system based on free exchange. Hence, Hegel perceptively captures the imperialist nature of the growth in the nation state as it goes beyond its boundaries in the search to satisfy ever more expanding needs. This is no solution to poverty, however, as the problems inherent in the system are simply exported to the new country. The system of needs therefore contains deep antagonisms that cannot be mediated. The incipient presence of the working class – which Hegel grasps within the estates – suggests further rupture, not less. Even the institutions of the police and corporation find themselves ill-equipped to overcome such contradictions. The poor themselves can gain no recognition in the corporation. Without a trade they remain outside this institution. Hegel offers considerable intervention in society to try to overcome these problems, but the possibility of a successful solution is not clear.

To criticise Hegel for not offering a fully integrating system for all, and failing to resolve the contradictions in his system, is to misunderstand Hegel's aim. Hegel analyses '*what is*' to stress how the search for freedom is an ongoing process through the moments of universal and particular. This is why he can say that the state, the supposed end point of his theory, is actually 'subordinate' to 'world spirit'.[7] So the will can develop beyond the edifice of the state to freedom. Either Hegel was a poor philosopher for leaving so many contradictions within his system or he was trying to suggest something else with the contradictions he highlights. My contention is that Hegel is speculatively analysing the various forms in which the Will satisfies its needs through its constant search for freedom.

For Marx, the circuit of needs is a circuit of antagonism. Workers satisfy their 'natural needs' in capitalism through the mediation of labour. Workers pump out a surplus, which the capitalist appropriates, and the workers then posit their needs as 'necessary' through the mediation of the wage. Marx emphasises the tendency for the circuit to produce severe inequalities through this pumping out of the surplus. Some people are reduced to satisfying their needs at a very rudimentary level. Others can actually satisfy their needs through the form of 'luxury needs', which may at times be the preserve of the capitalist class. 'True social need' encapsulates the inability of the market to satisfy people's needs because the market only recognises the 'social need' of effective demand. For Marx, the contradiction between the needs of workers and the needs of capital is fought out on this terrain of need and labour. The overcoming of the realm of natural necessity allows Marx to focus on higher needs in the alienated system of production that is capital.

In contrast to my emphasis on the very similar understanding Hegel and Marx have of needs, Christopher Berry suggests that an important difference does remain.[8] Berry argues that for Marx, the multiplication of needs results in further dehumanisation for people in capitalism. For

Hegel, in contrast, such multiplication is a reflection of the 'increasing liberation of mankind from the "strict natural necessity of need"'.[9] Yet as my analysis has shown, this is a clear misunderstanding of Marx in this respect. Marx is a dialectician who understands that need-satisfaction in capitalism has both negative and positive consequences. The dehumanisation Berry refers to is the negative consequence. The positive, however, which Berry ignores, is the self-valorising activity of individuals and the growth in technology. Both of these factors allow a diminishing of the realm of necessity, and an expansion in human freedom. Berry's reading of Marx on this matter is very one-sided, therefore, and posits a false contrast between Marx and Hegel. Marx looks to these positive moments that are present already within capitalism as moments of transcendence – the Hegelian positive within the negative.[10]

FREEDOM FROM NECESSITY

Hegel imaginatively displays the antipathy he feels towards the realm of necessity in his use of the Greek Promethean myth. For defying the authority of the god Zeus, Prometheus was chained to a rock and set upon by a vulture, which proceeded to eat his liver. Each day the liver grew again, the vulture returned, and Prometheus was plunged into a perpetual process of pain and suffering. For Hegel the implications of this myth were clear:

> What Prometheus taught men had reference only to such acquirements as conduce to the satisfaction of natural needs (*natürlicher Bedürfnisse*). In the mere satisfaction of these needs (*Bedürfnisse*) there is never any sense of satiety; on the contrary, the need is always growing and care is ever new.[11]

Just like Prometheus, we have to confront a 'pain which never ceases'.[12] Every day we face the prospect of having to satisfy our 'natural needs' in order for life to continue.

For Hegel, this stark image of man tied to the rock of natural necessity raises a particular problem. To stay at the level 'in which natural needs as such are immediately satisfied would merely be one in which spirituality was immersed in nature, and hence a condition of savagery and unfreedom'.[13] Freedom itself, therefore, consists in 'its distinction from the natural'.[14] Humans can only be free where they do not satisfy their 'natural needs' immediately. A man tied to the immediate satisfaction of his 'natural' needs is as unfree as Prometheus chained to his rock. For Hegel, Prometheus did give humans fire and skills and the capacity to master things in nature, but he offered nothing spiritually.[15] To be free, therefore, Prometheus and humankind itself must overcome this realm of necessity.

My contention on this matter has been that Hegel sees the onset of machinery and automation as a solution to this problem. Hegel, as an observer of the early development of capitalism, clearly captures the negative aspects of the introduction of machinery. Stultifying and deadening labour follows for those still within the labour process, whilst poverty and further degradation awaits those expelled. Speculatively, however, Hegel is also aware of the positive in the negative, which manifests itself even in this alien form. Tremendous increases in productivity also allow humans the possibility drastically to reduce the time they spend within the realm of natural necessity. Humans can then satisfy their more 'spiritual needs' free from their Promethean burden. Spirit, therefore, does exist as a moment within the realm of necessity. Hegel points to labour as a moment of liberation even with this unfree realm. Dialectically, therefore, the realm of the free is present in the realm of the unfree. The Will's development is a constant attempt to overcome nature and affirm spirit.

Marx clearly replicates Hegel's emphasis on the liberating aspect of technological developments in his own writings.[16] Marx also realises how the introduction of machinery means that the worker 'steps to the side of the production process', and eventually allows the 'general reduction of the necessary labour of society to a minimum'.[17] Marx, like Hegel, links this possibility with the human need to escape the realm of natural necessity and enter the true realm of freedom, where 'labour determined by necessity and external expediency ends'.[18] In this realm, the saving of labour time now becomes 'equal to an increase in free time – time for the full development of the individual'.[19] Only with the defeat of natural necessity can an individual be a 'real' individual and, as such, be free.[20]

Both Hegel and Marx were fully aware, therefore, that the achievement of freedom increases dramatically with the onset of advanced technological developments. Such technological innovations can offer humans the chance of surpassing the Promethean level of natural necessity.[21] The escape from the realm of natural necessity, and humans' capacity to satisfy their 'spiritual needs', now becomes a real possibility.

Hegel's and Marx's argument, that humans can only have freedom when they are not involved in the immediate satisfaction of their 'natural needs', has important political implications for the organisation of society today. If the realm of necessity is seen as the realm of unfreedom, then attention has to focus on how best we can use productive developments to limit such a realm. The satisfaction of our 'spiritual needs' thus becomes dependent on how best we can reduce the time we have to put into satisfying our 'natural needs'. The emphasis then centres on the diminution and eventual abolition of necessary labour through the introduction of machinery. Looking into their own society, Hegel and Marx clearly perceived this possibility. As we approach the end of the twentieth century, fully automated production processes are clearly evident, and in some sectors of the economy actually present. However, technological developments contain the same contradictions today as they did in Hegel's and Marx's time. Increases in productivity have been used not to free people, but to imprison them. Workers are tied to the machine or have to 'step aside', not to allow the development and satisfaction of their 'spiritual needs', but to face the painful prospect of unemployment and poverty. Only with a more rational use of technology will it be possible for Prometheus to lose his chains of natural necessity and enter the realm of freedom. Only then will he be free from need and thereby satisfy his need to be free.

The importance attached to overcoming the realm of natural necessity also highlights Hegel's and Marx's emphasis on human 'spiritual needs'. The spiritual exists even in the realm of necessity and unfreedom. However, Hegel uses the human/nonhuman animal distinction to emphasise how the spiritual must eventually overcome the level of natural necessity. At this level, humans are no different from nonhuman animals. Humans become different through deferred gratification and labouring to satisfy 'natural needs'. For Hegel, 'spiritual needs' arise out of humans' objectification of themselves in the world. They make their emotions and feelings manifest through their creative activity. They externally realise themselves and do so in many different forms; from throwing a stone in a river, to producing an artistic masterpiece. Analysing forms allows us to grasp how Hegel can see the inner connection between the seemingly irreconcilable moments of the human need for self-realisation. Few people would associate a work of art with the innocuous and unimportant activity of tossing a stone into a river. For Hegel, however, both are expressions of the human need to externalise themselves and make a mark on the world. So even in the realm of unfreedom, moments of the spiritual exist. Labour, as a form of self-realisation in the realm of necessity, is a moment of liberation because it contains a spiritual aspect within itself. This self-realisation feeds into the need for recognition. Others recognise your contribution to their need through your labour, and you reciprocate this by recognising their contribution to your needs. All these moments of 'spiritual need' – externalisation, creative labour, recognition – are present as moments within the realm of necessity. Their proper satisfaction takes place beyond that realm.

For Marx, there is a similar emphasis on the importance of human spiritual needs and their contradictory presence in the realm of necessity and the system of capitalist production. Marx also uses the human/nonhuman animal distinction to demarcate 'human needs' from nonhuman animal needs, which he sees as being unfree and tied to necessity. Just as Hegel argues for the presence of universal needs in the form of particular or subjective needs, Marx also sees 'human needs' as existing in the mode of 'egoistic needs'. In the individual's most subjective considerations there exist higher moments which link her or him with other people and allow her or him to reach the true realm of freedom. Humans make their spiritual aspect manifest through these 'human needs', which take the form of self-realisation. Marx, just like Hegel, sees this need for self-realisation as the external manifestation of the human essence. This self-realisation also leads to the important moment of recognition between people as the individual realises how her or his own existence is inseparable from that of others. The individual's 'egoistic needs', therefore, take the form of 'human needs'. Labour is a further form of self-realisation and a vital human need. It allows humans to express their creativity and objectify their individuality as truly human beings. Again, for Marx, just as for Hegel, these moments of spirit exist in an alienated form within capitalism and the realm of necessity. Moments of the true realm of freedom and spirit are present even in the degrading world of capital. Overcoming the tyranny of necessity, and the contradictions inherent in that system, will allow humans to satisfy their 'spiritual needs' properly.

MODERN NEED THEORY

One of the main issues that arose from the discussion of modern need theory in Chapter 1 was the conflict between universal and particular notions of need. Some modern need theorists have a tendency to privilege universal conceptions of need against particular conceptions and *vice versa*. The search for objective, universal needs often results in the neglect of the particular needs of minority cultures. Similarly, the attempt to secure the particular needs of a minority culture often ignores the diversity of needs within such a culture and the similarity of needs beyond. Attention to form in Hegel's and Marx's understanding of need suggests how we might overcome this dichotomy.

Hegel and Marx both understand universal and particular needs in their movement and transition from one to the other, not as distinct and separate. Such a dialectical understanding of need provides the possibility of grasping both the needs of a particular culture and the potential mediation of those needs with other cultures. We can then comprehend needs, therefore, in their difference and their unity within and between cultural groups. Consequently, an Hegelian and Marxist understanding of need can make an enlightened contribution to contemporary debates about needs and their satisfaction in a culturally diverse world.

Some modern need theorists are keen to distinguish between needs and wants. They do so by identifying needs as objective and wants as subjective. Needs are then understandable in relation to some universal standard, whereas wants are psychological and depend on the beliefs of particular individuals. Such theorists emphasise how wants statements are referentially opaque and intentional, whilst needs statements are referentially transparent and extentional. Applying such an analysis to Hegel's and Marx's understanding of need produces some interesting observations.

Modern need theorists would see Hegel's and Marx's concept of 'natural needs', such as food, drink, etc., as needs because they are objective – all humans have to satisfy such needs to continue existing. They would interpret the 'contingent needs' or 'egoistic needs' as wants because they are subjective, particular and differ from person to person. When needs take the form of 'opinions', modern need theory would suggest that they are also wants and not needs. This is because 'opinions' become subordinate to the dictates of subjective 'fancy'. Similarly, they would not treat Marx's concept of 'luxury need' as a need, because it relates more to the wishes and desires associated with a want, rather than to the objectivity and urgency of a need.

As the detailed examination of need in Hegel's and Marx's writings would suggest, however, they would reject the attempt to hold needs and wants so rigidly distinct. If Hegel were to hold needs and wants apart, he would be committing the errors of the understanding. Similarly, Marx would be operating within a bourgeois mode of theorising which sees concepts as static and separate instead of being internally related. Rather, a focus on the movement between need concepts is what is essential to understand properly the forms needs take in society. So modern need theorists would miss the movement from 'universal need' to the particular 'opinion' or want. They would not see that wants are the mode of existence of 'universal needs'. Wants or 'opinions' are a form 'universal needs' can take in society. This, for Hegel, is the dialectical development of 'universal needs'. Similarly, treating 'luxury needs' in Marx's schema as something superficial neglects how the working class can posit such needs as 'necessary', or how 'necessary needs' can take the form of 'luxury needs' in certain circumstances. By understanding needs in this way, Hegel and Marx are giving due attention to the subjective needs of individuals whilst also recognising the objective 'universal needs' they have to satisfy. Need theorists who desire to keep needs distinct from wants are therefore guilty of interpreting the wants of individuals as something superficial.[22]

The development of a distinction between 'thick' and 'thin' conceptions of need is therefore a useful addition to modern debates. The advantage of this distinction is that an attempt is being made to recognise the importance of subjective need by actually rejecting the use of the term 'want'. A 'thin' theory of need aims at universalising need without reference to cultural content and subjectivity. A 'thick' theory, on the other hand, focuses on needs as particular cultures or particular individuals experience them. It is the 'thin' theory that is attempting to see needs as objective, while the 'thick' is stressing the importance of subjectivity. As we have just seen, certain need theorists particularly attack the suggestion that a need can be subjective. They have argued that once subjectivity arises, wants rather than needs are at issue. The way the 'thick' and 'thin' debate is conducted, however, means that the subjective aspect is treated not as a want but as a need. On the terms of this debate, a need can be either objective ('thin') or subjective ('thick'). Those adhering to the latter inevitably stress the culturally relative or subjective nature of needs, and reject the imposition of universal, objective needs on ordinary people. A major advantage, therefore, of the 'thick' theory of need is that it focuses on what people think are their needs instead of dictating to them what it has been decided they need.

Applying this distinction to Hegel's and Marx's own analysis suggests that 'universal needs' are a 'thin' conception of need. They are objective and true for all human beings in all cultures. A 'thick' conception of need is captured in 'contingent needs' and needs as 'opinions' for Hegel, and the 'egoistic' and 'luxury' needs for Marx. These needs are subjective, and differ from individual to individual and from society to society. However, to keep 'thick' and 'thin' distinct, just as to keep need and want distinct, would again be committing the errors of the understanding and bourgeois thought. Hegel's and Marx's analysis suggests that it is the movement in and between these concepts that should be the primary focus of investigation. We have to understand the 'thin', 'universal need' through its movement to 'thick' or subjective satisfaction. The 'universal need' for food, for instance, takes the form of a particular need – the need for meat. This need multiplies through taste and refinement, so we get the particular need for certain types of meat cooked in many different ways. Universal thereby becomes, and exists as, particular. It follows, however, that the particular can also become universal. The universal need for meat certainly manifests itself in different forms, but these particular forms can become universal too.

Hegel's and Marx's emphasis on understanding the mediation between universal and particular needs suggests a degree of flexibility in trying to reconcile the conflicts that can often arise between the two. The obvious concern of need theorists is to establish objective theories of needs in order to secure a level of human flourishing for all human beings across all societies. The problem is in making this universal sensitive to particular need-satisfaction within different cultures. I would argue that Hegel's and Marx's discussion of universal and particular needs offers such a sensitivity. Their analysis makes us realise the contingency of 'universal needs' within and across cultures. What is universal or particular today may not be so tomorrow. As societies develop and tastes change, new universals are created along with new particulars. Our object of investigation when examining need-satisfaction in and between cultures, therefore, should be the dialectical mediation between universal and particular needs. It is Hegel's and Marx's understanding of needs based on analysing forms that we can put to such fruitful use in this endeavour.

NOTES

1. That Marx had Hegel in mind when discussing 'natural needs' in *The German Ideology* can be gleaned by his reference to Hegel in a marginal note as follows: '*Hegel*. Geological, hydrographical, etc., conditions. Human bodies. Needs, labour'. K. Marx, and F. Engels, *Collected Works*, Volume 5 (Lawrence and Wishart, London, 1976), p. 42.
2. G. W. F. Hegel, *System of Ethical Life and First Philosophy of Spirit*, (trans.) H. S. Harris and T. M. Knox (State University of New York Press, Albany NY, 1979), p. 102; G. W. F. Hegel, *Elements of the Philosophy of Right*, (trans.) H. B. Nisbet (Cambridge University Press, Cambridge, 1991), paras 11 and 11R. Hereafter cited as PR.
3. Hegel, *System of Ethical Life*, p. 104.
4. Hegel, PR, paras 17 and 17A.
5. K. Marx, 'Economic and Philosophical Manuscripts', in K. Marx, *Early Writings*, (trans.) R. Livingstone and G. Benton (Penguin, Harmondsworth, 1992), p. 390.
6. Hegel, PR, 63A.
7. Hegel, PR, para 33A.
8. C. J. Berry, 'Need and Egoism in Marx's Early Writings', *History of Political Thought*, VIII, 3, Winter, 1987.
9. Berry, 'Need and Egoism', p. 472.
10. As Springborg rightly suggests: 'It is not difficult to see Marx's socialist revolution as a culmination of the Hegelian principle of social transformation as the test of rational necessity.' P. Springborg, *The Problem of Human Needs and the Critique of Civilisation* (Allen and Unwin, London, 1981), p. 108.
11. G. W. F. Hegel, *The Philosophy of Religion*, Volume 2, (trans.) E. B. Speirs (Kegan Paul, London; Trench, Trubner, 1895), p. 237; G. W. F. Hegel, *Werke*, Volume XVII (Suhrkamp Verlag, Frankfurt, 1970), pp. 107–8.
12. Hegel, *Philosophy of Religion*, Vol. 2, p. 237.
13. Hegel, PR, para 194R.
14. Hegel, PR, para 194R.

15. G. W. F. Hegel, *Aesthetics. Lectures on Fine Art*, Volume I, (trans.) T. M. Knox (Clarendon Press, Oxford, 1974), p. 462.

16. Cf. A. Schmidt, *The Concept of Nature in Marx* (New Left Books, London, 1971); D. MacGregor, *The Communist Ideal in Hegel and Marx* (George Allen and Unwin, London and Sydney, 1984), pp. 217–18, 245.

17. K. Marx, *Grundrisse*, (trans.) M. Nicolaus (Pelican, Harmondsworth, 1973), pp. 705–6.

18. K. Marx, *Capital*, Volume 3, (trans.) D. Fernbach (Penguin, Harmondsworth, 1991), p. 959.

19. Marx, *Grundrisse*, p. 711.

20. For a discussion of the notion of the individual in Marx's thought see I. Forbes, *Marx and the New Individual* (Unwin Hyman, London, 1990).

21. I hasten to add here that I am not depicting Hegel as a technological determinist in the way Cohen attempts to do for Marx. G. A. Cohen, *Karl Marx's Theory of History: A Defence* (Clarendon Press, Oxford, 1991). My emphasis on the agency of the Will suggests that it is its interaction with other Wills that causes change in society. Technological developments are the product of such interaction. In this sense, it is not the 'productive forces' that are primal but humans in their social relations with each other. Neither Hegel nor Marx, therefore, subscribes to technological determinism.

22. The value of this dialectical understanding of needs is ignored by writers such as Wiggins. He states that 'neither Marx nor Hegel says what a need is, or indicates what it really turns on in a given case whether this or that is needed by someone'. D. Wiggins, *Needs, Values, Truth* (Blackwell, Oxford and Cambridge MA, 2nd edition, 1991), p. 3. Yet Hegel and Marx do capture whether something is 'needed by someone' through the universal concept and general abstraction of 'natural need'. However, they understand this concept not statically but dialectically, in that 'natural needs' can take many forms of satisfaction within and between different societies and cultures. It is the analysis of these universal and particular forms that can allow needs to be discerned out of the self-activity of human beings.

9

POLITICAL IMPLICATIONS OF
THE NEED-FORM

After the aborted workers' and students' revolt in Paris, 1968, one eminent Marxist decided that a return to Hegel was necessary but posed the rhetorical question: 'Why Hegel? Why now?'[1] The answer was that delving into Hegel would shed light on the new beginnings of concrete struggles for the 1970s. Consequently, at times of crisis and transition Marxists turn to Hegel. Lenin, for example, the arch-activist who always maintained that it was far more enjoyable participating in a revolution than writing about it, responded to the outbreak of World War I and the crisis in the *established* Marxism' of German social democracy by devoting three months to the study of Hegel's *Logic*.[2] Irrespective of the flaws in Lenin's reading of Hegel, we should not forget how struck he was by the materialist basis of Hegel's supposed idealism. This led Lenin to remark famously that 'intelligent idealism is nearer to intelligent materialism than is stupid materialism'.[3] The relevance of Hegel for grasping the material problems of society could not therefore be doubted.

As the twentieth century draws to a close, then, we too must ask: 'Why Hegel *and* Marx? Why now?' The answer, more so than ever as the attempt to close off Marxism is at its height, is that, as this book has tried to show, Hegelian-Marxism is crucial for grasping the contradictions and moments of transcendence in and against systems of domination. Hegelian-Marxism roots its analysis in the material struggles of human beings, who constitute and satisfy their needs through a process of struggle. Focusing on the forms that the antagonistic basis to need-satisfaction takes reveals the rupturing potential of subjects against a monstrous system of need that they themselves have created and can defeat. The movement to a better society, where needs are properly satisfied away from immediacy and strife, is at the heart of Hegelian-Marxism's emphasis on the importance of freedom.

Against this view are paradigms that accept the parameters and assumptions of the capitalist system and which inevitably dominate contemporary political discourse. These paradigms are liberalism, communitarianism and social democracy. The weaknesses of these approaches are revealed here by considering the relationship between rights and needs and the role of the state. Whilst liberalism is shown to over-emphasise rights against needs, communitarians and social democrats are guilty of ignoring the insidious nature of the modern state in trying to achieve their supposed end of communal values and optimal need-satisfaction respectively. I begin this concluding chapter, however, by considering the failed paradigm of the twentieth century that has generally been seen as resulting in a tyranny over needs and leading to the false perception that Marxism is indeed dead. That paradigm is, of course, Soviet communism.

SOVIET COMMUNISM

Soviet communism offers some empirical evidence of the problems associated with satisfying needs from a Marxist perspective. Indeed, for Francis Fukuyama an important reason for the demise of Soviet-style communism and the supposed success of capitalist democracy was the failure of the former to satisfy properly its people's needs.[4] Although rejecting such a glorified view of capitalism, there is little doubt, as Callinicos rightly asserts, that it is essential for any Marxist analysis to 'grapple with the embarrassment of association with the shipwreck of "existing socialism"'.[5]

The form of centralised economic planning adopted in the Soviet Union is now generally regarded as an unviable mechanism for satisfying people's needs. The inefficiency, poor quality of products and general shortages of both consumer and producer goods were indicative of the problems that plagued the system.[6] Moreover, the overemphasis on developing productive forces, whilst neglecting production relations, was instrumental in justifying the Five-Year Plans along with 'all the human misery that this entailed'.[7]

There are two main responses when trying to come to terms with the Soviet experiment. The first is to deny that there was anything distinc-tively socialist about the system at all and regard it as merely 'an extreme and highly autarkic version . . . of militarised state capitalism'.[8] The second, more realistic view suggests that the socialist epithet cannot be dismissed so easily. Socialism may have been 'distorted and deformed' but it was not 'purely rhetorical'.[9] Indeed, fundamental socialist values were encapsulated in a number of measures, such as the rejection of private ownership of the means of production; a commitment to an egalitarian distribution of income; the planned development of the forces of production; the provision of welfare services on the basis of social need;

job security; guaranteed employment; and the forms if not the substance of working-class power.[10] These values were 'deeply embedded' in the working class of the Soviet Union and were important in producing moments of resistance in, against and beyond that system. The very degeneration of the Russian revolution stems, therefore, from the mistaken project of trying to impose socialism from above through the alienated form of the state and not from the self-organisation of the working class itself.[11] Consequently, the degeneration of socialism in the Soviet Union emitted circuits of domination and control that attempted to stifle the self-determination of the working class. The elite tried to satisfy people's needs through an overbearing planning system, which resulted in the tyranny of the universal over the particular.

Ferenc Fehér, Agnes Heller and György Márkus captured the intensity of such domination in a trenchant critique of how 'actually existing socialism' erred so fundamentally in trying to satisfy people's needs. For them, the Soviet Union and east European states imposed what they call a 'dictatorship over needs'.[12] The only relatively succinct definition of this term appears towards the end of the book, where they refer to it as the 'idea that the subjection of the "rebellious" and "individualistic" private person to a "superior wisdom" has to be started at the level of his needs system'.[13] Such a conception of 'dictatorship over needs' seems to imply, therefore, that the Soviet system was about 'total control' over bodies, souls and the ways in which people satisfied their needs.[14] However, their emphasis on 'dictatorship' raises a distinct problem.[15] They suggest that the 'dictatorship over needs' was actually 'a dynamic and modernising society'; however, if this is the case then how is such a dictatorial stranglehold over needs ensured?[16] This can only be either by the rupturing of the relationship between the satisfaction of existing needs and the emergence of new needs; or by the fact that needs are formed but prevented from being gratified. The authors are not specific on either of these points, and the reason seems to be that they overemphasise the dictatorial nature of Soviet-type societies in relation to needs. This is not to deny the tyrannical nature of such regimes, but an Hegelian-Marxist understanding of needs would emphasise the contradictions of such a tyranny. Focusing on the self-constitution of people's needs even within alienated structures indicates the possibility of transcendence against a seemingly all-powerful and controlling system.

An Hegelian-Marxist approach, therefore, focuses on the particular or determinate form that the general abstraction or universal concept of 'natural need' – needs that humans have to satisfy in order to subsist – assumed in Soviet society. As in capitalism, the mediation of the satisfaction of 'natural needs' was through the compulsion of having to work and the expenditure of labour-power.[17] However, unlike in capitalism, workers in the Soviet system did not fully surrender control over the expenditure of labour-power, giving them a considerable degree of power over the production process.[18] Such control indicates that the Russian working class were not simply passive victims of a dictatorship over their needs, as Fehér *et al.* suggest. Instead, the workers self-constituted their needs antagonistically in and against the Soviet system. These needs were 'radical' because they offered moments of rupture within a system of domination. I will now illustrate how these 'radical needs' became manifest under the regimes of Stalin, Khrushchev and Brezhnev – regimes that were quite open to analysis by Fehér, Heller and Márkus when writing the *Dictatorship Over Needs*.

To interpret Stalinism as having a complete stranglehold over the needs of the Russian working class, as Fehér, Heller and Márkus contend, is simply too one-sided and ignores how the insubordination of labour was rife during the implementation of the first two Five-Year Plans (1928–37) in the Soviet Union.[19] Such insubordination up to the middle of the second Five-Year Plan had involved the 'major weapon' of strikes and mass protests.[20] The most common form of resistance, however, was the go-slow, because more overt forms of insubordination were far too dangerous for those involved. This was especially the case given the lack of trade unions or political organisations that could have allowed workers to organise more widely and collectively to gain greater strength and support.[21] Even so, workers still acted 'consciously and collectively' on many occasions and conducted negotiations with managers ' "in a crowd"' to avoid any victimisation of particular individuals.[22] Ironically, the most vociferous in their protests were Communist Party activists themselves.[23]

The Soviet regime had to defeat this collective power of a seemingly powerless Russian working class, but it did not stop the problem of insubordination. Instead, the inability of workers to continue with collective action meant that individual disruption was the only option.[24] Attempts by the emerging elite to break collective resistance simply resulted in further contradictions that caused moments of rupture. These contradictions were in the planning system itself and its stated purpose of trying to improve the satisfaction of people's needs.[25] Proper democratic planning assumes a 'community of needs' between all members of society.[26] Agreeing on the general goals for producing to satisfy needs but leaving their achievement to local jurisdiction is the correct way to proceed. In the Soviet Union, however, the regime could not allow any such local control and initiative to occur. Instead, planners tried to force workers to implement their instructions. However, attempts to stop collective insubordination by breaking up collective methods of work and payment simply resulted in individual workers working at their own speed. The outcome was unpredictability in the quantity and quality of their outputs.[27] Any rational calculation for production was therefore impossible with such uncertainty. Consequently, the need to meet unrealistic production targets and the existence of a labour shortage forced managers to make concessions to workers. '[H]olding down production norms, illegally padding workers' earnings or tolerating poor use of work time' were the usual responses.[28] Moreover, such practices continued even under more authoritarian countermeasures up to 1940.

Such insubordination at the supposed height of Stalinist tyranny clearly indicates moments of 'radical needs' that offered the possibility of rupture and transcendence in and against the Soviet system. The failure of Stalinist policies of naked coercion led the regime to find new ways to assert control over workers and ensure the production of surplus product. Khrushchev, for example, proposed a policy of supposed democratisation of the workplace.[29] One aspect of this policy was to give greater rights to workers in terms of reducing unfair dismissals, improving working conditions, and allowing unions to have a veto over norm rises within a factory.[30] The end result, not surprisingly, was actually to make labour discipline even more difficult to enforce, precisely because of the legalisation of workers' rights.[31] The only possible response of the elite to the failure to increase surplus extraction during the 1950s and 1960s would have been to use mass unemployment to discipline labour. Such a policy was untenable, however, because it could have 'provoked possibly uncontrollable protest and disorder' – a likely event given that uprisings had already occurred against the threat of less severe measures such as an increase in food prices.[32]

During the Brezhnev era the same contradictions and antagonisms generated by the manifestation of 'radical needs' were still very evident. In this, as in previous periods, 'all problems go back to labour'.[33] The Brezhnev reign again saw managers having to concede to workers over factors such as limiting the introduction of new technology, egalitarianism in pay and overstaffing. 'Social peace' typified the Brezhnev years due to the reluctance of the elite to attack the power of the Russian working class. Those economic reforms that were introduced were so 'half-hearted' that they had no chance of success.[34] The Shchekino experiment introduced in 1968, for instance, which attempted to increase output in an enterprise whilst reducing the number of producers, was 'unevenly adopted' throughout the economy.[35] Moreover, the policy of reducing the number of workers in an enterprise was not enacted. Supposedly redundant workers were actually 'absorbed within the enterprise' rather than forced to find work outside.[36]

The crisis of the Soviet system, then, was a consequence of the insubordination of labour and the manifestation of 'radical needs'. Hence, 'the history of the USSR is a history of . . . [the] attempt[] to dominate labour'.[37] Stalin tried to do this by direct force, Khruschev by organisation and Brezhnev through peace, but none succeeded in his objectives.[38] Evidence of the increasing power of the Russian working class is therefore irrefutable. First, as we have seen, workers exhibited a 'high degree of control' over their own work processes, because factory managers and workers colluded in order to ensure 'an orderly result' in terms of goods produced.[39] Consequently, the actual rate of work itself became determined by the worker, who established norms over labour-time. Such control allowed workers to challenge the system collectively by demanding better working conditions and increases in consumer goods.[40] Such power was also manifest through the wage-form, with wages in industry, for instance, experiencing an annual growth rate of 2.41 per cent from 1960 to 1986.[41]

From an Hegelian-Marxist perspective these workers were self-constituting moments of their 'radical needs' in and against the domination of the bureaucratic Soviet system. Fehér, Heller and Márkus ignore these forms of resistance and constitution of needs. They fail to focus on the dialectical or contradictory basis of need-satisfaction even in a seemingly all-dominating system such as the Soviet Union. Indeed, in an essay published only four years before the revolutions in 1989, Fehér and Heller concluded that there was little possibility of a challenge against the Soviet system materialising.[42] They excluded the potential for resistance by overemphasising the 'dictatorship over needs' and underestimating the contradictions of need-satisfaction in and against such a dictatorship. For example, as Callinicos correctly contends, Fehér and Heller completely missed the constitution of ecological needs that had an important role in mobilising movements for these revolutions in the USSR and eastern Europe.[43] Moreover, they failed to see that a number of other groups riddled the system with moments of resistance in their attempt to constitute their own needs. Such groups ranged across non-conformist intellectuals, non-Russian nationalities, youth movements and feminists, to name but a few.[44]

Such a failure to capture moments of 'radical needs' on Heller's part is particularly noticeable. As we saw in Chapter 7, Heller argued that the satisfaction of 'radical needs' was only possible in the society of 'associated producers' and not in capitalism. She argued that workers' struggles over wages, for instance, were not 'radical', because they failed to go beyond the capital/wage relation. I argued then that this was to miss important moments of rupture and possible transcendence even within the contradictions of the alienated system of capital. In terms of the Soviet Union, therefore, Heller did not recognise the importance of such struggles and their effect of causing an endemic crisis in the Soviet system. Even stranger is that in her *Theory of Need in Marx*, she allows for the possibility of a communist society occurring after capitalism. When collaborating with Fehér and Márkus in *Dictatorship Over Needs*, however, no such possibility is forthcoming for the Russian working class. Apparently, the Russian workers were doomed to a fate against which they could do little. Yet, as we have seen, focusing on the form 'natural needs' take in the Soviet Union reveals immense antagonisms in the satisfaction of needs. These antagonisms have resulted in moments of rupture and transcendence in and against the Soviet system. Attention to form from an Hegelian-Marxist perspective is the way to expose such moments of need-satisfaction.

LIBERALS AND COMMUNITARIANS

This section considers the relationship between needs and rights. Within contemporary political theory, liberals such as John Rawls have emphasised the fundamental importance of rights over any other value in providing a framework in which needs are likely to be met in a just way. Against this emphasis on rights has appeared the communitarian critique, which is more concerned to emphasise the importance of need. What I want to do in this section is to outline and examine the liberal emphasis on right, the critique of this by communitarians, and the attempted fusion of rights and needs by socialist writers such as Doyal and Gough.

Rawls bases the idea of individual rights on his conception of 'primary goods, that is, things that every rational man is presumed to want' to pursue his life plans.[45] There are two types of 'primary goods' that Rawls assumes individuals will need: social primary goods and natural primary goods. Natural primary goods refer to health, intelligence, vigour, imagination, and natural talents that are affected by social institutions but are not directly distributed by them. Social primary goods are defined as income and wealth, opportunities, powers, rights and liberties which are distributed by social institutions.[46]

As is now well known, Rawls's theory of justice posits individuals in an 'original position' which is the 'initial status quo which insures that the fundamental agreements reached in it are fair'.[47] A 'veil of ignorance' ensures that these individuals do not know what their position will be in society in terms of class, social status or natural abilities. A lack of such knowledge means that they will therefore devise principles of justice to ensure all people have the best possible access to those primary goods distributed by the social institutions.[48] Although they could choose many different principles of justice, Rawls argues that they will in fact adopt two if they are acting rationally.

The first principle of justice is the liberty principle, which states that all individuals should have an equal right to basic liberty. The second is the difference principle, which states that inequalities are allowed if they benefit the worst-off in society and if all positions in society are open to everyone through a policy of equality of opportunity. The principles of justice offer guidelines on what courses of action are just in particular situations. Inequalities are only allowed if they benefit the least well-off in society. So for Rawls, any individual in an 'original position' under the 'veil of ignorance' would develop these two principles of justice.[49] Rawls arranges these principles in lexical order, with the principle of liberty taking precedence over all other social goods. So equal liberty is of a higher priority than equality of opportunity, for example. The right to liberty takes priority because Rawls thinks that all individuals desire the protection of their basic liberties to function as individuals. As a defender of liberalism, Rawls interprets such liberty politically in terms of the right to vote; eligibility for public office; free speech and assembly; freedom of conscience and thought; the right to personal property; and freedom from arbitrary arrest under the rule of law.[50]

As regards the difference principle, two points need to be noticed to see why Rawls thinks this would be adopted by individuals in the 'original position'. He assumes first that the individuals are rational and second that they are risk averse; that is, if the choice is to play safe or take a risk then they will choose to play safe. Rawls argues that if individuals are risk averse and rational then they will have to choose the difference principle as a principle of justice. This is because the individuals do not know what social position they will be in when the 'veil of ignorance' is lifted and they are in society. It makes sense, therefore, to devise a principle of justice which benefits the worst-off in society as anyone could be one of them. So Rawls argues that the rational thing to do is to adopt what he calls a maximin strategy. This means that individuals maximise what they would receive in the minimum, worst position in society. Risk aversity, therefore, makes individuals pick that distribution which benefits the worst-off. So individuals in the 'original position' will opt for the difference principle.[51] For Rawls, then, any individual in an 'original position' under the 'veil of ignorance' will opt for these two principles of justice as long as they are rational and risk averse.

Rawls's theory has been particularly attacked by communitarian thinkers. One focus of their critique, which is of concern to this study, is their rejection of Rawls's use of right and its prioritisation over the good. The wholesale rejection of the validity of rights stems from the fact that their existence cannot be demonstrated. Consequently, any belief in such a concept is akin to nothing more than a belief in 'witches and unicorns'.[52]

Rawls's attempt to prioritise right over all other values and as distinct from the good is also rejected. In contrast, the good is actually prior to the right because the good 'gives the point of the rules which define the right'.[53] The formulation of principles of justice is not separable from our moral intuitions about what is or is not good. In fact, we actually have to 'draw on the sense of the good that we have . . . in order to decide what are adequate principles of justice'.[54] Consequently, the good cannot come as an afterthought to the primacy of right but is inextricably bound up with it.

Another aspect of the communitarian critique is on the very notion of 'primary goods' themselves. Walzer, for example, argues that Rawls's conception of primary goods is so 'thin' – i.e. abstracted from cultural content and subjectivity – as to be of little relevance to concrete or particular circumstances of need-satisfaction in different societies.[55] On the basis of the approach to needs developed in this book, Walzer is highlighting how Rawls dichotomises universal ('thin) and particular ('thick') need-satisfaction. The Hegelian-Marxist approach emphasises the importance of mediation between universal and particular and not their separation. In this sense, communitarian thinkers such as Walzer are quite correct to reject Rawls's argument here on the universal applicability of his 'primary goods'.

SOCIAL DEMOCRACY

Although not explicitly responding to the communitarian critique of Rawls directly, Doyal and Gough attempt to revise Rawls's *Theory of Justice*. They do so by linking the importance of individual rights to needs, and hence some notion of the good, whilst also, as we saw in Chapter 1, offering a universal conception of need that is applicable across all societies and cultures.

In their revision of Rawls's argument, Doyal and Gough attempt to combine the best aspects of classical liberal and socialist thought.[56] They argue that the classical liberal aspect relates to the priority of the right of liberty, whereas the social aspect relates to the difference principle's aim of ensuring access to 'primary goods' for the least well-off. Additionally, they suggest that equality of opportunity acts as a guide for measuring whether any surplus created by the difference principle has been distributed properly.[57]

For Doyal and Gough, Rawls minimises the importance of 'primary goods' by opting for a 'thin' theory of the good, in his desire to have competing visions of the good coexisting within his constitutional democracy.[58] However, this leaves individuals in the 'original position' in so much ignorance that they may decide to gamble in their choice of principles to be amongst the better-off in society. For Doyal and Gough, this will in no way ensure that the least well-off in society will therefore flourish as Rawls expects.[59] To rectify this problem, Doyal and Gough argue that Rawls requires their own theory of need. This will ensure that the calculations of those in the original position will result in optimal health and autonomy for all once they emerge from the 'veil of ignorance'. Hence, Doyal and Gough amend the difference principle to allow for inequalities only if they benefit the least well-off by providing them with the goods for optimising need-satisfaction.[60] Not surprisingly, Doyal and Gough therefore reject Rawls's lexical prioritising of the liberty principle. They argue that this can easily lead to a situation where formal freedom coexists with people being in extreme poverty.[61] For this to be avoided, Doyal and Gough propose a reading of Rawls which puts forward not two principles but one principle of justice with three components.[62] The first is the right to basic need-satisfaction in terms of health, autonomy and civil liberties. The second justifies inequalities for the optimum satisfaction of such needs. The third is procedural and defines the legal constraints on producing social inequalities.

For Doyal and Gough, then, the only way 'of ensuring that effective participation in the economic and political process can be guaranteed in principle . . . will be through the optimal satisfaction of basic needs'.[63] They therefore develop the moral right to optimal need-satisfaction into constitutional rights that must be guaranteed by the public authority. In this way classical liberal values of rights become 'compatible with' and 'dependent upon the creation and/or success of certain socialist-inspired institutions of the welfare state'.[64] Consequently, Doyal and Gough argue that the least advantaged in society will have their need-satisfaction prioritised through the emphasis on basic need-satisfaction.[65] Doyal and Gough are therefore trying to link rights with needs to overcome Rawls's dichotomisation of these two concepts. They are grounding the classical liberal notion of right on the basis of their own more socialist need theory. For them, it appears that the right is not prior to the good but inextricably bound up with it, as the communitarian critiques suggested.

HEGELIAN-MARXISM

Using the language of rights is important to Doyal and Gough because
they want to ensure the satisfaction of basic needs for all. This inevitably
entails the acceptance of the use of the institutions of the state to ensure
that all have the right to satisfy these basic needs. The introduction of the
concept of right necessitates a brief discussion of Hegel's and Marx's
understanding of the concept.

For Hegel, rights emerged from the self-activity of human beings in
their interaction with each other and through the satisfaction of their
needs.[66] Indeed, rights came into existence as law on the basis of the
initial satisfaction of needs. By focusing on the dialectical development of
need, Hegel revealed a monstrous, wild beast of a system which various
institutions could not tame. Rights within institutions did not apply to
everyone in society. The excluded poor and an incipient working class
existing antagonistically within the estates were not protected by any
notion of right and remained as a moment of rupture in and against a
dominating system. Hegel's system of need contains deep antagonisms,
therefore, which cannot be mediated through the institutions which are to
assert notions of right.

For Marx, rights are either to be rejected wholesale or, in another
interpretation, valued but not in the form of bourgeois rights.[67] However,
the key issue for Marxists in relation to rights is that rights should be
analysed to reveal the 'real functions and the bourgeois interests that lie
'behind' them.[68] The role of need in Marx's writings, as we have seen,
presents the worker as an antagonistic force in and against the capitalist
system. Consequently, any rights that emerge within the state are the
result of class struggle and the insubordination of labour, which the state
has to try and control. The state itself, therefore, must be grasped as an
antagonistic form of social relations.[69] The state is a capitalist state whose
own existence depends on reproducing and maintaining the capital/labour
relation. By definition this is a process of incessant struggle which
involves the attempts to discipline both capital and labour to ensure
the continued existence of capitalist society. Social democrats and
bourgeois theorists fail to acknowledge or even grasp this antagonistic
basis to the state, which raises problems for their attempt to use the state
for their own objectives. How though should rights be understood within
an Hegelian-Marxist perspective?

The presence of rights within the constitution of the state is an outcome
of class struggle. Principles of right must be comprehended not as a 'set of
independent rational standards by which to assess social relations' but 'as
arising from and controlling those relations'.[70] These rights are a mode of

existence or form of the satisfaction of needs by human beings in and against a dominating system. The antagonistic basis to need-satisfaction by human beings is constitutionalised through the law, which is itself the source of right. Right, therefore, has to be understood dialectically as the legal recognition of the insubordination and power of labour within the state.[71] The state itself, then, is not a neutral entity but an antagonistic form, which has to regulate the social relations of production and ensure the continued existence of capitalism.

Understood in this way, Doyal and Gough's desire for the constitutionalisation of the right to basic need-satisfaction seems problematic. Their approach, although concerned to avoid an overemphasis on the top-down administration of needs, still sees the necessity for a strong state. Moreover, they are particularly critical of the viability of a more bottom-up approach to need-satisfaction.[72] Similarly, communitarian thinkers fail themselves to grasp the problematic nature of the state because they see it as a vehicle for promoting communal values and shared identities. Indeed, that some of their number could see some of the reactionary exhortations of the Reagan administrations on moral and family values as a positive attempt to create a 'common life of larger meanings' shows the dangers in communitarian thinking.[73] Community quickly becomes a byword for the exclusion of those who do not fit into the 'common life' that exists in the heads of a privileged elite. Hence, communitarians ignore how the state itself can become tyrannical in imposing conceptions of the good and needs on those who want to assert a different form of existence. In contrast, an Hegelian-Marxist approach focuses on the antagonistic self-constitution of needs by human beings in society. This cannot be imposed from above through the alienated form of the state, but must be democratically devolved into communities to allow the greatest participation possible once the state power has been destroyed.

The degree to which theorists such as Doyal and Gough ignore the class nature of the modern state is evidenced in their affirmation of Sweden as the 'global leader' for 'most closely approximating optimum need-satisfaction'.[74] In passing, they are careful to suggest that this means not that there are no 'inadequacies' or cases of 'outright suffering' there, but simply that Sweden does 'better on average' than any other country.[75] Additionally, they also recognise that this 'global leader' is 'not necessarily the best conceivable model' for ensuring optimum need-satisfaction because of the problems of 'generalisability and sustainability'.[76] Despite such reservations, however, there is no mention of the problems of the state itself as a regulator of the social relations of production.

The Swedish case is indeed an interesting one. The high point of social democratic success seemed to offer a society where capital and labour mediated by the Swedish state could exist in a corporatist harmony. However, the capital/labour relation is not simply national but must be understood as a 'moment of the global capital relation'.[77] The development of the Swedish state must, therefore, be comprehended against the development of global capitalist social relations. Indeed, one of the reasons for the failure of the Swedish model by 1990 was that the antagonisms could no longer be contained within the structures of the corporatist state. The debate over 'wage earner funds', which attempted to stop excessive profit making and increase workers' participation within enterprises, began to rupture corporatist arrangements from the mid-1970s.[78] The role of the state here was of crucial importance because it had to regulate the social relations of production and ensure capital accumulation. Trying to maintain a corporatist consensus was severely weakened by the response of large employers, particularly exporters, who attempted to subvert collective bargaining by threatening to relocate abroad.[79] Not surprisingly, then, even a state that was 'thoroughly permeated' by social democrats succumbed to adopting policies which threatened its welfare ethic by creating an environment which would attract capital investment and secure capital accumulation.[80]

As a moment of the global capital relation, Sweden, like any other nation state, has to compete to induce and retain within its own territory a 'share of the global surplus value produced'.[81] This implies tremendous constraints on the role of the state in achieving the type of social justice and need-satisfaction that Doyal and Gough think is possible – constraints that are not faced up to in their analysis precisely because of their concern to propose 'an extension of the power of the state' to secure the 'conditions for human liberation'.[82]

The Hegelian–Marxist approach cannot offer clear blueprints for the satisfaction of needs beyond capital. Both Hegel and Marx were loath to build castles in the air. Instead, they concentrate on exposing the contradictions inherent in a system of domination by analysing the forms of need that emerge as people make and shape their world. They highlight moments of transcendence, real moments within existing society, by focusing on the antagonistic satisfaction of needs in, against and ultimately beyond a dominating system on the road to freedom. One of the most potent moments of freedom that Hegel and Marx both recognise is the possibility of machines replacing humans within the realm of natural necessity. The positive use of technological developments to reduce and abolish the realm of natural necessity is far from a forlorn hope. Marx himself was well aware of the positive productive capacities within capitalism, but was horrified by its inability to use such resources for the benefit of all.

Capitalism at the end of the twentieth century remains a system of exploitation which results in poverty for millions of people around the globe. The tyranny of work imposed through the commodity-form sums up the daily grind for those 'lucky' enough to sell their labour-power. Yet amidst these ruins, Hegelian-Marxism focuses on the antagonistic presence of people asserting their 'radical needs' as a rupturing potential in and against such a seemingly dominating system. To avoid any charge of wishful thinking, Hegel and Marx root their analysis in '*what is*' – the material circumstances of ordinary people as they develop and satisfy their needs in the search for freedom. As Hegel himself said: 'when individuals . . . have once got in their heads the abstract concept of full-blown liberty, there is nothing like it in its uncontrollable strength'.[83] The fragile nature of capital's existence, its inherent tendency to lurch from crisis to crisis, and the resistance it meets from those it would like to dominate day after day is indicative of this 'uncontrollable strength'. That both Hegel and Marx exposed how this 'strength' emerges so potently through the self-constitution and satisfaction of needs indicates, therefore, their continued relevance for understanding the contradictions of contemporary capitalism.

NOTES

1. R. Dunayevskaya, *Philosophy and Revolution* (Columbia University Press, New York, 1989), Part One.
2. Dunayevskaya, *Philosophy and Revolution*, p. xxx; V. I. Lenin, *Collected Works*, Volume 38 (Lawrence and Wishart, London, 1963).
3. Lenin, *Collected Works*, Vol. 38, p. 276.
4. F. Fukuyama, *The End of History and the Last Man* (Hamish Hamilton, London, 1992).
5. A. Callinicos, 'Premature Obituaries: A Comment on O'Sullivan, Minogue, and Marquand', in A. Shtromas (ed.) *The End of 'Isms'?*, Special Issue of *Political Studies*, XLI, 1993, pp. 64–5.
6. A. Callinicos, *The Revenge of History: Marxism and the East European Revolutions* (Polity Press, Cambridge, 1991), p. 43.
7. J. Townshend, 'Has Marxist Politics a Future?', *Contemporary Politics*, 1, 2, 1995, p. 84.
8. Callinicos, 'Premature Obituaries', p. 62.
9. S. Clarke, 'Crisis of Socialism or Crisis of the State?', *Capital and Class*, 42, 1990, p. 19.
10. Clarke, 'Crisis of Socialism', p. 20.
11. Clarke, 'Crisis of Socialism', p. 29.
12. F. Fehér, A. Heller and G. Márkus, *Dictatorship Over Needs* (Blackwell, Oxford, 1983).
13. Fehér *et al.*, *Dictatorship Over Needs*, pp. 227–8. As I. Szelenyi, 'Review-Symposium on Soviet-Type Societies', *Telos*, 60, Summer, 1984, p. 167, indicates, one has to scour the whole book to decipher what the term means.

14. Z. Bauman, 'Review-Symposium on Soviet-Type Societies', p. 173.

15. G. Poggi, 'Review Symposium: Dictatorship over Needs', *Thesis Eleven*, 12, 1985, p. 167.

16. Fehér *et al.*, *Dictatorship Over Needs*, p. 243; Poggi, 'Review Symposium: Dictatorship over Needs', p. 167.

17. H. Ticktin, *Origins of the Crisis in the USSR: Essays on the Political Economy of a Disintegrating System* (M. E. Sharpe, New York and London, 1992), p. 83.

18. Ticktin, *Origins of the Crisis in the USSR*, pp. 83, 87.

19. D. Filtzer, *Soviet Workers and Stalinist Industrialisation: The Formation of Modern Soviet Production Relations, 1928–41* (Pluto, London, 1986), pp. 85–6.

20. Filtzer, *Soviet Workers and Stalinist Industrialisation*, p. 85.

21. Filtzer, *Soviet Workers and Stalinist Industrialisation*, p. 86.

22. Filtzer, *Soviet Workers and Stalinist Industrialisation*, p. 86.

23. Filtzer, *Soviet Workers and Stalinist Industrialisation*, p. 87.

24. Filtzer, *Soviet Workers and Stalinist Industrialisation*, p. 116.

25. Filtzer, *Soviet Workers and Stalinist Industrialisation*, p. 117.

26. Filtzer, *Soviet Workers and Stalinist Industrialisation*, p. 118.

27. Filtzer, *Soviet Workers and Stalinist Industrialisation*, p. 118.

28. Filtzer, *Soviet Workers and Stalinist Industrialisation*, p. 119.

29. D. Filtzer, *Soviet Workers and De-Stalinization: The Consolidation of the Modern System of Soviet Production Relations, 1953–1964* (Cambridge University Press, Cambridge, 1992), pp. 231–2.

30. Filtzer, *Soviet Workers and De-Stalinization*, p. 232.

31. Filtzer, *Soviet Workers and De-Stalinization*, p. 233.

32. Filtzer, *Soviet Workers and De-Stalinization*, p. 234.

33. Ticktin, *Origins of the Crisis in the USSR*, p. 116.

34. Ticktin, *Origins of the Crisis in the USSR*, p. 116.

35. D. Lane, *Soviet Labour and the Ethic of Communism: Full Employment and the Labour Process in the USSR* (Wheatsheaf, Brighton, 1987), p. 147.

36. D. A. Dyker, 'Planning and the Worker', in L. Schapiro and J. Godson (eds) *The Soviet Worker: Illusions and Realities* (Macmillan, London, 1982), p. 60.

37. Ticktin, *Origins of the Crisis in the USSR*, p. 119.

38. Ticktin, *Origins of the Crisis in the USSR*, p. 128.

39. Ticktin, *Origins of the Crisis in the USSR*, p. 85.

40. Ticktin, *Origins of the Crisis in the USSR*, p. 87.

41. Ticktin, *Origins of the Crisis in the USSR*, p. 144.

42. F. Fehér and A. Heller, *Eastern Left, Western Left: Totalitarianism, Freedom and Democracy* (Polity Press, Cambridge, 1986), p. 56, cf. Callinicos, *Revenge of History*, p. 42.

43. Callinicos, *Revenge of History*, p. 42.

44. See E. Mandel, *Beyond Perestroika: The Future of Gorbachev's USSR* (Verso, London, 1992), Ch. 2. However, this is not to deny the reactionary basis to some of these needs.

45. J. Rawls, *A Theory of Justice* (Oxford, Oxford University Press, 1990), p. 62.

46. Rawls, *Theory of Justice*, p. 62.

47. Rawls, *Theory of Justice*, p. 17.

48. Rawls, *Theory of Justice*, p. 12.

49. Rawls, *Theory of Justice*, pp. 302–3.

50. Rawls, *Theory of Justice*, p. 61.

51. Rawls, *Theory of Justice*, pp. 152–3.

52. A. MacIntyre, *After Virtue: A Study in Moral Theory* (Duckworth, London, 1981), p. 67.

53. C. Taylor, *Sources of the Self: The Making of the Modern Identity* (Cambridge University Press, Cambridge, 1992), p. 89; cf. S. Mulhall and A. Swift, *Liberals and Communitarians* (Blackwell, Oxford, 2nd edition, 1997), pp. 119–20.

54. Taylor, *Sources of the Self*, p. 89.

55. M. Walzer, *Spheres of Justice* (Basic Books, New York, 1983), p. 8; cf. Mulhall and Swift, *Liberals and Communitarians*, pp. 132–4.

56. L. Doyal and I. Gough, *A Theory of Human Need* (Macmillan, London, 1991), p. 130.

57. Doyal and Gough, *Theory of Human Need*, pp. 130–1.

58. Doyal and Gough, *Theory of Human Need*, p. 131.

59. Doyal and Gough, *Theory of Human Need*, p. 132.

60. Doyal and Gough, *Theory of Human Need*, p. 132.

61. Doyal and Gough, *Theory of Human Need*, pp. 132–3.

62. Doyal and Gough, *Theory of Human Need*, pp. 133–4.

63. Doyal and Gough, *Theory of Human Need*, p. 134.

64. Doyal and Gough, *Theory of Human Need*, p. 134.

65. Doyal and Gough, *Theory of Human Need*, p. 135.

66. See above, p. 73.

67. For a discussion of these issues see R. G. Peffer, *Marxism, Morality and Social Justice* (Princeton University Press, Princeton NJ, 1990), pp. 324–8.

68. S. Lukes, *Moral Conflict and Politics* (Clarendon Press, Oxford, 1991), p. 185.

69. J. Holloway, 'Global Capital and the National State', *Capital and Class*, 52, 1994, pp. 26–9.

70. Lukes, *Moral Conflict and Politics*, pp. 184–5.

71. See M. Hardt and A. Negri, *Labour of Dionysus: A Critique of the State-Form* (University of Minnesota Press, Minneapolis, 1994), particularly Ch. 6.

72. Doyal and Gough, *Theory of Human Need*, p. 308.

73. M. Sandel, 'Democrats and Community', *New Republic*, 22 February 1998, pp. 20–3, quoted in Hardt and Negri, *Labour of Dionysus*, p. 255.

74. Doyal and Gough, *Theory of Human Need*, p. 290.

75. Doyal and Gough, *Theory of Human Need*, p. 291.

76. Doyal and Gough, *Theory of Human Need*, p. 296.

77. Holloway, 'Global Capital and the National State', p. 32.

78. L. Wilde, 'Swedish Social Democracy and the World Market', in R. Polan and B. Gills (eds) *Transcending the State-Global Divide: A Neostructuralist Agenda in International Relations* (Lynne Rienner, Boulder Co and London, 1994), pp. 191–2.

79. Wilde, 'Swedish Social Democracy and the World Market', p. 199.

80. Wilde, 'Swedish Social Democracy and the World Market', p. 197.

81. Holloway, 'Global Capital and the National State', p. 35.

82. Doyal and Gough, *Theory of Human Need*, p. 300.

83. G. W. F. Hegel, *Philosophy of Mind*, trans. W. Wallace (Clarendon Press, Oxford, 1894), p. 238.

BIBLIOGRAPHY

WORKS BY G. W. F. HEGEL

ORIGINAL GERMAN

Gesammelte Werke 6: Jenaer Systementwürfe I, (eds) Düsing, K. and Kimmerle, H. (Felix Meiner Verlag, Hamburg, 1975).

Gesammelte Werke 8: Jenaer Systementwürfe III, (eds) Horstman, R.-P. with Trede, J. H. (Felix Meiner Verlag, Hamburg, 1976).

'System der Sittlichkeit', in *Sämtliche Werke VII: Schriften zur Politik und Rechtsphilosophie*, (ed.) Lasson, G. (Felix Meiner Verlag, Leipzig, 1913).

Werke (Suhrkamp Verlag, Frankfurt, 1970), Volumes IV, VII, XIII, XIV, XV and XVII.

ENGLISH TRANSLATIONS

Aesthetics. Lectures on Fine Art, (trans.) Knox, T. M. Volumes I and II (Clarendon Press, Oxford, 1974–75).

Elements of the Philosophy of Right, (trans.) Nisbet, H. B. (Cambridge University Press, Cambridge, 1991).

Hegel and the Human Spirit, (trans.) Rauch, L. (Wayne State University Press, Detroit, 1983).

The Logic of Hegel, (trans.) Wallace, W. (Clarendon Press, Oxford, 1892).

Phenomenology of Spirit, (trans.) Miller, A. V. (Oxford University Press, Oxford, 1972).

The Philosophy of History, (trans.) Sibree, J. (Dover, New York, 1956).

Philosophy of Mind, (trans.) Wallace, W. (Clarendon Press, Oxford, 1894).

The Philosophy of Religion, Volume 2, (trans.) Speirs, E. B. (Kegan Paul, London; Trench, Trubner, 1895).

Philosophy of Right, (trans.) Knox, T. M. (Oxford University Press, Oxford, 1973).

Philosophy of Spirit, (trans.) Wallace, W. and Miller, A. V. (Oxford University Press, Oxford, 1971).

The Science of Logic, (trans.) Miller, A. V. (Allen and Unwin, London, 1969).

System of Ethical Life and First Philosophy of Spirit, (trans.) Harris, H. S. and Knox, T. M. (State University of New York Press, Albany NY, 1979).

WORKS BY MARX

ORIGINAL GERMAN (WITH F. ENGELS)
Gesamtausgabe (MEGA), I.2 (Dietz Verlag, Berlin, 1982).
Gesamtausgabe (MEGA), II.1.1 (Dietz Verlag, Berlin, 1976).
Gesamtausgabe (MEGA), II.1.2 (Dietz Verlag, Berlin, 1981).
Gesamtausgabe (MEGA), II.5 (Dietz Verlag, Berlin, 1983).
Gesamtausgabe (MEGA), IV.2 (Dietz Verlag, Berlin, 1981).
Werke, Volume 4 (Dietz Verlag, Berlin, 1969).
Werke, Volume 25 (Dietz Verlag, Berlin, 1964).

ENGLISH TRANSLATIONS
Capital, Volume 1, (trans.) Moore, S. and Aveling, E. (Lawrence and Wishart, London, 1961).
Capital, Volume 1, (trans.) Fowkes, B. (Penguin, Harmondsworth, 1988).
Capital, Volume 2, (trans.) Fernbach, D. (Penguin, Harmondsworth, 1992).
Capital, Volume 3, (trans.) Fernbach, D. (Penguin, Harmondsworth, 1991).
'A Contribution to the Critique of Hegel's Philosophy of Right. Introduction', in Marx, K. *Early Writings*, (trans.) Livingstone, R. and Benton, G. (Penguin, Harmondsworth, 1992).
A Contribution to the Critique of Political Economy, (trans.) Ryazanskaya, S. W. (Progress Publishers, Moscow, 1977).
'Critique of Hegel's Doctrine of the State', in Mark, K. *Early Writings*, (trans.) Livingstone, R. and Benton, G. (Penguin, Harmondsworth, 1992).
'Economic and Philosophical Manuscripts', in Marx, K. *Early Writings*, (trans.) Livingstone, R. and Benton, G. (Penguin, Harmondsworth, 1992).
'Excerpts from James Mill's *Elements of Political Economy*', in Marx, K. *Early Writings*, (trans.) Livingstone, R. and Benton, G. (Penguin, Harmondsworth, 1992).
Grundrisse, (trans.) Nicolaus, M. (Pelican, Harmondsworth, 1973).
'On the Jewish Question', in Marx, K. *Early Writings*, (trans.) Livingstone, R. and Benton, G. (Penguin, Harmondsworth, 1992).
Texts on Method, (trans. and ed.). Carver, T. (Blackwell, Oxford, 1975).
Theories of Surplus Value, Part II, (trans.) Simpson, R. (Lawrence and Wishart, London, 1968).
Marx, K. and Engels, F. *Collected Works*, Volume 4 (Lawrence and Wishart, London, 1975).
Marx, K. and Engels, F. *Collected Works*, Volume 5 (Lawrence and Wishart, London, 1976).
Marx, K. and Engels, F. *Collected Works*, Volume 6 (Lawrence and Wishart, London, 1976).
Marx, K. and Engels, F. *Selected Correspondence* (Progress Publishers, Moscow, 1975).

OTHER WORKS

Agger, B. 'Marcuse's "One-Dimensionality": Socio-Historical and Ideological Context', *Dialectical Anthropology*, 13, 4, 1988.

Althusser, L. *For Marx* (New Left Books, London, 1969).

Althusser, L. *Montesquieu, Rousseau, Marx* (New Left Books, London, 1982).

Apffel Marglin, F. 'Smallpox in Two Systems of Knowledge', in Apffel Marglin, F. and Marglin, S. A. (eds) *Dominating Knowledge: Development, Culture and Resistance* (Clarendon Press, Oxford, 1990).

Apffel Marglin, F. and Marglin, S. A. (eds) *Dominating Knowledge: Development, Culture and Resistance* (Clarendon Press, Oxford, 1990).

Archibald, W. P. *Marx and the Missing Link: Human Nature* (Humanities Press, Atlantic Highlands NJ, 1989).

Arendt, H. *The Human Condition* (University of Chicago Press, Chicago and London, 1958).

Arthur, C. 'Introduction', in Marx, K. and Engels, F. *The German Ideology* (Lawrence and Wishart, London, 1991).

Arthur, C. 'Hegel's *Logic* and Marx's *Capital*', in Moseley, F. (ed.) *Marx's Method in Capital: A Reexamination* (Humanities Press, Atlantic Highlands NJ, 1993).

Arthur, C. 'Review of Shamsavari's *Dialectics and Social Theory: The Logic of Marx's Capital*', *Capital and Class*, 50, Summer, 1993.

Avineri, S. *Hegel's Theory of the Modern State* (Cambridge University Press, Cambridge, 1972).

Avineri, S. 'The Discovery of Hegel's Early Lectures on the Philosophy of Right', *Owl of Minerva*, 16, Spring, 1985.

Avineri, S. 'The Paradox of Civil Society in the Structure of Hegel's View of Sittlichkeit', *Philosophy and Theology*, 3, Winter, 1988.

Barry, B. *Political Argument* (Harvester Wheatsheaf, Hemel Hempstead, 1990).

Bauman, Z. 'Review-Symposium on Soviet-Type Societies', *Telos*, 60, Summer, 1984.

Bay, C. 'Human Needs, Wants and Politics: Abraham Maslow, Meet Karl Marx', *Social Praxis*, 7, 1980.

Benhabib, S. 'The "Logic" of Civil Society: A Reconsideration of Hegel and Marx', *Philosophy and Social Criticism*, 8, Summer, 1981.

Benton, T. 'Humanism = Speciesism: Marx on Humans and Animals', *Radical Philosophy*, 50, 1988.

Benton, T. *Natural Relations: Animal Rights and Social Justice* (Verso, London, 1993).

Berry, C. J. 'Need and Egoism in Marx's Early Writings', *History of Political Thought*, VIII, 3, Winter, 1987.

Blackburn, S. *The Oxford Dictionary of Philosophy* (Oxford University Press, Oxford, 1994).

Boella, L. 'Radicalism and Needs in Heller', *Telos*, Fall, 1978.

Boger, G. 'On the Materialist Appropriation of Hegel's Dialectical Method', *Science and Society*, 55, 1, Spring, 1991.

Braybrooke, D. *Meeting Needs* (Princeton University Press, Princeton NJ, 1987).

Brod, H. *Hegel's Philosophy of Politics: Idealism, Identity, and Modernity* (Westview Press, Boulder Co, San Francisco and Oxford, 1992).

Bungay, S. *Beauty and Truth* (Oxford University Press, Oxford, 1984).

Callinicos, A. 'Introduction: Analytical Marxism', in Callinicos, A. (ed.) *Marxist Theory* (Oxford University Press, Oxford, 1989).

Callinicos, A. *The Revenge of History: Marxism and the East European Revolutions* (Polity Press, Cambridge, 1991).

Callinicos, A. 'Premature Obituaries: A Comment on O'Sullivan, Minogue, and Marquand', in Shtromas, A. (ed.) *The End of 'Isms'?*, Special Issue of *Political Studies*, XLI, 1993.

Caplan, A. L. *The Sociobiology Debate: Readings on Ethical and Scientific Issues* (Harper and Row, New York, 1978).

Carver, T. 'Commentary', in Marx, K. *Texts on Method*, (trans. and ed.) Carver, T. (Blackwell, Oxford, 1975).

Carver, T. 'Marx – and Hegel's *Logic*', *Political Studies*, XXIV, 1, 1976.

Chitty, A. 'The Early Marx on Needs', *Radical Philosophy*, 64, 1993.

Clapham, J. H. *The Economic Development of France and Germany, 1815–1914* (Cambridge University Press, Cambridge, 1955).

Clarke, S. 'Crisis of Socialism or Crisis of the State', *Capital and Class*, 42, 1990.

Cleaver, H. *Reading Capital Politically* (Harvester, Brighton, 1979).

Cleaver, H. 'The Inversion of Class Perspective in Marxian Theory: From Valorisation to Self-Valorisation', in Bonefeld, W., Gunn, R. and Psychopedis, K. (eds) *Open Marxism. Volume II: Theory and Practice* (Pluto, London, 1992).

Cohen, A. 'Marx – From the Abolition of Labour to the Abolition of the Abolition of Labour', *History of European Ideas*, 17, 4, 1993.

Cohen, G. A. *Karl Marx's Theory of History: A Defence* (Clarendon Press, Oxford, 1991).

Cohen, J. 'Review of Agnes Heller, *The Theory of Need in Marx*', *Telos*, 33, Fall, 1977.

Colletti, L. *Marxism and Hegel* (New Left Books, London, 1973).

Cowling, M. 'Marx's Conceptual Framework from 1843–5: Hegelian Dialectic and Historical Necessity versus Feuerbachian Humanistic Materialism?', *Studies in Marxism*, 2, 1995.

Cullen, B. *Hegel's Social and Political Thought: An Introduction* (Gill and Macmillan, Dublin, 1979).

Dallmayr, F. R. *G.W.F. Hegel: Modernity and Politics* (Sage, London, 1993).

Descartes, R. 'Discourse on Method', in Descartes, R. *Discourse on Method and Other Writings*, (trans.) Wollaston, A. (Penguin, Harmondsworth, 1966).

Descombes, V. *Modern French Philosophy* (Cambridge University Press, Cambridge, 1980).

Dickey, L. *Hegel: Religion, Economics and the Politics of Spirit, 1770–1807* (Cambridge University Press, Cambridge, 1987).

Doyal, L. and Gough, I. *A Theory of Human Need* (Macmillan, London, 1991).

Doyal, L. 'Thinking About Human Need', *New Left Review*, 201, September/October, 1993.

Dunayevskaya, R. *Philosophy and Revolution* (Columbia University Press, New York, 1989).

Dunayevskaya, R. *The Philosophic Moment of Marxist Humanism* (News and Letters, Chicago, 1989).

Dyker, D. A. 'Planning and the Worker', in Schapiro, L. and Godson, J. (eds) *The Soviet Worker: Illusions and Realities* (Macmillan, London, 1982).

Fehér F. and Heller, A. *Eastern Left, Western Left: Totalitarianism, Freedom and Democracy* (Polity Press, Cambridge, 1986).

Fehér, F., Heller A. and Márkus, G. *Dictatorship Over Needs* (Blackwell, Oxford, 1983).

Filtzer, D. *Soviet Workers and Stalinist Industrialisation: The Formation of Modern Soviet Production Relations, 1928–41* (Pluto, London, 1986).

Filtzer, D. *Soviet Workers and De-Stalinization: The Consolidation of the Modern System of Soviet Production Relations, 1953–1964* (Cambridge University Press, Cambridge, 1992).

Fitzgerald, R. (ed.) *Human Needs and Politics* (Pergamon, Ruschcutters Bay NSW, 1977).

Forbes, I. *Marx and the New Individual* (Unwin Hyman, London, 1990).

Fraser, N. *Unruly Practices: Power, Discourse and Gender in Contemporary Social Theory* (Polity Press, Cambridge, 1989).

Fukuyama, F. *The End of History and the Last Man* (Hamish Hamilton, London, 1992).

Geras, N. *Marx and Human Nature: Refutation of a Legend* (Verso, London, 1983).

Griffin, J. *Well-Being: Its Meaning, Measurement and Moral Importance* (Clarendon Press, Oxford, 1988).

Gunn, R. 'Marxism and Mediation', *Common Sense*, 2, 1987.

Gunn, R. ' "Recognition" in Hegel's *Phenomenology of Spirit*', *Common Sense*, 4, 1988.

Gunn, R. 'Against Historical Materialism: Marxism as a First-Order Discourse', in Bonefeld, W., Gunn, R. and Psychopedis, K. (eds) *Open Marxism. Volume II: Theory and Practice* (Pluto, London, 1992).

Gutman, A. 'The Challenge of Multiculturalism in Political Ethics', *Philosophy and Public Affairs*, 22, 3, 1993.

Halliday, R. J. 'Human Nature and Comparison', *Australian Journal of Politics and History*, 36, 3, 1990.

Hardt, M. and Negri, A. *Labour of Dionysus: A Critique of the State-Form* (University of Minnesota Press, Minneapolis, 1994).

Harris, H. S. 'Hegel's *System of Ethical Life*. An Interpretation', in Hegel, G. W. F. *System of Ethical Life and First Philosophy of Spirit*, (trans.) Harris, H. S. and Knox, T. M. (State University of New York Press, Albany NY, 1979).

Harris, H. S. *Hegel's Development: Night Thoughts (Jena 1801–1806)* (Clarendon Press, Oxford, 1983).

Harris, H. S. 'Hegel's Intellectual Development to 1807', in Beiser, F. C. (ed.) *The Cambridge Companion to Hegel* (Cambridge University Press, Cambridge, 1993).

Heller, A. *The Theory of Need in Marx* (Allison and Busby, London, 1976).

Hobsbawm, E. J. *The Age of Revolution: Europe 1789–1848* (Weidenfeld and Nicolson, London, 1962).

Hollander, S. *The Economics of Adam Smith* (Heinemann, London, 1973).

Holloway, J. 'Crisis, Fetishism, Class Composition', in Bonefeld, W., Gunn, R. and Psychopedis, K. (eds) *Open Marxism. Volume II: Theory and Practice* (Pluto, London, 1992).

Holloway, J. 'Global Capital and the National State', *Capital and Class*, 52, 1994.

Hook, S. *From Hegel to Marx: Studies in the Intellectual Development of Karl Marx* (Humanities Press, New York, 1958).

Houlgate, S. *Freedom, Truth and History: An Introduction to Hegel's Philosophy* (Routledge, London, 1991).

Ilting, K.-H. 'The Structure of Hegel's *Philosophy of Right*', in Pelczynski, Z. A. (ed.) *Hegel's Political Philosophy* (Cambridge University Press, Cambridge, 1971).

Ilting, K.-H. 'Hegel's Concept of the State and Marx's Early Critique', in Pelczynski, Z. A. (ed.) *The State and Civil Society: Studies in Hegel's Political Philosophy* (Cambridge University Press, Cambridge, 1984).

Inwood, M. *A Hegel Dictionary*, (Blackwell, Oxford, 1992).

Jacoby, R. 'The Myth of Multiculturalism', *New Left Review*, 208, November/December, 1994.

James, C. L. R. *Notes on Dialectics* (Allison and Busby, London, 1980).

Kant, I. *Critique of Pure Reason*, (trans.) Kemp Smith, N. (Macmillan, London, 1992).

Karelis, C. 'Hegel's Concept of Art: An Interpretative Essay', in *Hegel's Introduction to Aesthetics*, (trans.) Knox, T. M. (Clarendon Press, Oxford, 1979).

Kelly, G. A. 'Notes on Hegel's "Lordship and Bondage"', in MacIntyre, A. (ed.) *Hegel: A Collection of Critical Essays* (University of Notre Dame Press, London and Notre Dame, 1976).

Kitcher, P. *Vaulting Ambition: Sociobiology and the Quest for Human Nature* (MIT Press, Cambridge MA, 1985).

Kojeve, A. *Introduction to the Reading of Hegel* (Basic Books, New York, 1969).

Lane, D. *Soviet Labour and the Ethic of Communism: Full Employment and the Labour Process in the USSR* (Wheatsheaf, Brighton, 1987).

Lebowitz, M. 'Heller on Marx's Concept of Needs', *Science and Society*, 3, Fall, 1979.

Lebowitz, M. *Beyond Capital: Marx's Political Economy of the Working Class* (Macmillan, London, 1992).

Lederer, K. *Human Needs* (Oelgeschlager, Gunn and Hain, Cambridge MA, 1980).

Lefebvre, H. *Critique of Everyday Life*, Volume 1 (Verso, London, 1991).

Leiss, W. 'Marx and Macpherson: Needs, Utilities, and Self-Development', in Kantos, A. (ed.) *Powers, Possessions and Freedom* (University of Toronto Press, Toronto, Buffalo and London, 1979).

Lenin, V. I. *Collected Works*, Volume 38 (Lawrence and Wishart, London, 1963).

Lukács, G. *The Young Hegel. Studies in the Relation Between Dialectics and Economics* (Merlin, London, 1975).

Lukács, G. *History and Class Consciousness* (Merlin, London, 1990).

Lukes, S. *Moral Conflict and Politics* (Clarendon Press, Oxford, 1991).

MacGregor, D. *The Communist Ideal in Hegel and Marx* (George Allen and Unwin, London and Sydney, 1984).

MacIntyre, A. *After Virtue: A Study in Moral Theory* (Duckworth, London, 1981).

Mandel, E. *Beyond Perestroika: The Future of Gorbachev's USSR* (Verso, London, 1992).

Marcuse, H. *One-Dimensional Man* (Beacon Press, Boston, 1964).

Marglin, S. A. 'Towards the Decolonization of the Mind', in Apffel Marglin, F. and Marglin, S. A. (eds) *Dominating Knowledge: Development, Culture and Resistance* (Clarendon Press), Oxford, 1990).

Maslow, A. *Motivation and Personality* (Harper and Row, New York, Evanston and London, 2nd edition, 1970).

Mathias, P. *The First Industrial Nation: An Economic History of Britian 1700–1914* (Methuen, London and New York, 1983).

Mattick P. Jr, 'Marx's Dialectic', in Moseley, F. (ed.) *Marx's Method in Capital: A Reexamination* (Humanities Press, Atlantic Highlands NJ, 1993).

McLellan, D. (ed.) *Karl Marx: Selected Writings* (Oxford University Press, Oxford, 1977).

Mendus, S. 'Human Rights in Political Theory', *Political Studies*, 43, Special Issue, 1995.

Midgley, M. *Beast and Man* (Methuen, London, 1978).

Miller, D. *Social Justice* (Clarendon Press, Oxford, 1976).

Minogue, K. 'Ideology after the Collapse of Communism', in Shtromas, A. (ed.) *The End of 'Isms'?*, Special Issue of *Political Studies*, XLI, 1993.

Mobasser, N. 'Marx and Self-Realization', *New Left Review*, 161, January/February, 1987.

Mulhall S. and Swift, A. *Liberals and Communitarians* (Blackwell, Oxford, 2nd edition, 1997).

Murray, P. *Marx's Theory of Scientific Knowledge* (Humanities Press, London, 1990).

Murray, P. T. *Hegel's Philosophy of Mind and Will* (Edwin Mellen Press, Lewiston, Queenston and Lampeter, 1991).

Neocleous, M. *Administering Civil Society: Towards a Theory of State Power* (Macmillan, London, 1996).

Nicolaus, M. 'Foreword', in Marx, K. *Grundrisse* (Pelican, London, 1973).

Norman, R. *Hegel's Phenomenology: A Philosophical Introduction* (Sussex University Press, London, 1976).

Nussbaum, M. 'Human Functioning and Social Justice: In Defence of Aristotelian Essentialism', *Political Theory*, 20, 2, May, 1992.

O'Connor, J. *Accumulation Crisis* (Blackwell, Oxford, 1986).

Okin, S. M. *Women in Western Political Thought* (Princeton University Press, Princeton NJ, 1979).

Ollman, B. *Dialectical Investigations* (Routledge, London and New York, 1993).

Peffer, R. G. *Marxism, Morality and Social Justice* (Princeton University Press, Princeton NJ, 1990).

Petry, M. J. 'Hegel and the *Morning Chronicle*', *Hegel-Studien*, 11, 1976.

Plant, R. 'Hegel and Political Economy I and II', *New Left Review*, 103 and 104, May/June and July/August, 1977.

Plant, R. 'Hegel and the Political Economy', in Maker, W. (ed.) *Hegel on Economics and Freedom* (Mercer University Press, Georgia, 1977).

Plant, R. *Modern Political Thought* (Blackwell, Oxford and Cambridge MA, 1991).

Poggi, G. *The Development of the Modern State: A Sociological Introduction* (Hutchinson, London, 1978).

Poggi, G. 'Review Symposium: Dictatorship over Needs', *Thesis Eleven*, 12, 1985.

Poggi, G. *The State, its Nature, Development and Prospects* (Polity Press, Cambridge, 1990).

Rachels, J. 'Darwin, Species and Morality', *Monist*, 1, 70, 1987.

Rawls, J. *A Theory of Justice* (Oxford University Press, Oxford, 1990).

Reeve, A. *Property* (Macmillan, London, 1986).

Reuten, G. and Williams, M. *Value-Form and the State* (Routledge, London and New York, 1989).

Roemer, J. (ed.) *Analytical Marxism* (Cambridge University Press, Cambridge, 1989).

Rorty, R. 'Human Rights, Rationality and Sentimentality', in Shute, S. and Hurley, S. (eds) *On Human Rights: The Oxford Amnesty Lectures* (Basic Books, New York, 1993).

Rose, G. *Hegel Contra Sociology* (Athlone, London, 1981).

Sandel, M. 'Democrats and Community', *New Republic*, 22 February 1998.

Sayers, S. 'The Actual and the Rational', in Lamb, D. (ed.) *Hegel and Modern Philosophy* (Croom Helm, London, 1987).

Sayers, S. 'The Need to Work', *Radical Philosophy*, 46, 1987.

Sayers, S. 'Work, Leisure and Human Needs', in Winnifrith, T. and Barrett, C. (eds) *The Philosophy of Leisure* (Macmillan, London, 1989).

Scanlon, T. M. 'Preference and Urgency', *Journal of Philosophy*, 72, 1975.

Schmidt, A. *The Concept of Nature in Marx* (New Left Books, London, 1971).

Schmidt, J. 'A Paideia for the "Burger als Bourgeois": The Concept of "Civil Society" in Hegel's Political Thought', *History of Political Thought*, II, 3, Winter, 1981.

Shamsavari, A. *Dialectics and Social Theory: The Logic of Capital* (Merlin Books, Braunton, 1991).

Singer, P. *Animal Liberation* (Jonathan Cape, London, 1976).

Smith, S. B. 'What is "Right" in Hegel's *Philosophy of Right?*', *American Political Science Review*, 83, 2, 1989.

Smith, S. B. *Hegel's Critique of Liberalism: Rights in Context* (University of Chicago Press, Chicago and London, 1991).

Smith, T. *The Logic of Marx's Capital: Replies to Hegelian Criticisms* (State University of New York Press, Albany NY, 1990).

Soper, K. 'The Needs of Marxism', *Radical Philosophy*, 15, 1977.

Soper, K. *On Human Needs: Open and Closed Theories in a Marxist Perspective* (Harvester Press, Brighton, 1981).

Soper, K. *Troubled Pleasures* (Verso, London and New York, 1990).

Soper, K. 'A Theory of Human Need', *New Left Review*, 197, January/February, 1993.

Springborg, P. *The Problem of Human Needs and the Critique of Civilisation* (Allen and Unwin, London, 1981).

Ste Croix, G. E. M. de *The Class Struggle in the Ancient Greek World* (Duckworth, London, 1983).

Szelenyi, I. 'Review-Symposium on Soviet-Type Societies', *Telos*, 60, Summer, 1984.

Taylor, C. *Sources of the Self: The Making of the Modern Identity* (Cambridge University Press, Cambridge, 1992).

Thompson, G. *Needs* (Routledge and Kegan Paul, London, 1987).

Ticktin, H. *Origins of the Crisis in the USSR: Essays on the Political Economy of a Disintegrating System* (M. E. Sharpe, New York and London, 1992).

Toews, J. E. *Hegelianism: The Path Toward Dialectical Humanism 1805–1841* (Cambridge University Press, Cambridge, 1990).

Townshend, J. 'Has Marxist Politics a Future?', *Contemporary Politics*, 1, 2, 1995.

Waldron, J. 'Minority Cultures and the Cosmopolitan Alternative', in Kymlicka, W. (ed.) *The Rights of Minority Cultures* (Oxford University Press, Oxford, 1995).

Walker, S. *Animal Thought* (Routledge and Kegan Paul, London, 1985).

Walzer, M. *Spheres of Justice* (Basic Books, New York, 1983).

Waszek, N. *The Scottish Enlightenment and Hegel's Account of Civil Society* (Kluwer Academic, Boston, 1988).

Westphal, K. 'The Basic Context and Structure of Hegel's *Philosophy of Right*', in Beiser, F. C. (ed.) *The Cambridge Companion to Hegel* (Cambridge University Press, Cambridge, 1993).

Westphal, M. 'Hegel's Theory of the Concept', in Steinkraus, W. E. and Schmitz, K. I. (eds) *Art and Logic in Hegel's Philosophy* (Harvester, Brighton, 1980.

White, A. *Modal Thinking* (Blackwell, Oxford, 1971).

Wicks, R. 'Hegel's Aesthetics: An Overview', in Beiser, F. C. (ed.) *The Cambridge Companion to Hegel* (Cambridge University Press, Cambridge, 1993).

Wiggins, D. *Needs, Values, Truth* (Blackwell, Oxford and Cambridge MA, 2nd edition, 1991).

Wilde, L. *Marx and Contradiction* (Avebury, Aldershot, 1989).

Wilde, L. 'Logic: Dialectic and Contradiction', in Carver, T. (ed.) *The Cambridge Companion to Marx* (Cambridge University Press, Cambridge, 1991).

Wilde, L. 'Marx's Concept of Human Essence and its Radical Critics', *Studies in Marxism*, 1, 1994.

Wilde, L. 'Swedish Social Democracy and the World Market', in Polan, R. and Gills B. (eds) *Transcending the State-Global Divide: A Neostructuralist Agenda in International Relations* (Lynne Rienner, Boulder Co and London, 1994).

Williams, H. *Hegel, Heraclitus and Marx's Dialectic* (Harvester Wheatsheaf, Hemel Hempstead, 1989).

Wilson, E. O. *Sociobiology: The New Synthesis* (Harvard University Press, Cambridge MA, 1975).

Wilson, E. O. *On Human Nature* (Harvard University Press, Cambridge MA, 1978).

Witheford, N. 'Autonomist Marxism and the Information Society', *Capital and Class*, 52, Spring, 1994.

Wood, A. W. *Hegel's Ethical Thought* (Cambridge University Press, Cambridge, 1990).

Wood, A. W. 'Hegel and Marxism', in Beiser, F. C. (ed.) *The Cambridge Companion to Hegel* (Cambridge University Press, Cambridge, 1993).

Wood, E. M. *The Pristine Culture of Capitalism* (Verso, London, 1991).

INDEX

Where notes are indexed, they appear in the form, for example, 64n.37.

state capitalism, 177
strikes, 159, 179
structuralism, 2
Steuart, Sir James, 58
subsistence, 58, 85, 126, 130–2, 134
surplus, 4, 33, 54–6, 57, 59–60, 61, 128, 165,
    166, 167, 180, 185
Sweden, 187–8

taxation, 60
technology, 3, 5, 92, 143, 168, 170, 180
theory and practice, 24, 28–9, 35, 37, 100,
    102, 156–7
Thompson, G., 11–12, 14, 51
tool, 2, 47, 48, 49, 50, 53, 61, 62, 114, 115,
    165
trade, 55, 107
    international, 86
trade unions, 179
transcendence, 1, 124, 149, 154–5, 168, 176,
    178, 180, 181–2, 188

understanding, 24–7, 31, 52, 87, 172, 173
unemployment, 159, 170, 180
unfreedom, 4, 81, 92, 108
utility, 70, 77–8, 91, 107, 147

value, 32, 38, 54, 59, 70–1, 72, 127, 130, 131,
    132, 137
    abstract, 70, 72, 83, 91
    exchange, 32, 37, 38
    global surplus, 188
    surplus, 126, 128, 129, 133
    use, 37–8

wage, 14, 130, 131, 132, 133, 135–6, 137–8,
    149, 154, 156, 167
wage earner funds, 188
wants, 9, 11, 13–15, 18–19, 51–2, 80, 153, 172–3
wealth, 38, 60, 82, 86, 110, 128, 129, 130, 146,
    182
    accumulation of, 85
    inequalities in, 57, 60, 85
welfare, 71, 73, 84–5, 86, 87, 149, 177, 185, 188
Will, 2, 23, 28–32, 34, 35, 37, 39, 40, 41, 68–
    74, 80, 81, 88, 92, 117, 165, 167, 169
Wood, A., 57
work, 11, 34, 48, 54, 55, 57, 58, 60, 63, 75,
    76, 81–2, 83, 85, 86, 87, 88, 89, 90, 102,
    103, 104, 105, 110–11, 129, 145, 148,
    155, 170, 178, 180, 181, 189
working day, 147–9
Zeus, 112